JOHN WILMOT

INSPIRED PRINCIPLES OF PROPHETIC INTERPRETATION

*God means what He says
and says what He means*

JOHN WILMOT, D.D.

PASTOR, HIGHGATE ROAD CHAPEL, LONDON, 1924-1959
SPECIAL LECTURER, TORONTO BAPTIST SEMINARY

FOREWORD BY

DR. D. M. LLOYD-JONES

WESTMINSTER CHAPEL, LONDON

REINER PUBLICATIONS

SWENGEL, PA.
U. S. A.

1967

FOREWORD

I was glad to hear that it was proposed to put these "Prophetic Studies" by Dr. John Wilmot into permanent book form. I believe they will make a valuable contribution to such studies.

Nothing has been more gratifying during the past twenty years or so than the way in which the old dogmatic and intolerant attitude, which too frequently characterized many interested in these matters, has given way to a new spirit of humility and honest reexamination of the position.

What adds value to this study by Dr. Wilmot, over and above its inherent worth, is the fact that he himself has changed his position as the result of further study and thought. It is not merely an exposition of one particular attitude, therefore, but at the same time an appraisal of other points of view with which he has been long familiar over the years.

The reading of this book can do nothing but good because of its scriptural character and its careful argumentation.

All will not be convinced, but all should be helped and edified.

D. M. LLOYD-JONES

Westminster Chapel,
London,
December, 1965.

PREFACE

The chapters in this volume appeared as separate articles in The Gospel Witness of Jarvis Street Baptist Church, Toronto, from May 1963 to January 1965 under the general title, Inspired Principles of Prophetic Interpretation.

Dr. T. T. Shields, for forty-five years pastor and editor, and founder of the Toronto Baptist Seminary, is no longer with us, but my sense of indebtedness to him lives on. By his introduction I have been privileged on a number of occasions to serve the Seminary in special lectureship in several theological subjects.

I am grateful also to Dr. H. C. Slade, to the Senate and Faculty of the Seminary, who assigned to me, among other subjects during my visit in 1960, that of Predictive Prophecy.

Knowing the mind of Dr. Shields, as I had reason to do, I am sure he would have commended the unbiased consideration of these extended studies. I thank the present editors of The Gospel Witness for the generosity of space in that paper, and for their preparation for print and proof-reading of my copy supplied from England.

Many readers have encouraged reproduction in this present form. Some inquiries which the articles provoked have been replied to in private correspondence. To the critical review given in instalments in a prophetic magazine my limited reply which also appeared in The Gospel Witness is here given as a supplement.

Though an index of texts was recommended and prepared, I have thought it unnecessary. There has been a repetition of passages considered in several relations, and scripture references are supplied in the chapter content. My experience is that proof-texts in themselves are not satisfactory in establishing truth. The scripture, like the law, is an unity (James 2.10; John 10.35). A thoughtful, cumulative examination is desirable.

The closing articles were composed of copious excerpts on Origins. Readers will make their own comparisons. Were the prophetic opinions of such as J. N. Darby and B. W. Newton developed from the seed-plot of Irvingism? In the controversy between pre- and post-tribulation adventists, Newtonians have ascribed Darby's theory to the contemporary phenominal Irvingite revivalist movement, where, they have affirmed, it was first given forth in an "utterance" under the "power". It may be observed that certain views which Newton propagated were also "uttered" in the same context.

The Reiner Publications have readily undertaken the publication of this volume. Mr. Donald Reiner to whom I am indebted, I first met at the Toronto Baptist Seminary when we had profitable conversation on doctrinal and eschatological subjects. By occasional correspondence the contact has been maintained over many years.

Lastly, I record my gratitude to Dr. D. M. Lloyd-Jones, whose grace and kindness in contributing the Foreword, and whose estimation and commendation of these studies as a scriptural re-examination of popular dispensational and millennial positions, are highly valued.

J. W.

CONTENTS

INSPIRED PRINCIPLES
OF PROPHETIC
INTERPRETATION

"God means what He says,
And says what He means".

WE propose some considerations resulting from re-examination of dispensational and futuristic interpretations of predictive prophecy. It would appear that truth concerning "the power and coming of our Lord Jesus Christ" (2 Pet. 1) may be endangered by "cunningly devised fables." There is the further warning not to "wrest the scriptures" (2 Pet. 3). Peter, who avers that Paul's writings agree with his own on this subject, in rebuking scoffers at "the promise of His coming", affirms that the fulfilment of that "promise" will be catastrophic, simultaneous with the "day of judgment"; and the creation of "new heavens and new earth" for which the pilgrim church on earth, "according to His promise", expectantly waits, even hastening the arrival of that "day of God" by her holy behaviour and godliness. Surely, any foredating of the Second Coming, any interpolation of intervening events, millennial or other, involving an earlier fulfilment of the "promise", is to be questioned.

THE GOSPEL WITNESS may not commit itself to theories of prophetic interpretation, neither would it hesitate to challenge what may appear to be contrary to Scripture testimony. Dr. Shields in preaching again and again affirmed his expectation of the personal, visible, audible Coming of the Lord. There are sermons on file wherein also he boldly

1

challenged details in charts or programmes proposed by popular and speculative teachers.

In early years I embraced what is known as the Pre-tribulation and Pre-millennial Advent, as closing the present and introducing a future and final dispensation in Time's course. The Church has not always heeded the forewarning against regarding phenominal events as a sign of the End. The views mentioned had their origin in a time of crisis more than a century ago. So later, the First World War was considered a sign of "the Day approaching", the Second Coming being spoken of as imminent. In London thronged meetings were addressed by prominent evangelical preachers. The Advent Testimony and Preparation Movement was formed. About the same time the Scofield Reference Bible appeared, the prophetic notes in which are based on dispensationalism. Further developed views were represented in The Companion Bible with its "dispensational plan". The Sovereign Grace Advent Testimony differs from the A.T.P.M. mainly in that, while still dispensational and futuristic and pre-millennial, it holds the *post*-tribulation Coming. On these variant points of view "chief men among the brethern" (to borrow Luke's phrase: Acts 15:22), as John Nelson Darby and Benjamin Wills Newton, separated at the inception of the "Brethren" movement. It would appear, however, that these hitherto unknown prophetic teachings sprang from slightly earlier sources, accompanied with "manifestations" which, though remarkable and impressive at the time, proved unreliable and calculated even to deceive. The invented order of events, presented in chart and diagram and with selected proof-texts, can be very attractive though superficial. I have referred to Dr. Shields: he would say, "They suppose that the Mind of the Infinite can be reduced to a mathematical proposition"! On the American Continent the same outline and ordering of things to come are widely held and propagated. Indeed, by some they are regarded as fundamental to orthodoxy as any historic and well-established doctrinal tenet. Their acceptance has even been made a condition of Christian fellowship and affiliation.

It is not an adversely critical enquiry to ask whether any devout student of Scripture, following our Lord and the apostles as his guide, by humanly unaided search, could discover for himself these dispensational divisions, detailed outlines and arrangement of events. It is claimed that at "the commencement of the nineteenth century" (the time of origin) "God had mercy on the Church's ignorance and more light on prophetic truth was given". But that has been claimed for other religious innovations. And what if the light that is thought to be in us prove to be darkness?

MOMENTISM

Almost two millenniums have falsified the view that the Church was to expect the return of her Lord "at any moment", and the one hundred and thirty years since the error which has become so popular (in superficial talk but not in accordant behaviour!) originated, has no different answer to give. We may well again enquire, When did an any-moment possibility of the Second Coming begin? It could not have been expected between our Lord's ascension and Pentecost, for He had straitly instructed His disciples to wait for the Holy Spirit, which they did. They could not then have expected His return at any-moment.

It was equally impossible between the Pentecostal enduement and the completion of the Scriptures through His promised Spirit for the comfort, edification, direction and service of His Church during His heavenly absence. Upon completing their work the apostles died. Paul and Peter both wrote of this issue, yet they loved the "blessed hope" of the Lord's appearing. "The time of my departure", wrote Paul, not of the Lord's return, "is at hand". And Peter wrote for future believing generations "after my decease". No any-moment expectation there.

Moreover, before ascending the Lord committed to His Church their evangelizing mission among all nations "unto the uttermost part of the earth". He assured them of His spiritual presence until the consummation of the world. He could not be expected to return until that task should be completed. Upon His ascending the Davidic prophecy was fulfilled, "Sit Thou at My right hand until I make Thine enemies Thy footstool" (Ps. 110), and there He is enthroned in majesty "expecting" their subjugation (Heb. 10) and "the last enemy that shall be destroyed is death" (1 Cor. 15). At no moment prior to that universal victory will He come again.

It would appear, therefore, that these two proceed simultaneously, the evangelization of all nations by the continuing Church on earth until the last redeemed sinner is ingathered (Matt. 28) and the liquidation of all enemies by the triumphant Lord and Head of His Church in heaven, until the last is destroyed. The apostle's explanation of apparent delay is precisely accordant with this, for together with the assurance that the total victory shall come with the arrival of "the day of judgment and perdition" and the creation of the new universe, there is this, His "longsuffering to usward is salvation, He being not willing that any should perish but that all should come to repentance", and we are bidden to reason or "account" for the situation thus (2 Pet. 3).

The facts then are clearly testified: Christ shall remain in heaven, withal exercising "all authority in heaven and in earth"; the Church shall continue on earth taking the Gospel to all nations, the Jews included. Enemies betimes in force and again in defeat, but always restrained under His supreme governing power, will eventually and finally fall at His feet, for "every knee shall bow of things in heaven and things in earth and things under the earth, and every tongue shall confess that Jesus Christ is Lord to the glory of God the Father" (Phil. 2).

MILLENNIALISM

The forthcoming articles may be regarded as in continuation of a small treatise of mine entitled "Millennial or Perennial?" reproduced in THE GOSPEL WITNESS by Dr. Shields (June 28th, 1951) with his generous commendation as follows: "We publish the whole article in this one issue so that our readers may the more easily preserve it. We have never read anything on this subject more satisfactory. We believe it ought to be read by tens of thousands. It is enough for us to add, THE GOSPEL WITNESS says Amen to the principles here enunciated. We suggest that our readers put this article aside for future reference, and not only read it but study it diligently with the references Dr. Wilmot gives."

Dispensationalism and Millennialism as popularly received, though differing on points as already indicated, have this in common, some gratuitous comment or qualification is often added directing the reader or hearer to the dispensation to which the Scripture in question is alleged to belong, when the Scripture itself is silent. Mr. B. W. Newton, maintaining a rigidly literal outlook, writes that "the prophecies of the New Testament cannot be interpreted in opposition to those of the Old Testament," that "they are professedly supplemental to those already given in the Old Testament", and "it is important to receive the instruction of the prophets if we wish to apprehend the additional lessons of the apostles". The rule would be sound if the Testaments were reversed, that is to say, the prophecies of the Old Testament must not be interpreted in opposition to the New Testament. The supplementary lessons of the apostles are expository and meaningful; and it is important to receive the lessons of the apostles if we wish to understand the instruction of the prophets. Our Lord and His apostles were exponents of Moses and the prophets. By such guidance we find that a spiritual meaning is given and a Gospel and evangelical fulfilment intended. On the other hand, the judgment of the able writer quoted leads him to postpone fulfilment to "the millennial period", and so to "millennial interference", "millennial blessing", "human life in the millennium", "the millennial heavens and millennial earth", and choice words of psalmist and prophet are said to be those of the Israel Nation when the Lord shall come. The fact is, no such millennial qualifications are mentioned in the Old Testament and human judgment, therefore, forces the text to fit the theory. The one millennial occurrence in the New Testament (and in the whole Bible) makes mention of none of the earthly characteristics so arbitrarily placed within that thousand years (Rev. 20).

That "God means what He says and says what He means" we have no doubt; yea, we solemnly believe it, for He is immutable. But when and how does God say what He means is a matter for enquiry. We made some enquiry when on the last occasion I was invited to serve the Toronto Baptist Seminary in a lectureship, and Predictive Prophecy was assigned to me. Profitable seasons they were, with discussion and interrogation, and some edifying controversy. Let us all and always keep company with C. H. Spurgeon who wrote:

"I will follow the Scripture wherever it may lead me, and I will renounce the most cherished opinion, rather than shape or alter a single syllable of God's Book. It is not mine to make God's Word consistent, but to believe that it is so. When a text stands in the road I drive no further. The Romans had a god they called Terminus, the god of landmarks. Holy Scripture is my sacred landmark: woe is me if I remove it".

HOW GOD SAYS WHAT
HE MEANS

"**G**OD means what He says and says what He means" is a criticism commonly used in the attempt by some to dismiss that which they label "spiritualizing", as a handling of God's Word unworthily. It is sometimes repeated in such confident manner as to give the impression that this is the final word of argument, an indisputable maxim, an end to all controversy. Like everything else touching the Scriptures, however, it should be given serious examination, for it is not irrelevant to any aspect of the main contents, types, prophecies, doctrines. There will be no disputing among those who hold the Divine Being in reverence and respect His Book, that God does indeed mean what He says. "He cannot deny Himself". "It is impossible for God to lie". He will not alter the thing which is gone out of His lips. Upon His Word unreserved reliance may be placed. But the enquiry arises, Does God in making His will known by selecting earthly things (John 3:12), and expressing His will in "words of earth" (Ps. 12), "words which the Holy Spirit teacheth" (1 Cor. 2:13), and admittedly meaning what He says — Does God thereby restrict His meaning to the earthly and literal? He means what He says, but does He fix a rigid literal limitation to His meaning? Or, in what God says, are His chosen literal objects intended to represent, to reveal and to direct to the spiritual?

Therefore, is it not in this latter objective that we may discover what He means?

It will be acknowledged that the Author is the final exponent of His own thoughts expressed in what He says, and that what He meant, though not disclosed at the time of His speaking, determined His selection of the subjects and terms He used. Therefore, what He says will befit the spiritual complement disclosed in what He means. Must the Spirit's exposition of a subject be confined to our human understanding of the matter? Is there not such a thing as an earthly story with a heavenly meaning? Would it not be our wisdom to follow the counsel contained in the ancient couplet: "The New is in the Old concealed; the Old is by the New revealed"? What God said in the Old Testament is given His meaning in the New Testament. Yet contentment with the finality of spiritual meaning as supplied in the New Testament is met with the criticism: "Mysticizing or vaporizing glosses called interpretation". We are accustomed to sing of God's providence, "God is His own interpreter, and He will make it plain". Is not this equally true of His Word? Examples of the spiritual purpose and the spiritualizing principle abound in the teaching of our Lord and His apostles. Surely *their* manner of expounding what God says should be our guide in seeking to know what God means. If spiritualization is unwarranted we shall find ourselves in danger of placing our Lord and His apostles themselves, if reasoning be consistent, under criticism!

It is acknowledged, however, that types and shadows have their spiritual complement in Christ and His church. The real differences concern the predictive element in Scripture. It is recognized, of course, that many examples of spiritualizing intention are not written in the form of direct prediction. They were ordinances and provisions of God for His people of old time, having literal importance and obligation for them. They contained in themselves the selected and suitable representation of spiritual things to come. They were types of a futuristic nature, awaiting the predicted advent of the Messiah Redeemer. They served an appointed purpose in the economy of God unto the well-being

of His people while observed according to His laws.
But they were a foreshadowing of future events of
a spiritual and evangelical nature, and for this
reason any infringement of regulations was met
with censure. If what is historical. being also typical had this spiritual complement in view, may not
prediction also be expected to have spiritual fulfilment?

A precious illustration of what God said in prediction and what He meant in fulfilment is found
on the first page of the New Testament.

Isaiah's prophecy of the Incarnate Messiah, the
virgin's Son, is quite definite as to His name: "Thou
O virgin shall call His name Immanuel" (mg),
which name is repeated to inspire confidence when
combined enemies were challenged to defeat the
purpose of God: impossible, indeed, "because of
Immanuel" to appear in "Immanuel's land" (Isa.
8:8-10). It is here declared that whereas Immanuel
would be "a stone of stumbling and a rock of
offence to both the houses of Israel" (the judgment
of Isa. 6:9-10) yet would He be as a sanctuary
to "disciples" separated unto Him whom alone He
acknowledges saying, "Behold I and the children
whom God hath given Me are for signs in Israel",
for these are they who "Set apart in their hearts
Christ as Lord" (see Rom. 9:33; Heb. 2:13; 1 Pet.
3:15). Such are acknowledged as God's people and
He is with them, hence Immanuel. Doubtless, when
God through Isaiah pronounced, "Thou shalt call
His name Immanuel" He meant what He said, and
the fulfilment at Bethlehem is recorded (Matt.
1:21). Yet "Jesus" and not "Immanuel" is the
name there divinely announced and given, while it
is affirmed that "all this was done that it might be
fulfilled which was spoken by the prophet, Isaiah,
they shall call His name Immanuel, which, being
interpreted is, God with us". Where is the sequence of precise literality here? Two different
titles are announced in the two Testaments, nor
are they synonymous in that they bear the same
significance. Isaiah is emphatic about Immanuel
and Matthew is emphatic about Jesus. Is not this
an example and an explanation of the fact that
whereas God meant what He said through Isaiah,

He did not then precisely explain what He meant? He meant what He said in Immanuel, but He said what He meant in Jesus. The prophet said His name should be Immanuel because that name would indicate the presence of God with His people and all the deep meaning that such presence would hold, the ultimate and eternal fellowship. The evangelist says His name shall be Jesus, because in Him His people would be saved from their sins, the immediate and essential condition. The holy presence cannot be with a sinful people, but a people saved from sin are assured of that presence. His name is both Immanuel and Jesus, and Jesus is the realization of Immanuel.

Leaven is a physical commodity used in bread making, but the New Testament uses it of doctrine, thus spiritualizing a material substance about which there is nothing of mysticism or vaporism unless doctrine or morality be so regarded. By the apostle leaven is spiritualized as malice and apostasy (1 Cor. 5:8; Gal. 5:9) and the church is warned because of its permeating nature. When the Lord Jesus warned His literalist disciples to beware of the leaven of the Pharisees and Sadducees, they could think only of bread possibly overlooked, but He remonstrated that their faith, not bread, was lacking, for in such event He could remedy the deficiency by His creative power, as He reminded them (Matt. 16:6). When the Lord charged Israel to beware of leaven in their feast — a memorial, not necessarily of evil but of their having been redeemed from Egypt in haste (Ex. 12:39; Deut. 16:3) for the permeating process of leaven required time — He meant what He said and they searched their dwellings when they kept the feast. But in Christ's warning it was explained that by leaven spiritualized He meant evil doctrine and conduct in their permeating influence. In whatever manner the parable of the woman hiding leaven may be understood, whether of evil corrupting Christendom or the Gospel spreading throughout the world, the same idea of a spiritual or moral entity is intended, a slow process whether of good or of evil (Matt. 13:13). God's meaning is moral and spiritual.

Similarly the Lord reminded the sceptical generation of His time that God gave their fathers in the wilderness bread from heaven, manna, which sustained them physically and temporarily only, and they knew it to have been a historical and literal experience. God meant what He said through Moses, "I will rain bread from heaven for you". But not until the fulness of time arrived when God sent forth His Son was the spiritual meaning made clear; although Moses had anticipated it when he said: Man doth not live by bread only but by every word of God". These followers of His exposed themselves as still hardened literalists who could not accept the truth that He in His sacrificial ministry was to be their spiritual sustenance through faith, that He was Himself the real bread which came down from heaven — bread symbolized also in His recent miracle of the wilderness by His own miraculous multiplication by which He admonished them: "Labour not for the meat which perisheth (the literal) but for that meat which endureth unto life eternal (the spiritual) which the Son of Man shall give unto you" (John 6:27). Thus it was that the natural and literal experiences of Israel's history had their spiritual counterpart in the person of the Lord Jesus Christ, and from the typical literalness He directed to the spiritual realities. In this manner are we not guided to look beyond the "shadows" of what God said, literal though they were, to the "good things to come", the spiritual substance explaining what God meant, comprehended in our Lord Jesus Christ?

In the historical record concerning Abraham and Sarah and Hagar and Isaac and Ishmael and Sinai and Jerusalem, all may identify the actual persons and places about which God spoke. Yet it was not until He gave the Spirit of illumination to His apostles that they explained how God designed in these a spiritual allegory (Gal. 4:22-31). He meant what He said in all the historical associations and experiences, but He did not say what He meant until Paul was inspired to write: "These are the two covenants, the one from Mount Sinai which is Hagar, for this Hagar is Mount Sinai in Arabia, and answereth to (is in the same rank with) Jerusalem which now is" historically associated with David and not with Abraham and Moses, thus uniting the Patriarchs, the Law and the Kingdom in the divine spiritual meaning; and we learn that the Mosaic covenant was intended and foreshadowed in the events of Abraham's life. However, there is no mention of any future restored exalted rank for Jerusalem; she represents the bondage of the law. The only means of release is of higher origin, a spiritual birth from above of which the Lord had earlier spoken to Nicodemus (John 3), for "Jerusalem which is above is free and is the mother of us all". What a comprehensive commentary is this in which the apostle reasons that from Abraham the progenitor of the nation, throughout the earthly kingdom of Israel represented by Jerusalem, there is not nor can there be any emancipation from the bondage occasioned by sin and the condemnation of the law, save through the Gospel of the Lord Jesus, the word of God by which sinners are born anew (1 Pet. 1:23). This then is the inspired allegory, the spiritualization of Old Testament persons, places and events — one thing being spoken and actual, the literal; and a different thing being meant, the spiritual, of which the literal is the emblem or representation.

A remarkably emphatic example of spiritualization is given in Paul's conception of a Mosaic commandment. He has no compunction about it, there is no forcing of terms, no fancifulness attaching to his understanding and interpretation of the intention of Moses' injunction addressed to the nation of Israel, though Paul transferred the divine objective from Israel to the Church. He even asserts that so far from his conveniently applying an Israelitish provision which suited his purpose, God illustrated in the literal Mosaic appointment for Israel a spiritual principle intended for the Church (1 Cor. 9: 7-8). "It is written in the law of Moses, Thou shalt not muzzle the ox that treadeth out the corn." Did God mean what He said? Of course He cared for oxen as for all His creatures, and the Israel farmer respected the injunction so that the unmuzzled ox ate the corn (Deut. 25:4). But, Paul asked, "Doth God take care for oxen, or saith He it altogether for our sakes?" And his answer is emphatic: "For our sakes, no doubt, this is written", that is, written by Moses in the Law of Israel, for God meant what He said about the oxen, but intended for the Church as interpreted by the apostle, through whom God said what He meant. Even then in Moses' day and in Israel's industry God had in mind and in meaning the ministers of His Gospel. It is *altogether* thus says Paul. There is *no doubt* about it, he says. "It is written" by Moses, but "for our sakes". And thereupon Paul spiritualizes the ploughing, and sowing and threshing and reaping, the whole literal process. So that although God meant what He said about oxen ploughing when Israel farmed, His spiritual meaning, then undisclosed, awaited the inauguration of the New Testament Church to and for which the apostle was inspired to explain what God meant.

Does not this example of the unforced and spontaneous apostolic understanding of the Old Testament, and the relation of both Testaments, instruct us concerning the principle that the ordered temporal economy of Israel had in view the higher spiritual calling of the Church; that Moses and the Prophets ministered for the sake of the Lord and His Apostles; that whereas the revelation of God in the former was in things substantial and of the earth, they were nevertheless designedly selected as a guide in things spiritual?

"Now all these things happened unto them for ensamples, and they are written for our admonition upon whom the ends of the world are come" (1 Cor. 10). This verse, and others like it, bear convincing witness to this principle. The things which *happened* unto Israel from the time of the nation's inception by redemption from Egypt's bondage onwards did not occur fortuitously. They were types of divine intent (v. 6). They were patterns prepared objectively by the Designer. So intimate is the relation between the figure and the reality that the context actually describes Israel in the wilderness as receiving in the manna "spiritual meat", and in the water "spiritual drink", from "that spiritual rock",

and he emphatically says "that Rock was Christ".
This course of Israel's history, then, was not considered after the events, as an afterthought found suitable for Christian application — like an observant preacher may light upon some "happenings" as convenient illustrations for a sermon — but all took place according to plan, and not only for the benefit of those involved at the time, but for the edification of the Church of the New Testament "upon whom the ends of the world are come", the goal of God's purpose, the Church in which all believers from the beginning of time are incorporated (Heb. 11:39-40), the one body "where there is neither Greek nor Jew, but Christ is all and in all" (Col. 3:11), the "eternal purpose which He purposed in Christ Jesus", toward the accomplishment of which He providentially directs and administers all events. Further, it is stated that when these "happenings" were recorded in the Scriptures they "were written" by divine prescription "for our admonition" — they were written for the future. So that the events occurrent in Israel and recorded in the Scriptures, what God said and did in Israel, were for the sake of the Church in this age of the Gospel.

This is supported by similar testimonies. "Whatsoever things were written aforetime were written for our learning" (Rom. 15:4). The embrace is inclusive, nothing in the Old Testament is excluded here. "Whatsoever" allows no distinction between types, psalms, prophecies, all is for the benefit of the Church, "that we through patience and comfort of the scriptures might have hope". From a single prediction about the sufferings of Christ (v. 3) the apostle enlarged upon this general declaration: "Whatsoever things were written aforetime" are for believers now.

Similarly the Apostle Peter writes of the ministry of the Prophets. Their subject, he says, was "the sufferings of Christ and the glory that should follow" (or glories, plural of majesty). These they testified beforehand by the Spirit of Christ Who was in them. Their writings which concerned our salvation by grace and the manner of time signified by the Spirit, that is, how and when this should be accomplished, they afterwards diligently searched. For it was revealed to them that their ministry was not to their own but to a future generation. But not however, a millennial future beyond the calling of the Church, but now to those to whom the Gospel is preached "with the Holy Ghost sent down from heaven", that is to the generations from the enduement of the Spirit at Pentecost, to the Church which Christ now glorified will present to Himself.

He had Himself graciously rebuked the tardy faith of some when expounding Moses and the prophets saying, "Ought not the Messiah to have suffered these things and to enter into His glory?" and may not Peter have had this in mind (1 Pet. 1:12; Luke 24)? How clear it seems, then, from these several witnesses that while God spake all these words by His prophets, and meant what He said, it was reserved for His apostles to say what He meant. The Spirit of Christ inspired both the Scriptures of the prophets and their sense as explained by the apostles; and because the Spirit of *Christ* testified of Christ in Israel's prophets, it were more according to truth to describe the Old Testament Scriptures as "Christian" rather than "Jewish". They were not of Jewish origination though the Jews were advantaged in that the oracles of God were committed unto them (Rom. 3); their Author was "the Spirit of *Christ*". The New Testament also is the "Word of Christ" which came unto the Church and is not of her origination (1 Cor. 14:36). No prophecy is of the prophet's own unfolding but of the Spirit (2 Pet. 1:19). And because the Lord Jesus Christ is the one Mediator Whose Spirit does not speak from Himself but take of the things of Christ, whether they be things already written in the older Scriptures or things (then) to come, therefore, He, the Lord Jesus Christ, is rightly the Author and Finisher of the entire Scriptures. "The testimony of Jesus is the Spirit of prophecy" (Rev. 19:10).

When God chose and called the people of Israel He did so because He would make them His instruments. Two advantages were theirs—they were the custodians of the Scriptures, for "unto them were committed the oracles of God", and "of them, as concerning the flesh, the Christ came, Who is over all God, blessed forever" (Rom. 3 and 9). Israel left to herself, reverted to type; she went back to Paganism. When God hid His face from them, what did they but copy the idolatries and immoralities of the nations around, importing paganism into their own land and corrupting the pure religion of Moses? This was abomination to the Lord, and this was "Jewish". But God's pure Word committed to Israel of which they were the custodians, and the later Scriptures committed to the Church have been preserved by His superintending providence amidst all the vicissitudes of both Israel and the Church by the same Spirit Who originally gave them by His inspiration.

These Testaments are complementary. In the former, God meant what He said, and "every transgression and disobedience received a just recompense of reward" (Heb. 2), for in diverse manners they forecast the Christ and the predictive type must not be marred. In the latter, God said what He meant, for, to quote Dr. Charles Hodge of Princeton: "The quotations given in the New Testament from the Old Testament are not *mere* quotations, but authoritative expositions. The apostles, in their use of Old Testament passages, tell us what the Holy Spirit *meant*".

THE DIVINE ORDER:
FIRST THE NATURAL
AFTERWARDS THE
SPIRITUAL

HOLY Scripture, the written Word of God, was given for spiritual purposes. Even the record of the material creation is no exception for "by faith we understand that the worlds were framed by the word of God, so that things which are seen were not made of things which do appear" (Heb. 11:3). Faith is a God-given spiritual quality. It is described as "the faith of God's elect" and "precious." By it we perceive the fact of the world's creation by God, though we saw neither Him nor the acts of creation as described in the first chapter in the Bible. The same Word by which the worlds were prepared is that by means of which faith is conveyed (Rom. 10:17). The Creator Himself is unseen. Moses endured "as seeing Him Who is invisible". "God is a Spirit". First in the created universe and fully in His incarnate Son He was revealed. "No man hath seen God at any time; the only-begotten Son Who is in the bosom of the Father, He hath declared Him" (John 1:18). Hence He said, "He that hath seen Me hath seen the Father" and "No man cometh unto the Father but by Me." But the physical universe itself is a partial disclosure of the invisible Creator, "for the invisible things of Him from the creation of the world are clearly seen, being understood by the things that are made, even His eternal power and godhead" (Rom. 1:20). Both origin and objective are spiritual.

Are we not, therefore, introduced to a spiritual intention at the very opening of the Scriptures? The record itself is historically and scientifically accurate, yet it was written subsequent to the ruination occasioned by the Fall and the entrance of sin. We may believe, therefore, that it was written with a view to salvation, and is, with the rest of Scripture, spiritually profitable (2 Tim. 3:15-17). The Redeemer, Who also was the Creator, we read, "was foreordained before the foundation of the world but was manifest in these last times" (1 Pet. 1:20). "The Spirit moved" as indeed He does when the spiritually dead are quickened; and the commanding word of the first day had in view the initial spiritual illumination in the new creation (2 Cor. 5:17; 4:6; John 1:4-5). Adam himself was a "figure of Him that was to come", the last Adam, (Rom. 5:14). Christ was to come, therefore was Adam so created, even as the reality at least in purpose precedes the figure. There can be no figure or type or model without the reality. The last Adam was no afterthought; He was the first and last. And the dominion with which Adam was invested prefigured the universal authority of Christ the Redeemer (Ps. 8; Heb. 2). The very words used at the uniting of Adam and Eve which might convey nothing but a natural sense, the apostle uses of a spiritual union, saying, "This is a great mystery, but I speak concerning Christ and the Church". (Gen. 2:24; Eph. 5:31); while the words, "Let us make man in our image, after our likeness" cannot but forecast the ultimate in redemption when we shall be "conformed to the image of His Son", and seeing Him, "shall be like Him", and even "the body of our humiliation shall be fashioned like unto His glorious body" (Rom. 8; 1 John 3; Phil. 3). Moreover, the expectation of believers will be realized in the new heavens and the new earth, for the habitation of which, doubtless, they, the new creation, are destined. The Sabbath rest, wherein God rested from all His works, beholding them "very good", pointed forward to the "rest that remaineth" over and beyond "to the people of God"; a rest into which neither the people under Moses or Joshua or David did enter, but is theirs who believe the Gospel of Christ Jesus, for "we who believe do enter into rest" (Heb. 4). These spiritual and eternal benefits are obtained through the conflict and triumph of the Seed of the woman, announced in the first prophecy, Who by His death and resurrection "bruised the serpent's head", (John 12:31; Col. 2:15; Heb. 2:14). These initial Biblical chapters, therefore, are for spiritual purposes, and are designed to direct us by the divine record of the material creation to a new creation, spiritual and eternal, through the redemption which is in Christ Jesus.

We may understand, therefore, that literal existences created and ordered in the divine activity are themselves intended to serve spiritual ends, and that there is a purposed sequence as when it is written, "That was not first which is spiritual, but that which is natural; and afterward that which is spiritual" (1 Cor. 15:46). It has been well said that error is truth pressed too far, which would indeed apply to some forms of what is called spiritualizing, or fancifulness. On the other hand, is there not a danger of pressing too far when literalizers extend the succession beyond the stated spiritual terminal of fulfilment? For this interpretation would appear to require a revision or addition, thus: First that which is natural; afterward that which is spiritual, but again, after that which is spiritual has come, a reintroduction of that which is natural or literal. Does not the "afterward" denote the arrival of finality and permanency with the spiritual? Thus it is with the earthly and heavenly things of which our Lord spoke; and with the natural and spiritual birth (John 3).

The argument that persons, places, events, within the divine plan, which have appeared in the first instance in natural or literal form, being again spoken of futuristically, must have a repeated natural subsistence, is no sound premise in the light of the order of succession quoted above. In this eschatological chapter the statement appears to explain the principle of divine design. Throughout the apostle's argument there is no suggestion that a reversion to the natural state of things following the spiritual is to be expected. We notice, for instance, the first Adam and the last Adam; the first man and the second Man; Christ the resurrection firstfruits and they that are His; the natural body and the spiritual body, the earthly and the heavenly; corruption and incorruption; mortality and immortality; this life and the life to come; death and victory; with no reappearance of the former either in a millennial age or the eternal state (1 Cor. 15). Very generally in Scripture we come upon this balancing or placement of opposites, such as The First and the Last; the Beginning and the End; this world and the world to come; the time past and the last days; the old covenant and the new covenant; take away the first and establish the second; glory done away and glory that excelleth; one man's disobedience and the obedience of One; the law of works and the law of faith; the curse incurred and the curse removed; the law by Moses and grace and truth by Jesus Christ; Israel after the flesh and the Israel of God; born of the flesh and born of the Spirit; the letter killeth but the Spirit giveth life; the ministry of condemnation and the ministry of righteousness; the reign of sin and death and the reign of grace through righteousness unto eternal life; the heavens and earth which are now and the new heavens and new earth.

There are spiritual existences as well as natural, and we find them described in the very same terms. The original creation record, for instance, has been shown to anticipate the new creation, agreeable to the principle that Adam, the crown of God's creation, was "the figure of Him that was to come", in and for Whom all creation exists (Rev. 4:11). Is it not, therefore, a reasonable subject for enquiry, not to be repulsed by superficial literalizers as spiritualizing, whether persons, places and events, in God's historical revelation, as Canaan, Jerusalem, Zion, Israel, David, the Priesthood, the Temple, the Throne, the Kingdom, the Reign, etc., may not be intentionally invested with a spiritual or spiritualized meaning and with finality, though natural and literal in their original existence; and especially in view of the fact that the context of these futuristic references in the Old Testament is evangelical, and largely in symbolical terms, and in the New Testament by quotation and adaptation they are so employed?

In support of the protest against spiritualizing it is said: "Scripture must be taken literally; at the same time every scripture has a spiritual meaning: God's literal is spiritual" and "the farthest from the literal is usually the worst". This is not the case if a "literal" is intended in the natural sense of the text above, for there it is distinguished from the spiritual. Of course, every true preacher of the Word of God will seek for the spiritual meaning, otherwise how could his hearers be profited? Divine truth devoid of spiritual energy is impotent. The contention here, however, is otherwise. It is that while spiritual lessons may be drawn or illustrations found, the literal still remains to be re-introduced into this world in tangible material form; a reinstitution of the past, though, perhaps, with additional accompaniments not originally present; the natural temporarily ennobled, not the spiritual eternally established; the promises materially fulfilled to the Jews in a re-established earthly kingdom in a world of carnal satisfaction, after the Church has received the spiritual complement of those promises and the Lord Jesus shall have appeared the second time without sin unto salvation.

Accordingly it is reasoned that promises and blessings named predictively in the Old Testament, suited for evangelical illustration, are but their *application* in this present age of the church, but awaiting their *fulfilment* realistically in a millennial age to come. The spiritual complement which the Scripture says supersedes the natural, and the spiritual application deduced from it, are, therefore, to give place to the natural and literal once again. This lacks New Testament support both in direct teaching and in principle, and renders void the text and its context above (1 Cor. 15). This method of "accommodation" is also fraught with danger. Modern Criticism, for example, explains away New Testament "fulfilment" of Old Testament prediction by this use of "application". The words of Isaiah are to be "applied" to the birth of Jesus, whereas Matthew used the word "fulfilled". In like manner the critics regard fulfilled prophecies generally — the New Testament writer found a convenient Old Testament statement and *applied* it to his case! Should not this kind of accommodation be avoided, and the "fulfilment" be accepted, rather than an "application" now but an allied fulfilment later?

As an example, reference may here be made to the New Covenant which, it is said, is *applied* to the Christian Church in the Epistle to the Hebrews but will be fulfilled to Israel and Judah in the Millennium!

Notwithstanding the fact that Biblically recorded history of Israel is the ground of Gospel doctrine, quotations and references abounding in the New Testament where Moses and the Prophets are appealed to as the authority showing the natural superseded by the spiritual, it is averred that after this, when the Church shall have entered upon her heavenly state in glory, there will be a reintroduction in this world of what the NT describes as "the beggarly elements"; when "that which is perfect is come" a returning to "that which is in part"; when "the true light shineth" the "shadows" are to fall again; when God shall have established the "better" a retrogression to the "beginnings"; instead of a going on unto maturity a laying again of the foundations; when the "true" has arrived a reinstatement of the "figures". It is written, however, as of finality: "He *taketh away* the first that He may *establish* the second" (Heb. 10:9, see also 9:9, 10). As Dr. T. T. Shields remarked, "God does not walk backwards." And Paul wrote, Thus to build again is transgression (Gal. 2).

Another criticism of spiritualization is this: "Even if figurative language is used, what is thus figured will be literally fulfilled." Does literally here mean materially? It would be more in keeping with Scripture to say that what is figured will be spiritually fulfilled, for the figures themselves are the substantial objects. It should be noted that spiritualization is found in the OT.; the prophets, for instance, thus interpreted Moses. Thus it was with the temporal redemption of Israel from Egypt and the consequent commemorative institution and its spiritual complement. And so the Old Testament supplies a key to New Testament spiritualization from the nation's beginning; for example, Israel's enemies, those very substantial enemies of Pharaoh and his hosts, literally drowned in the waters, represented their sins and iniquities overwhelmed in oblivion by a pardoning God. Here is an undoubted case where physical experience in history had a spiritual design and fulfilment through the Gospel. (Micah, 7:18-20). Moreover, the introduction to this spiritual evangelical object is given in the words: "According to the days of thy coming out of the land of Egypt will I show unto him marvellous things". Marvellous things indeed, for as the prophet exclaimed, "Who is a God like unto Thee that *pardoneth* iniquity, and *passeth by* the transgression of the remnant of His heritage". The very terms used of the literal event of the exodus are here given a spiritual meaning. This, therefore, may also be the significance of "the second time" in the passage by the evangelical Isaiah. The second deliverance may be spiritual through the Gospel with Messiah's rest in glory (Isaiah 11:10, 11; cf. Isa. 61; Luke 4: Rom. 15:12).

Thus it is also with Israel's annual feasts forecasting redemption in Christ Jesus. They receive in the New Testament a Gospel fulfilment. It is evident that three of these were especially important (Deut. 16:16; Lev. 23). It is further evident that with a marked precision as to time the fulfilment may be observed. Passover, Firstfruits, Pentecost it is recognized were spiritually answered in Christ's death and resurrection and the enduement of the Holy Spirit, the Gospel and the Church. And therefore Trumpets, Atonement and Tabernacles likewise and consistently share this fulfilment. For "the trumpet of the gospel sounds with an inviting voice", and the blessings of the Atonement are ours through penitence and faith, while Tabernacles representing the wilderness provisions is fulfilled in Gospel benefits through the Spirit upon Christ's glorification. While the first three of these Feasts of Jehovah are acknowledged to have received their spiritual implementation, is it consistent to suppose that those remaining which complete the Redemptive programme await the millennium, and a reinstitution after the original literal fashion? This not only mars the continuity and the spiritual principle, but fails to recognize the New Testament declaration of our Lord and the later explanation given by the Spirit.

The realization, historically prefigured in the events of the wilderness, is to be found in Christ by faith. It was when this final feast of the year was observed in our Lord's time that He delayed until the "last day", the "great day", that is, the eighth day, and cried "If any man thirst, let him come to me and drink". For the people in their ceremonialism had commemorated the water given from the smitten rock (Ex. 17; 1 Cor. 10) to the chanting of Isa. 12, and the pouring out of the water from the golden pitcher filled from the pool of Siloam. The waters of the earth had failed, the carnal could not satisfy, and they were spiritually thirsty still. And amidst the illuminations from the candelabra commemorating the Shekinah light the Pillar of Fire, which led them in their journeyings, the Lord Jesus added, "I am the light of the world: he that followeth Me shall not walk in darkness but shall have the light of life" (John 7:37, 39; 8:12). This was the last of the Annual Feasts, and of its spiritual fulfilment the apostle wrote: "This spake Jesus of the Spirit which they that believe on Him should receive; for the Holy Spirit was not yet then given because that Jesus was not yet glorified" (John 7:39).

This final feast of the year is the memorial of wilderness supplies until the Canaan settlement (and was observed in the land for Canaan herself also was typical). It befits the pilgrim church until her Lord returns to receive her to Himself. Language could not be more decisive in determining the meaning, that the fulfilment is not millennial and Jewish and in the future, but evangelical and Christian in this present time.

At the very consummation of divine revelation, concerning the city which John saw descending out of heaven from God, figuratively displaying the glory of the bride the Lamb's wife, it will be observed that what is thus figured will be spiritually realized. Or, since what is figured here is the bride of the Lamb, is she expected to be a literal bride? Or does not this represent a spiritual relationship beyond all human capacity to imagine, and which being heavenly is not of the earth, but exceedingly surpassing all that is known or can be known in this world? Hence the prodigious dimensions, glory and general description of the city and the Lamb Himself, Who is "all the glory of Immanuel's land." It may be answered, therefore, that "the farthest from the literal is the best."

"In form", writes Dr. Albertus Pieters, "prediction and fulfilment are diverse, in essence they are the same. This principle applies to the New Testament no less than the Old. We are promised eternal life in heaven, and to make us realize it we read of many mansions, of white raiment, of harps of gold, of a river of life to quench our thirst, of the fruit of the tree of life for food, of medicinal leaves of healing, of golden streets, and a heavenly city that has a wall and twelve gates. Such things are needed to convey to us the purpose of God to supply every need and to cause us to dwell in perfect peace and safety, but in what form the reality will be enjoyed we cannot tell, because we do not know what our situation and needs will be in the disembodied state, or after the soul has been reunited to the body in resurrection. Only we do know that whatever such things would mean to us now, of abundant provision, perfect security and glorious existence, shall be fulfilled, and more than fulfilled".

WORLD, AGE, DISPENSATION, TIMES

IN the usage of Scripture we come upon futuristic terms such as "the latter days" in the Old Testament and "the last days" in the New Testament. We also meet with "the fulness of the times", "dispensation", and descriptions of human habitation as "world", and "age" (usually translated in the A.V. "world"). The significance and application of such expressions are used sometimes with an emphasis of differentiation, in setting forth different theories respecting the second coming of Christ and related events, both antecedent and consequent. Knowledge of the origin and use, as well as the distinguishing dictionary meaning of Scripture terms, which we choose to apply to eschatological subjects, as all will concede, is not without importance.

The researches and findings of Dr. Gerhardus Vos as given in his book *"The Pauline Eschatology"* are a rewarding contribution to this great subject. He has very carefully surveyed and examined all instances of the occurrence of such terms in the Scriptures. "Eschatology", he begins "is the doctrine of the last things. It deals with the teaching or belief that the world movement, religiously considered tends towards a definite, final goal, beyond which a new order of affairs will be established; frequently with the further implication that this new order of affairs will not be subject to any further change, but will partake of the static character of the eternal". The book should be studied; the subject is involved, but a few quotations and conclusions may be of service.

"The latter days" is applied to space as well as to time in the sense of 'the hindmost part'. An example of the application to space is 'the uttermost parts of the sea' (Ps. 139:9). Applied to time, it would proximately signify, 'the farthermost parts of the days'. The note of epochal finality is never missing in it. The idea is elastic as to its extent, no less than movable as to its position. The principal question is whether the static outcome, the permanent state of blessedness predicted, is actually included sometimes at least, in the latter days. If so, then this would extend it indefinitely; in fact, render it synonymous with what the New Testament considers the state of eternity, although, of course, the language of time would still be employed to describe it. While generally the term deals with the fortunes and destinies of the people, a possible exception is that of Balaam (Numb. 23:10) where 'my last end' refers to the death of the righteous person, and, therefore, to the future after death (compare the reverse in 2 Sam. 2:26). The term covers the resulting permanent eschatological estate."

Referring to the significance of "last" (the last days in the New Testament) we read: "Most significant is the designation of Christ as 'the last Adam' (1 Cor. 15:45), the fountain-head of the resurrection, a quickening Spirit, of heaven and heavenly, all this referring to the final celestial state and the conditions pertaining thereto. As backward of the first Adam there was no other, so forward of the last Adam there is none other." Would not this same significance, therefore, attach to the qualifying "last" wherever used, in respect of days, time, hour, trumpet, enemy, etc. allowing for none other succeeding of the thing described?

It is shown that 'age' (aion) and 'world' (kosmos) are used of space as well as time. "As is well known these languages (the Hebrew or the Aramaic vernacular) originally possessed no word for 'world' (compare Gen. 1:1, 'the heavens and the earth'). In later times, through the contact with and influence of other languages and modes of thought, it was found necessary to employ a single word for the concept of 'the world'. The word that entered into this vacant place of speech was a *time*-designation. The choice of precisely this word for that particular use cannot have been purely arbitrary; there must have been some reason in the *time*-meaning that invited the transition to the *world* meaning. Belief in a fixed nature and a temporal duration of the present order of things is inherent in the 'aion' (age) where it inclines to pass over from the time into the world category. From that point on an age and a world had become so closely cognate as to be well-nigh inseparable, both being expressible by the same word. Originally a pure time-concept 'age' now became an all-comprehensive space concept as well. *'Aion'* may mean 'age' in the New Testament, and it may mean 'world'. In some cases the sense may be difficult, in other cases the sense 'world' is unmistakable. 'Aion' in its time sense stood in the Semitic idiom not seldom in the plural because the concept was subject to pluralization for the sake of stressing endlessness or plurality. In Jewish and Christian literature *'aion'* was made to render double service for 'age' and 'world', traces of which are discoverable with Paul (e.g. Rom. 12:2; 1 Cor. 2:6-8; 3:18; 2 Cor. 4:4; Gal. 1:4; 1 Tim. 6: 17). The A.V. has rendered *'aion'* everywhere by 'world' except Eph. 2:2 where *'aion'* and *'kosmos'* occur together in the same phrase, 'the course of this world'. (Walking according to the temporal nature of this world, rather than of eternity?) The reference 'foundation of the age' for 'foundation of the world' would yield no sense".

Dr. J. Norval Gildenhuys makes this remark: "In Rabbinic literature we often come across the expressions, 'this age' and 'the age to come'. The typical Johannine phrase, 'eternal life' actually means 'life of the age' (the coming age), and thus points to the life that is suitable to the age, the life of those who share in the coming age. Just as 'kingdom of God' is spoken of sometimes as a present fact and sometimes as something whose final manifestation lies in the future, so also is eternal life used with this double connotation, although the final consummation lies in the future; the age to come has already come in and through the Lord Jesus Christ, those who are united to Him in faith and love already possess the life eternal belonging to the final age. Eternal life is sometimes used as a synonym for the kingdom of God (compare Matt. 19:17; Mark 9:43-47)."

Dr. Vos remarks: "There is no place in the apostle's scheme for an earthly provisional kingdom of the Messiah. The great powers to be destroyed are sin and death, the victory to be won over them proceeds from grace and life. The proximate fruit of the ripening Christian experience consists in such hope as does not put to shame, inasmuch as the foretaste of the life to come is shed abroad in the believer's heart through the preliminary gift of the Holy Spirit (Rom. 5:4). The Christian is saved upon the basis of hope, for hope and the things upon which it terminates constitute the supreme goal of salvation (Rom. 8:24). The pre-Christian pagan state is characterized by the absence of God and of hope—the blessed hope and appearing of our great God and Saviour Jesus Christ, the hope of eternal life (Tit. 2:13; Tit. 3:7). The antithesis is between a world (age) that is and a world (age) that is to come."

In pursuance of dispensational teaching a difference is stressed between these terms which it would appear is not supported. The promised presence of the Lord in His commission is given emphasis as "I am with you even unto the end of the age," so differentiating between the material world and its temporal form. That is to say, according to this view, the end of the age brings us to that point of time when, the Church's world-wide mission finished, the Lord Jesus will return to establish His millennial kingdom, or "the age to come". The material world, therefore, is said to continue beyond the present age, and would incorporate the age to come, thereafter giving place to the new creation of heaven and earth or the eternal state. Thus the world, so understood, would cover at least two ages, whereas the examination (above referred to) would show that these are interchangeable terms for the selfsame subject, giving different aspects of the same thing, the world in its material and its temporal form. The present evil age, therefore, continues until the new creation, and the age to come, or in its pluralization, ages to come, describe eternity.

In common usage the term *dispensation* is applied to periods of time, the duration being determined by characteristics or events related to the mode of divine revelation and government. The Scofield Reference Bible proposes, evidently based on a numerical theory, seven successive dispensations of human history, five past, one present, and another to come, whereupon time shall be no more. Generally, however, it suffices to recognize two distinctions only, and upon these the Scriptures seem clear; namely, law and grace, broadly coincident with the Old and New Testaments, as when it is written: "the law was given by Moses but grace and truth came by Jesus Christ". Even so, the advent of the Lord Jesus Christ did not annul the law but fulfilled it. The word translated 'dispensation' might preferably be understood better by 'administration' or stewardship (compare Isa. 22:19; 1 Cor. 9:17), the principles of divine administration being as immutable as God Himself. Divine government, therefore, is not determined by time boundaries; we cannot say that the administration of the law ceased with the coming of Christ, or that grace was not sovereignly in exercise before His advent. Grace was shown to Abraham, to whom also the Gospel was preached (Gal. 3:8) and so to others who "waited for the consolation of Israel"; while the law is still operative against sin of all kinds, and is in accord with the ministry of the Gospel (1 Tim. 1:9-11). "By the law is the knowledge of sin" and even believers are "under the law to Christ." Dispensation, therefore, might more accurately signify operation than duration.

An instance of the occurence of dispensation, relevant to our subject, is found in Eph. 1:10, where, it would seem, the substitution of 'administration' would better suit the meaning of the verse. In His administration of "the eternal purpose which He purposed in Christ Jesus", embracing the heavens and the earth, God will bring into ultimate unity a world now dismembered through sin. The qualifying word is "in Christ", for He is Head of the redeemed and renewed race, and also of the universe for He is head of all principality and power. This, His good pleasure, is purposed in Himself (9) ; its realization is not in any wise contingent upon the assent or activity of angels or men: He is Himself the Operator, and blessed indeed are they who "have obtained an inheritance in Him" (11).

Dr. Charles Hodge favours the sense of 'economy' in this passage. Dispensation, therefore, as so loosely used, does not befit this passage as does 'administration' or 'economy,' either of which supposes and necessitates the sovereign achievement of the Lord Himself. "The expressions", says Dr. Hodge, " 'ends of the ages' (1 Cor. 10:11), 'end of days' (Heb. 1:2) 'fulness of the time' (Gal. 4:4) and 'fulness of times' (Eph. 1:10), are all used to designate the time of Christ's advent. By 'the economy of the fulness of time' is, therefore, to be understood that economy which was to be clearly revealed and carried out when the 'fulness of time' had come".

The fulness of times, therefore, covers the period of history between the first and second advents of Christ. Its administration is the operation of God in grace and in providence, or, in the terms of the context, "in all wisdom and prudence", whereby in His perfect knowledge and management of affairs, He shall have comprehended all things in Christ under His supreme headship. All, then, is moving onward to the final consummation when the redeemed race, the church, meet for the habitation of new heavens and earth in which righteousness will dwell, which are her expectation (2 Pet. 3:13), will be displayed as "the fulness of Him Who filleth all in all" (Eph. 1:23). Beyond the fulness of times is eternity.

In accord with this objective, and in confirmation of the present rather than an alleged future time-dispensation being the fulness of time, is the passage on the virgin birth of Christ (Gal. 4:4). Here it is written, "when the fulness of time was come"; that is, following upon the earlier legal times of preparation, as the context explains, the fulness of time entered by God sending forth His Son to redeem. The fulness here indicates the introduction with the Redeemer's advent of the present and final administration of God in time, upon completion to give place to the eternal state, the ages to come. "The fulness of time", says Dr. Vos "has nothing to do with the 'ripeness of the times'; it designates the arrival of the present dispensation of time at its predetermined goal of fulfilment through the appearance of the Messiah".

A further expression is used by Peter in Acts 3:21; namely, "the times of restitution". Is this restitution to be made during an earthly millennial reign of the Messiah, or are these "times" proceeding now, the risen Lord exercising "all authority in heaven and in earth" as He declared to be His prerogative, "angels and authorities and powers being made subject unto Him" Who "is able to subdue all things unto Himself"? The answer here is governed by the word "until" which denotes that *during* these times the Lord Jesus will remain in the heavens, having been there "received" upon His ascension, to the right hand of the majesty on high. This is the context. "Until", according to the lexicon, carries the meaning of, "continuedly, fixing attention upon the whole duration". Dr. E. Henderson in his work on the prophet Ezekiel says, "To this rule He was predestined, and if Israel failed to enjoy as a people the benefits of His government in the blessings of the new covenant, it was because they rejected His great salvation. The reign here and elsewhere predicted was not to be earthly and temporal but spiritual, on the throne of David in the spiritual world. Compare 2 Sam. 7:16; Ps. 110:

1; and Acts 3:21, where 'until' is to be rendered 'during' ". The review that Jesus Christ will yet again be "sent" to "bring in these times" (see e.g. Scofield) contradicts the sense of the passage and ignores the force of 'until' which makes the times of restitution simultaneous with Christ's mediatorial session in heaven. He will come again not to introduce the restitution predicted by the prophets, but because He shall then have completed it.

The restitution is surely the remedying of the universal ravages of the Fall of the first Adam by the last Adam's redeeming victory. The theory that Peter's language conditioned the second coming of Christ and millennial seasons of refreshing upon the nation's repentance is not supported by this passage. Times of refreshing (19) will always accompany or follow true repentance, and this the Lord Jesus is *now* exalted, Prince and Saviour, in heaven to give (Acts 5:31). The promise "He shall *send* Jesus Christ" (20) must be understood in the light of Peter's own explanation in the context; namely, "God, having raised up His Son Jesus, *sent* Him to bless you in turning everyone of you away from his iniquities" (26). This sending of Jesus Christ, being postresurrection, cannot refer to His earthly ministry among them terminated by His cross, nor is it declared to be still in prospect, conditioned upon their repentance, but that which has occurred and is present. It is not an assurance that God will send the Messiah to restore the nation's political economy by His earthly reign over them, but an announcement of what has taken place under His exalted Saviourhood, to bless them by turning them from their iniquities. Israel He favoured with priority. "Unto you *first*, God, having *raised up* His Son Jesus, *sent Him* to bless you". It is not to His future personal return, therefore, that reference is made, but to the preaching of His apostles in the power of the Spirit, of whom our Lord in His promise, said "I will come to you" (John 14:18). This is not to confuse the coming of the Spirit with His personal second coming, but it is to recognize that in this spiritual sense of the Spirit's presence, Christ comes and is present, as indeed He promised (compare Matt. 28:20; 18:20).

Paul wrote in terms accordant with this in what is probably the most comprehensive statement of the universal and effective supremacy of the Lord Jesus Christ attained upon His ascension (Eph. 1:21-23), in ratification of His finished work in life and in death. "He *came* and preached peace," writes Paul, "to you which are afar off and to them that were nigh" (Eph. 2:17). When and how did or does the risen Redeemer come and preach but through His apostles whom He commissioned in His name, and by His Spirit? "For through Him we both have access by one Spirit unto the Father" is the next verse. In sending forth His apostles our Lord said, "As My Father hath sent Me, even so send I you", and "He that receiveth you receiveth Me." Magnifying their office, the apostolic ambassadors besought their hearers "in Christ's stead" and "as though God did beseech you by us" (2 Cor. 5).

Repentance is enjoined *so that* "times of refreshing may come from the presence of the Lord". Convenient or opportune seasons of refeshing would be a certain limited portion of the duration of the times of restitution (19-21) during which the heavens must receive the ascended Lord, Whose presence there in person is the source of spiritual refreshing here. To this "all the prophets witnessed" through whom "God *before* had showed that Christ should suffer", in which sense the following word, "which *before* was preached unto you" must be understood. To Israel Christ in His suffering for their sins was *before* preached even as God *before* revealed by the mouth of His prophets. And the sending of Jesus Christ to bless them after His resurrection is fulfilled in the preaching of Peter and the apostles. These "times of restitution" have been the subject of prophetic ministry "since the world began" (21).

The chosen language of Scripture attributes to the first advent of Christ a victory and glory more momentous than is ascribed to His second advent. Consider, for example, the embrace, the strength, the grandeur, of such passages as Eph. 1:19-23;

Col. 1:16-20; Phil. 2:6-11; Heb. 2:10-15. In another passage the apostle writes of the wisdom and princes of this world "that come to nought" (1 Cor. 2:6). It is to be noted that the time element in these words is simultaneous with that respecting other terms or statements considered above. When will He bring these princes and their wisdom to nought? The wisdom and power of Christ as having been crucified will accomplish this. It is not said that this negation awaits His second coming. The amazing fact is that even now, in consequence of His victory on Calvary and from the tomb, His opponents are being annulled unto eventual negation. They are thus being caused to cease and brought to an end —the princes of this world are *in process* of being brought to nought. When Christ gloriously returns it will indeed be to show the universal success of His administration (Eph. 1:10) and "Who is the blessed and only Potentate, the King of kings and Lord of lords . . . to Whom be honour and power everlasting" (1 Tim. 6:15-16).

THE WORLD TO COME

"**B**UT now, we see not yet all things put under Him" (Heb. 2:8). This testimony is as apposite today as to the apostles in their day. The total subjugation of the universe to Christ is not yet, but it is as certain as the complete salvation of His elect people. These both shall be His demonstrated accomplishments to be celebrated at His second coming. At His investiture the risen and ascended Son of Man "was given dominion and glory and a kingdom that all people, nations and languages should serve Him; His dominion is an everlasting dominion which shall not pass away, and His kingdom that which shall not be destroyed" (Dan. 7:14). The *vision* was given to Daniel and he recorded it; it is similar to unveilings given to John the apostle. A glance at the context will light upon repeated terms of everlastingness not only in reference to the exalted Son Himself, but to the saints of the heavenly places who are associated with Him. Daniel saw the victorious end, but also the conflicts which preceded it en route, for at last "the kingdom and dominion and the greatness of the kingdom under the whole heaven shall be given to the people of the saints of the Most High, Whose kingdom is an everlasting kingdom, and all dominions shall serve and obey Him". The reference is to the new earth which with the new heavens is the expectation of the saints. This will be the

possession and reward of Christ Jesus the Lord
because He is the Son of Man.

Not yet do we see this completed, it remains as
yet an unfinished work, but the Scripture assures
us that all will be in subjection to Him in the
"world to come". And it is of this coming world
that the apostle says, "whereof we speak". Our
sight of the universal triumph of Christ awaits His
appearing; we are not given to see it even in vision
as were Daniel and John. But "we walk by faith,
not by sight." By faith even now we see Him
"crowned with glory and honour", for He having
"gone into heaven . . . angels and authorities and
powers (are) made subject unto Him" (1 Pet.
3:22). "The world to come" is to be made subject,
not to angels, but to Man; that is, to the Man
Christ Jesus. In this connection the quotation is
made, "O Lord, our Lord, how excellent is Thy
Name in all the earth" (Ps. 8). "The world to
come", it is pointed out, is the habitable world or
earth. The verse obviously refers back to or takes
up the argument from the earlier words, "When
He again bringeth His Firstbegotten into the
world, He saith, And let all the angels of God worship Him" (Heb. 1:6). He is "the Firstbegotten
from the dead" and unto Him, as risen, and not to
angels, God hath said, "Thou are My Son, this day
have I begotten Thee" (Heb. 1:5; Acts 13:33;
Ps. 2:7).

WORLD WITHOUT END

What is this coming new world to which the Lord
Jesus Christ in meritorious resurrection has the
right of possession? Can it be this old world merely
renovated for a thousand years? Would not a new
creation the rather correspond to "newness of
life"? (see Rom. 6). Again, this world "lieth in the
evil one", and for how many millenniums has he
had the dominion? And is Christ the Conqueror to
wrest it from him for but a thousand years, and
then destroy it? Can this present evil world, though
renovated, be truly called, "the world to come"? Is
not "the world to come" to be distinguished altogether from "the world that now is", set in con-

trast with the new heavens and earth which the redeemed of the Lord await? (2 Pet. 3). That new creation will doubtless be in subjection to the Second Man, the Lord from heaven, with Whom will be blessed all who, being in Christ, are already new creatures awaiting their complete transformation at His coming (2 Cor. 5; Phil. 3). These are "the many sons He is bringing to glory" of whom, it is said, "He is not ashamed to call them brethren" (Heb. 2:10-11).

As this present inhabited world is also spoken of as this present age, so the habitable world to come is the age to come, or, in the use of the plural of majesty, the ages to come. It is in this age to come that eternal or everlasting life will be the full and crowning reward of grace unto Christ's faithful disciples (cf. Mark 10:30; Luke 18:30; cf. Matt. 12:32; Luke 20:34-36). And this qualifying "everlasting" agrees with the description of the endlessness of the coming kingdom and dominion (see Daniel above). Righteousness is the legal ground of this grace of eternal life (Rom. 5:21) and righteousness is said to "dwell" in the new heavens and earth. The superiority of the Son of God to men as well as to angels is here declared: "God, thy God, hath anointed Thee with the oil of gladness above Thy fellows" and the reason for the reward is given, "Thou hast loved righteousness and hated iniquity", and again, "to the Son, He saith, thy throne, O God, is for ever and ever: a sceptre of righteousness is the sceptre of Thy kingdom" (Heb. 1:8-9; Ps. 45). The language does not envisage a limited period of sovereignty in this world, but answers to the "years of the right hand of the Most High", as when again it is said, "Thou remainest", and when this world and its works "shall perish", and "as a vesture Thou shalt fold them up and they shall be changed: but Thou art the same and Thy years shall not fail" (Heb. 1). "We see not yet"; but whatever the ages to come unfold, this we are promised, the grace of God in Christ Jesus will eclipse all (Eph. 2:7).

"We see the Man Jesus, as Man, and therefore, as One risen from the dead, crowned with glory and honour", though we see not yet all things put under Him. Dominion over the original creation, the world which now is, was vested in the first man, Adam, who, mankind being viewed in him as its head, forfeited the privilege and right through sin, the race thereby falling with him. The dominion over the new creation is vested in the Second Man, and in Him as their Head, the "many sons He is bringing to glory", later called "the church of the Firstborn" (Heb. 12); for as He is the Son, so they are "many sons", and as He is the Firstborn from the dead, so they are firstborn ones, being related to Him in resurrection life.

It would appear that through the deception of the Evil One who compassed Adam's fall, the dominion of this world passed from man to angels, and to evil angels at that. "The devil and his angels" is Scripture's recognition of these powers, while Satan is called the god and prince of this world, and in his final identification, "the dragon, that old serpent, the devil and Satan" (Rev. 20). "The whole world lieth in the wicked one" (1 John 5). In God's providential administration His holy angels are commissioned in this present world to an invisible but effective ministry in the interests of His redeemed (Heb. 1). We further read of Michael and his angels, as though the archangel were in command, and we read of conflict between the holy and the evil powers. The Scriptures do not enlighten us in every particular, but we may conclude that God subjected this present world to angelic ministry, in some sense to the service and for the benefit of man (Psa. 103, 104; Dan. 10; Matt. 4; 1 Cor. 11, 10, etc.). But since the God-Man, Kinsman-Redeemer, has by His ransom price purchased the inheritance, and proved Himself alone the Man worthy to unseal its title-deeds and take the throne (Rev. 5), "not to angels hath He subjected the world to come" but to "the second Man, the Lord from heaven".

In consideration of the view that the evil usurper seized the dominion from man in accomplishing his fall, some further Scripture statements may be examined. Dispensationalism generally carries with

it, though not entirely, what has come to be called
"the gap theory" in respect to the creation of the
heavens and earth. This is that some unrecorded
prehistoric convulsion rendered the heavens and
earth of the beginning "without form and void"
(Gen. 1), and this is attributed to "angels that
sinned", thus placing the fall of Satan and his
angels prior to the events recorded in Genesis 1
from verse 2, but after the creation of verse 1, so
introducing the alleged "gap". Against this it is
reasonably held that the prophet's negative reference to this is balanced by his positive explanation
that "He formed it to be inhabited" (Isa. 45:18; cf.
42:5; 24:1, etc.). That would be to say the void and
formless state was not the consequence of some evil
eruption following an original creation unrevealed
and rendering a restoration necessary, but rather
marks the commencement of the Creator's work,
verse one being the title to the record which follows: "In the beginning God created the heavens
and the earth". How did He do it? "He spake and
it was done, He commanded and it stood fast"
(Ps. 33). "By the word of God the heavens were
of old, and the earth standing out of the water and
in the water" (2 Pet. 3). We read "And the earth
was without form and void" and some say the verb
holds the sense of "became". But the meaning may
be, as in the case of its repetition throughout the
chapter, "came to be, came into existence". It did
not so remain for that was but the Creator's first
act, and He proceeded, for He intended the world
should be habitable, to form it and to fill it until
His fiats ended with the creation of man. Inspecting
His handiwork He thereupon pronounced it "very
good". It scarcely seems, therefore, that the fall
of Satan was pre-Adamic, but rather followed the
appearance of the glorious being who resembled
the Creator Himself.

The Devil was "perfect" in the day of his creation, and as such was "in Eden the garden of God",
appointed to be "the anointed cherub that cover-
eth", possibly denoting his service to the newly
created earth and her inhabitants (Ezek. 28; Isa.
14). Then, we are told, "the morning stars sang

together, and all the sons of God shouted for joy" (Job. 38:7). Presumably Satan fell from his high estate through jealousy and pride when God made "man in His Own image and in His Own likeness", his role being, with that of the angels, to serve the interests of this more glorious creature of divine resemblance. This would agree with the teaching of Scripture as to the relative place and ministry of angels. Satan, thus fallen, aspired himself to vie with man and encompass his downfall. He has a number of titles. Lucifer, a day-star, is one of them. And, though truly the prince of darkness, is he not transformed into an angel of light? (2 Cor. 11; 14). Remonstrating with Lucifer, son of the morning, the prophet writes, "Thou hast said in thine heart, I will ascend into heaven, I will exalt my throne above the stars of God, I will sit also upon the mount of the congregation, I will ascend above the heights of the clouds, I will be like the most high". Adam in his primal majesty and holiness, in the image and likeness of his Creator, had been given dominion; all things had been put under his feet (Gen. 1:28; Ps. 8). But the being who by reason of his jealousy and pride became the evil tempter, occasioned Adam's fall, and in him, that of the whole race, the Evil One thus usurping the place of human sovereignty and dominion. Man, created supremely higher than Satan, became his slave, while Satan, intended to be the servant of man, became his master. (The words of Psalm 8:5, "Thou hast made him a little lower than the angels" are quoted in Heb. 2 of Christ, the Second Man in His overcoming condescension to regain the inheritance.)

God's purpose and His announcement and activity were perfectly to retrieve this fallen condition of His creation, and He has done so through His incarnate Son, as Redeemer, for the law of redemption required that He should be kinsman, the woman's Seed, the Man. Thus it is God's intention that "the habitable world to come" shall be subject, not to angels, but to Man, as at the first; yet to the Man Who as firstbegotten from death, in which He rendered the invaluable ransom (Ps. 49), is Himself the Firstborn of all creation and "the image of the invisible God" (Col. 1). Thus He by Whom in the beginning all things were made is recorded as "rejoicing in the habitable parts of the earth; and my delights were with the sons of men" (Prov. 8). Having redeemed unto Himself the inheritance, shall He not in the new creation and new world "see of the travail of His soul and be satisfied"? The new race then transformed into "His image and His likeness" and forever with Him, shall be the inhabitants of the new world.

The insistence with which we meet, namely, that the "world" spoken of having the meaning 'the habitable world' (Heb. 2:5) must refer to the world that now is in its final millennial form of administration under the supreme Messiahship of Jesus Christ as Man, does not appear to be compatible with the balanced and consistent teaching of Scripture that the present fallen creation in disobedience is to give place to a new creation in righteousness; that the first Adam and the sinful race are to be superseded by the last Adam and a holy race; that Paradise lost shall be Paradise restored; that repeated millenniums of evil rule by "the prince of this world" will give place to the eternal reign of the Prince of glory; that where sin abounded grace shall much more abound; that the new heavens and new earth will, as the old, not be formless and void, but suitably inhabited, the creature itself being delivered from the bondage of corruption into the glorious liberty of the children of God. For "(He) is the image of the invisible God, the firstborn of all creation; for by Him were all things created that are in heaven and that are in earth, visible and invisible, whether they be thrones, or dominions, or principalities, or powers; all things were created by Him and *for* Him. And He is before all things, and by Him all things consist. And He is the Head of the body, the church; Who is the beginning, the firstborn from the dead; that in all things He might have the pre-eminence: for it pleased the Father that in Him should all fulness dwell" (Col. 1:15-19).

MESSIAH-ISRAEL AND
THE ISRAEL NATION

"**I**SRAEL**"**, often used as synonymous with "Jews", figures largely, even essentially, in dispensational theory. "Israel" was a divinely chosen title. God meant what He said when He gave it to Jacob and his race, but did He then fully reveal what He meant in so re-naming the father of the nation? What may have been the purpose in changing the name of Jacob to Israel? The changing of Abram to Abraham was to denote that Abraham should be the father of many nations. It did not associate him with one nation in particular. Moreover, these "many nations" were not "after the flesh". The new covenant of saving grace and justifying faith was in view, Christ and believers in Him being Abraham's "seed". By Scripture foresight "the gospel was preached unto Abraham". In this connection he was to be "heir of the world," the world in foreview being composed of all believers from among all nations, for "God calleth those things which are not as though they were" (Rom. 4). In order to do this the miracle of Isaac was wrought, the child of "promise" not of the flesh, as are all the true children of God, but none others. The changing of the name, Abram, "exalted father", to Abraham, "father of a great multitude," signified no limited earthly Jewish commonwealth, as Jews in our Lord's day seemed proudly to expect (John 8:33), but a worldwide emancipation in

45

Christ, "a great multitude which no man can number out of all nations" brought to glory by the "God of glory" Who "appeared unto our father Abraham", and called him to that end (Acts 7). The people who sprang from Abraham through Isaac and Jacob, called Israel, were favoured to be the means but not the end.

Might not, therefore, the changing of Jacob's name to Israel have been with the intention of introducing the princely Seed Who should have power with God and with men and should prevail? That is, the title did not especially distinguish the race as such, but was conferred upon them vicariously because of Christ, Who as the true Israel, the true Isaac, was to come. A remarkable reference to the inception of the Israel nation, which indeed may serve as a key to the foreseen realization of the ideal and true Israel, the Messiah, is found in Hos. 11:1. The words are retrospective, for Hosea, contemporary with Isaiah, recalls the nation's redemption from Egypt. Yet, according to the New Testament, this historical event was prospective in that it anticipated the providential experience of the incarnate Redeemer Himself, being related to the early sojourn and exodus from Egypt of the infant Lord. The event, it is stated, occurred in the Israel nation's beginning "that it might be fulfilled", that is, not only the words but the incident, at the birth of the Incarnate Son of God Who was and is the real Israel in view (Matt. 2:15).

Admittedly, God meant what He said when through the prophet He recalled the centuries-old deliverance of Israel from Egypt: "When Israel was a child, then I loved him and called My son out of Egypt". But through those centuries past up to Hosea's day and onwards, continuing words of the prophet were verified concerning the nation: "My people are bent on backsliding from Me". The directive, therefore, is away from the disobedient Israel-nation to Messiah-Israel the obedient Servant, for "though He were a Son, yet learned He obedience by the things which He suffered" (Heb. 5:8). While, therefore, God meant what He said when referring historically to the nation whom He thus typically

redeemed to be His servant, He did not then say
that He meant a more important and fulfilling future event, when His incarnate Son, the personal
Israel, should as His true and perfect Servant enter
upon His redemptive mission. The ordering of
events touching the course of the elect nation doubtless was determined by His foreordination that of
Israel according to the flesh, Christ should come,
"My Servant, Mine elect, in Whom My soul delighteth" (Isa. 42:1).

Isaiah, contemporary with Hosea, in contrast
with the failure of the Israel-nation as God's servant and witness, pointedly sets forth Messiah as
the ideal Servant. The introduction of the nation-
servant is in these words: "Hear ye this, O house
of Jacob, *which are called by the name Israel,* which
sware by the name of the Lord, and make mention
of the God of Israel, *but not in truth nor in righteousness*" (Isa. 48:1). Such is the Israel-nation. But
in conspicuous contrast the world is summoned to
attend the declaration of the incarnate Servant,
Messiah-Israel: "Listen, O isles, unto Me; and
hearken, ye people, from far; the Lord hath called
Me from the womb; from the bowels of my mother
hath he made mention of My name . . . *And (He)
said unto Me, Thou art My Servant, O Israel,* in
Whom I will be glorified", as He was not glorified in
the nation. "And now, saith the Lord that formed
Me from the womb to be His Servant, to bring
Jacob again to Him, though Israel be not gathered,
yet shall I be glorious in the eyes of the Lord, and
My God shall be My strength. And He said, It is
a light thing that Thou shouldest be My Servant
to raise up the tribes of Jacob, and to restore the
preserved of Israel: I will also give Thee for a light
to the Gentiles that Thou mayest be My salvation
unto the end of the earth" (Isa. 49). These words
were used by the apostle Paul at Antioch when the
Jews by their rejection of the preaching of Christ
"judged themselves unworthy of eternal life", although it was necessary that the Gospel should *first*
be preached unto them, thereby bringing upon
themselves the judgment of the prophet: "Behold,
ye despisers, and wonder, and perish: for I work

a work in your days, a work which ye shall in no
wise believe, though a man declare it unto you"
(Acts 13). It is certain, therefore, that Isaiah did
not forecast the restoration of Jacob and Israel in
any national sense: these together with the Gentiles
being enlightened as to the salvation which is in
Christ Jesus. And who may be the "preserved of
Israel" among the tribes of Jacob but the remnant
set in contrast with the generally unbelieving nation; the remnant of which the first disciples gathered around our Lord in person, and later the "firstfruits" through the power of the Holy Spirit, which
Paul called "a remnant according to the election of
grace"?

In sharp contradistinction with the obedience of
Messiah-Israel from His birth unto His death upon
the cross (Phil. 2) is the treacherous conduct of the
Nation - Israel, the rejected servant, of whom it
is written in the context: "Yea, thou heardest not;
yea, thou knewest not; yea, from that time that
thine ear was not opened: for I knew that thou
wouldest deal very treacherously, and wast called
a transgressor from the womb" (Isa. 48:8, 18, 19).
The very terms in these chapters concerning the two
Israels appear to be designedly placed in opposition. Noticeable too is the repetition of emphasis
upon the Name in its vicarious merit, and the contrast in the true Servant with the mark of volun-
tary service readily yielded, thus: "The Lord God
hath opened Mine ear, and I was not rebellious,
neither turned away back" (like the nation-servant).
The Mosaic custom of boring the ear of the willing
servant is here referred to, and these verses (Isa.
48:8; 50:5), considered with Deut. 15:16, 17; Ps.
40:6; Heb. 10:5, illumine the meaning of the words
as used by Isaiah in contrast.

It is in this context setting forth the Messiah as
the Servant called Israel that we find such impressive statements as: "I am the Lord your holy One,
the Creator of Israel, your King: bring My sons
from far, my daughters from the ends of the earth,
everyone that is *called by My name.* I have created
him for My glory, yea, I have formed him. I have
made him. One shall say, I am the Lord's, and another shall call himself *by the name of the God of*

Jacob, and another shall subscribe with his hand unto the Lord, *and surname himself by the name of Israel"*. These are the chapters which name the Messiah-Israel, the First and the Last, the one universal Saviour Whose bidding is, "Look unto Me and be ye saved all the ends of the earth: for I am God, and there is none else" (Isa. 45:22).

The Lord Jesus, the obedient Servant of Jehovah, is the ideal and representative "Israel". By His name are called the remnant of Israel, repentant of their own failure and redeemed in Him. By His name also are called believing Gentiles from the ends of the earth. It is noteworthy that in this Hosean prophecy not only is Messiah anticipated as "Israel My Son", but the language encompasses the world-wide reach of the Gospel (as does the corresponding passage in Isaiah). Thus Paul upon this quotation reasons that all the "called" are God's true people, saying: "Even *us,* whom He hath called, not of the Jews only but also of the Gentiles". And Peter, in recognition of the same prophecy, writes of the chosen generation, royal priesthood, holy nation, peculiar people (doubtless having in mind the same context as Hosea: Ex. 19:5-6). Moreover, it is also made clear that the prophet's time directive, "In that day", is the present Gospel era, and he closes with a prediction of its completion in the final resurrection and redemption of the body. Messiah is both Saviour and King. "Israel", therefore, belongs to Christ and to all His people (Hos. 1:10, 2:23; 13:4, 10-14; Rom. 9:25-26; 1 Pet. 2:10; 1 Cor. 15:55). That they should be called Israel because they are Christ's corresponds with their being Abraham's seed for the same reason. "The Israel of God" like "the children of God" are all those, and only those, who are redeemedly and believingly related to the Lord Jesus Christ (Rom. 9:7-8; Gal. 6:16). They are Christians because they are Christ's. They are Israel because He is Israel and they are His. They are not all Israel who are of Israel, but they all are Israel who are Christ's. Although the nation was Israelized, not all may truly claim the name, even as not all in Christianized nations are truly Christian.

What God meant or had in view when He changed the name of Jacob to Israel, doubtless was the advent of Christ, the child to be born, the Son to be given, as revealed through the prophet Isaiah and supported in the Scriptures generally. But in the history of the notable event there are features which invite attention, for the incident involved a Christophany when "Jacob was left alone and there wrestled with him a Man till the breaking of the day" (Gen. 32:24-30). "What is thy name?" asked the heavenly Man, and he said, "Jacob". "Thy name shall be called no more Jacob, but Israel; for as a prince hast thou power with God and with men, and hast prevailed". The change is confirmed later, and the promises previously spoken to Abraham and to Isaac are repeated to Israel. Upon this announcement Jacob turned the question upon the Visitant: "Tell me, I pray thee, thy name". And he said, "Wherefore is it that thou dost ask after My name?" as though, had Jacob understood, it had been already disclosed! That no immediate confirmation was made is not uncommon in Scripture: "thou shalt know hereafter". Thus we simply read: "And He blessed him there."

Our understanding is assisted by another and later incident. When Manoah, apprised of the birth of Samson, similarly asked the Angel, "What is thy name?" he replied, "Why askest thou thus after my name seeing it is Wonderful?" . . . and the angel did wondrously and Manoah and his wife looked on (Judges 13:18-22). The name was not spoken but the characteristics of the visitation and the angel's answer were not without revealing relation to it. So, beholding, they may have discerned it for Manoah in some fear exclaimed, "We have seen God". Of the virgin's Son, Isaiah wrote later, "His Name shall be called Wonderful . . . the Prince of peace". Such instances would allow the conclusion that the name, "Israel", was transferred to Jacob from the Angel himself. Jacob, no longer expecting to prevail in his own strength, asked to be blessed by the Man with Whom he wrestled. That blessing was given; it was conveyed in the name. In the character of that new name, "a prince with God", there was signified "power with God and with men." The name of the Man Who wrestled with him was not directly announced nor was it refused, the interrogation being returned to Jacob, "Wherefore dost thou ask after My name?", as though the name was already disclosed, Jacob being changed to Israel because the Man, Messiah, was the true Israel, foreordained to come into this world incarnate and "of Israel as concerning the flesh". "And Jacob called the name of the place, Peniel, (that is, the face of God) for I have seen God face to face and my life is preserved."

The Man Who wrestled with him Jacob now recognized as the God-Man, Whom through the Gospel we know as God manifest in the flesh. In assuming our humanity it was sovereignly ordained that He should come of the people known as Israel, therefore, He justly bore that name. With this in view the name was called upon Jacob, surely regenerated Jacob; and upon his children, but strictly and in the determinate counsel of God, upon his regenerated children, "the children of the promise", for "they are not all Israel who are of Israel" (Rom. 9). Who, other than He, is worthy to bear the "Israel" title? Who else as a Prince has prevailing power with God and with men? He alone is the princely Mediator, for "Him hath God exalted with His right hand to be a Prince and a Saviour, for to give repentance to Israel and remission of sins" (Acts 5:31).

PRIORITY IN MERCY
AND JUDGMENT

T HAT the New Testament abounds in quotations
   from the Old Testament in support of its
evangelical doctrines and benefits assured to believers in the Church, it is very evident. In regard
to the supposed special case of the Jews, however,
it is said that "as the Church has entered into the
fulness of Israel's spiritual blessings, so Israel is
to share these with the Church in the age to come",
the age to come being regarded as an earthly millennial reign of Messiah over Israel in restored
nationhood. It is difficult to find in the New Testament confirmation of this. The Lord Jesus and His
apostles in their use of Old Testament promises
originally addressed to Israel, while regarding such
as fulfilled to the Church, made no promise that
national Israel would inherit these in an earthly
state after the Church shall have entered upon her
heavenly glory. Again, in this connection it may
be observed that God meant what He said in the
time of preparation through Moses and the Prophets, but said what He meant in the age of fulfilment in Christ and through His apostles. The
Church, of course, is composed of believers, both
Jewish and Gentile. In this the Jews were accorded
priority. Gentiles were added, becoming fellow-
heirs and of the same body and fellow-partakers of
His promise in Christ by the Gospel (Eph. 3:6).
The Gentiles, having been aliens from the common-

wealth of Israel and foreigners from the covenants of promise, were without God and without Christ, having no hope. But in Christ this middle wall of partition is removed, and Gentiles with Jews are through faith all one, and both have access in one Spirit unto the Father (Eph. 2:12; 3:14-18). To erect again a barrier which God has removed is transgression (Gal. 2:18). In Christ, distinguishing racial and religious privilege is nothing; a new creation is everything; that new creation is "the Israel of God" (Gal. 6:15; cf. 5:6).

"To the Jew first" was the principle governing the order of procedure, "and also to the Gentiles". The witness to this principle is impressive. "Let the children *first* be filled" (Mark 7:27). "Into any city of the Samaritans enter ye not, but go ye rather to the lost sheep of the house of Israel" (Mark 10:6). "There shall be weeping and gnashing of teeth when ye shall see Abraham, Isaac and Jacob, and all the prophets, in the kingdom of God and ye yourselves thrust out. And they shall come (the patriarchs and prophets already being in the kingdom) from the east and from the west and from the north and from the south and shall sit down in the kingdom of God. And, behold, there are last that shall be first, and there are first that shall be last" (Luke 13:28-30). The anticipation of this may be seen in the repetition of the Abrahamic promise to Jacob, whose name was changed to Israel in expectation of the Messiah Who should be God's salvation not only to the remnant of Israel but unto the ends of the earth (Gen. 28:14; Isa. 49:6). "He beheld the city and wept over it, saying, If thou hadst known, even thou at least *in this thy day,* the things which belong unto thy peace, but now they are hid from thine eyes . . . because thou knewest not *the time of thy visitation*" (Luke 19:41-44). "Last of all He sent unto them His Son . . . and they slew Him . . . Therefore the kingdom of God shall be taken from you and given to a nation bringing forth the fruits thereof" (Matt. 21:33-46). What nation can this be other than the only nation spoken of in the New Testament in the antitypical language of Israel; namely, the holy nation, the Church (1 Pet. 2:9)? "All the prophets from Samuel and those that follow after have told of *these days* (introduced by the Incarnation and further announced when Peter preached at Pentecost; compare also as an example the principle in John 7:39 and the antitypical fulfilment of the wilderness smitten rock). Ye are the children of the prophets and of the covenant which God made with our fathers, saying unto Abraham, In thy seed shall all the families of the earth be blessed (which Seed is Christ: Gal. 3:16). Unto you *first,* God, having raised up His Son Jesus, sent Him to bless you in turning away everyone of you from his iniquities" (Acts 3:18-26; cf. Rom. 11:26). This sending of the risen Christ is through His apostles, through Peter then addressing them, and in the power of the Spirit, for He said, "As My Father has sent Me, even so send I you" and "He that receiveth you receiveth Me and Him that sent Me" (John 20:21). Paul declared, "We are ambassadors for Christ, as though God did beseech you by us, we pray you in Christ's stead" (2 Cor. 5:19-20).

"It was necessary that the Word of God should first have been spoken unto you (said Paul to the Jews at Antioch): but seeing ye put it from you, and judge yourselves unworthy of everlasting life, lo, we turn to the Gentiles. For so hath the Lord commanded us". Why so "necessary" then if a later salvation is in store? In support, he quotes the passage from Isaiah concerning the prosperity of the Gospel of Christ, the obedient Servant, "Messiah Israel" (Acts 13:46-47; Isa. 49:6). Their rejection of the Lord Jesus Christ proclaimed first to them in His Gospel occasioned the apostle's solemn announcement from their own prophets of judgment full and final: "Behold, ye despisers, and wonder, and perish: for I work a work *in your days* a work which ye shall in no wise believe, though a man declare it unto you" (Acts 13:40-41; Hab. 1:5). The force of such language appears to allow of no opportunity other than that extended then and in God's longsuffering until He shall come the second time, but without even the hint of an-

other visitation and an age of blessing thereafter.
Indeed, Paul wrote that their apostasy was such
as "to fill up their sins alway: for the wrath is
come upon them to the uttermost" (1 Thess. 2:16),
in all probability a reference to the approaching
destruction of their city and temple and the scattering of the people among all nations as forewarned
by the Lord Himself (Matt. 24; Luke 21). The
"uttermost" would be the extreme, and unrepeatable.

That the opportunity and provision of salvation
for Israel and for all nations is limited to the age
that now is, is plainly declared by Paul in terms
which allow of no elasticity. The period is bounded
by the Advents of Christ. It arose from His coming
in humiliation to put away sin by the sacrifice of
Himself. prepared for in Israel's economy of old.
This sufficient and final sacrifice for sins secures
salvation to believers throughout those former
times (Rom. 3:25; Heb. 9:15). The period will be
concluded with His second coming, which will not
be with respect to the removal of sin or to give
repentance, or a second chance, or inaugurate a
millennial evangelizing of the nations; but unto salvation, that is, the "salvation ready" — made ready
by His cross — "to be revealed in the last time",
"salvation which is in Christ with eternal glory"
(Heb. 9:28; 1 Pet. 1:5; 2 Thess. 2:10). The one
and only solemn prospect beyond the present opportunity (and the word is addressed to the Hebrews)
is that of "the judgment" (Heb. 9:27; 2 Pet.
3:7-15).

"Behold", writes the apostle as though he would
alert the attention. "now is the accepted time, *now*
is the day of salvation"; Hence his earnest entreaty
in the context, "We pray you, we beseech you, be
ye reconciled to God". As his custom was, the Old
Testament being his authority, he quoted Isaiah's
evangelical prophecy, that God meant what He said
of Messiah, and announced the present Gospel administration as the appointed time of realization
to show how God meant what He said (2 Cor.
5:20: 6:2). Again, the quotation is from the
Messiah-Israel passage where the acceptable year
of the Lord and the good news of salvation are

assured in covenant to and through "the Lord thy Saviour and Redeemer, the mighty One of Jacob" (Isa. 49:8; 61:1). The embrace and this order of the saving grace in the ideal Servant and true Israel, as stated in this prophecy quoted by Paul to the disbelieving Jews at Antioch, account for his introduction that "*It was necessary* that the word of God should *first* be spoken to you", for thus the prophet had presented the case. In these words is the apostle's recognition of an ordered procedure in evangelization. Comprehending the entire mission of Christ, therefore, in Person and by His Spirit, "Now" and "To-day" with no hope of tomorrow and later, would impress the urgency of the saving opportunity for Jews and Gentiles alike, upon the neglect and despising of which nothing awaits save "a certain fearful looking for of judgment and fiery indignation which shall devour the adversaries" (Heb. 10:27).

The day of judgment will be ushered in by the second coming of Christ. That day is appointed (Acts 17:31). For the ungodly it will be a "day of perdition" (2 Pet. 3:7); for the righteous a day of salvation and reward (1 Cor. 4:5; 2 Tim. 4:1; Rev. 11:17-18). It would appear there is to be an arrangement, a sequence, according to privilege and advantage, even in the judgment day. The Lord seemed to indicate this in certain of His parables. To Paul, to whom it was given chiefly to declare the priority of the Jew in respect to the Gospel, it was also given to forewarn the Jew in regard to the execution of judgment. Instead of a popular supposition that in that day of Christ's coming, Israel is to be given another visitation in mercy, the apostolic testimony is the reverse. We read: "the Gospel is the power of God unto salvation to every one that believeth, to the Jew first and also to the Gentile"; but we also read: "To them that do not obey the truth but obey unrighteousness, indignation and wrath, tribulation and anguish upon every soul of man that doeth evil, to the Jew first and also to the Gentile: for there is no respect of persons with God" (Rom. 1:16; 2:9). And this, writes Paul, will be "in the day when God shall judge the secrets of men by Jesus Christ according to my Gospel" (Rom. 2:16).

"In the mouth of two or three witnesses every word shall be established" is a Scriptural principle, announced by Moses, confirmed by our Lord, and written for the Church. Paul in admonishing the Jews at Antioch expounded the same Scriptures as did Peter at Jerusalem, and independently, but by the same Spirit, gave the same meaning in fulfilment of what God had said. He insisted that "the promise which was made unto the fathers" (Acts 13:32) and renewed to David (23), God had fulfilled in Messiah's first advent, in His birth, life, death, resurrection and ascension to glory. Thus God had "raised unto Israel a Saviour" (23:33). This Saviour God promised, and the salvation is that announced in "the sure mercies of David", according to the "everlasting covenant", surely the new covenant (23-24: Isa. 55). Upon their embracing or refusing this Gospel depended their justification or judgment (38-39), in both respects fulfilling "that which is spoken of in the prophets" (27-40).

This repeated promise to the fathers and to David is condensed in one sentence; namely, that God would "raise unto Israel a Saviour". This is God's final word to Israel; It is His final word to every generation of the Israel people throughout this Gospel age. The Lord Himself declared it in the parable of the vineyard He addressed to their leaders, "last of all He sent unto them His Son" — there is no promise of a second or repeated "sending" — upon their rejection of Whom He would "miserably destroy those wicked husbandmen" (Matt. 21). Likewise Paul had no supplementary or additional promise or expectation to offer; he hinted no hope that a later generation of Jews would be nationally saved by the appearing of Christ; nothing but the doom of the impenitent, should they thus put the Word of God from them.

How solemnly at variance with the New Testament, and consequently how deceiving, is the sentimental suggestion met with frequently in the writings and speeches of dispensationalists, including missionaries to the Jews, that a future salva-

tion still awaits the Gospel-despising people at the
second advent of Christ! The apostle knew nothing
of this. Contrariwise he said, "Behold, ye despisers,
and wonder, and perish", which, be it noted, is the
Old Testament judgment of finality; it is not
Pauline!

"The sure mercies of David", Isaiah's anticipation of the Gospel which the apostles preached, is
associated with the assurance, "Behold, I have
given Him for a witness, a leader and a commander
to the people" (Isa. 55). Isaiah spake this of
"David", but the historical David was then deceased. Was David to have a resurrection, or was
the promise fulfilled in Christ? According to the
apostles, although through Isaiah God said David,
He meant "this man's seed", even Christ (Acts
13:23). These titles of Witness, Leader and Commander, correspond to the offices accorded Him in
the New Testament in His evangelical and mediatorial relations (Acts 5:31; Heb. 2:10; 6:20; 1
Pet. 3:22; Rev. 1:5, 18; 3:7, 14). He is nowhere
said to enter upon such relationship with the nation of Israel at His second coming in glory. Israel
had been specially advantaged or privileged in preparing the Gospel which later was to be first proclaimed to her. Her history from the call of Abraham to the advent of Christ was designed of God
as preparatory to its spiritual counterpart, the ultimate objective. His appointments, direction, superintendence, with the miraculous elements which
characterized the period and the people was with
a view to producing the revelation of His will
which we have in the Old Testament. Incidentally,
it may be noted that because the prophetic and
apostolic ministries were to provide the Scriptures
of truth, the Holy Spirit's inspiration was infallibly
operative, and all supernatural features are thus
sufficiently accounted for. which ceased upon the
completion of the holy writings. There is no ground,
therefore, for the perpetuation of the miraculous
in the general activity of the Church. "We walk
by faith, not by sight" and "faith cometh", not
through signs and wonders, but "by hearing the
Word of God" (Rom. 10:17).

Israel had this advantage: being chosen as God's instrument, she was supernaturally and providentially cared for in that the Scriptures were committed to her (Rom. 3:2). She had this related and simultaneous advantage, that through her means "as concerning the flesh", the Messiah should come, the very Subject of those Scriptures. Further, she was given this advantage and privilege, that the Gospel of salvation in Christ, written in those Scriptures, though for the whole world, was to "the Jew first". Does it not, therefore, appear altogether equitable that the privilege of priority in mercy should be balanced by the responsibility of priority in judgment (Rom. 1:16; 2:9-10)?

THE THRONE AND
TABERNACLE
OF DAVID

FROM the writings of the prophets it was known and expected that Messiah would be the Son of David. "In the city of David", was the confirming angelic announcement of His birth. The multitudes acclaimed Him as He entered Jerusalem, saying, "Hosanna to the Son of David: Blessed is He that cometh in the name of the Lord", reciting from Ps. 118 which thus prophetically related Messiah both to earth and to heaven, to David and to Jehovah. This even the children repeated as He entered the Temple. The people, astonished at His power, would ask, "Is not this the Son of David?"; and the needy sought His grace, crying, "Jesus, Thou Son of David, have mercy upon me".

The question of questions with which the Lord Jesus silenced His Pharisee critics was, "What think ye of the Messiah; whose Son is he? They say unto Him, the Son of David". The Lord thereupon quoted David's 110th Psalm, prefacing it with, "How then doth David by the Spirit call Him Lord, saying, The Lord said unto my Lord, Sit thou on My right hand until I make Thine enemies Thy footstool", and He asked the silencing question: "If David then call Him Lord, how is he his son?" (Matt. 22). Here we are introduced to the first of a number of occurrences of this quotation in the New Testament, the assurance that the son of David, who also is David's Lord, should be enthroned in His humanity and, therefore, subsequent to His incarnate birth, death and resurrection, on the right hand of God in heaven, otherwise described as "the Majesty on high". The apostles also observe that this exaltation as David's Son and Seed was His as the right and reward of His death, in virtue of which He confirmed the covenant and released "the sure mercies of David", fulfilling the promise to "raise unto Israel a Saviour" (Acts 13 etc.). Is it not of some note that all the fulfilling references to the enthronement of Christ as the Son and Seed of David are associated with His resurrection and ascension, and none with His second coming or millennial reign or an earthly throne or kingdom (e.g. Rom. 1:3-4; 2 Tim. 2:8)? Emphases are important. What might be the intended emphasis in these words, "Sit Thou on My right hand until I make *Thine* enemies *Thy* footstool"? Had not this vanquishing of all His enemies, assured to David's Son, already received a foreshadowing in that to David himself the Lord had said, "Moreover, I will subdue all thine enemies" (1 Chr. 17:10), which eventually came to pass when "the king sat in his house and the Lord had given him rest round about from all his enemies" (2 Sam. 7:1, 9, 11)? David sat upon "the throne of the Lord" as did Solomon after him, yet it was none the less the "throne of David" (1 Chr. 28:5; 29:23). Messiah was David's sovereign Lord, yet He was none the less David's Son. David therefore perceived by the Spirit that his promised Messiah-Son would be enthroned in heaven until His enemies also should be all subdued as his own had been.

Should not the choice of David, a man after God's own heart, and his regime, the setting up of his throne in the earthly Zion, and all that appertained to his kingdom, be regarded as in conformity with the general character of the Old Testament, to be expounded, therefore, as to its spiritual complement, in the New Testament? The manner in which Christ is described and His offices and ministry regarded in relation to David substantiates this. It is He of whom David spake by verbal inspiration in his last words, saying, "He that ruleth over man must be just, ruling in the fear of God. And He shall be as the light of the morning when the sun riseth, even a morning without clouds; as the tender grass springing out of the earth by clear shining after rain". David's own reign was not of this character, but he found in the predicted and expected Messiah, Son of David, "all my salvation and all my desire" guaranteed by "an everlasting covenant" (2 Sam. 23). How similar to the naturalistic symbolic language used of His birth and ministry; for instance, "the dayspring from on high hath visited us, to give light to them that sit in darkness and in the shadow of death", and "The people which sat in darkness saw great light; and to them which sat in the region and shadow of death light is sprung up" (Luke 1; Matt. 4)!

Speaking from the throne, the "right hand of the majesty on high", He has proclaimed this word: "I am the living One, Who became dead, and behold, I am alive for evermore, and have the *keys* of death and of hell." Enemies indeed! It is as Son of David that He thus speaks, "these things saith He that is holy, He that is true, He that hath the *key of David*, He that openeth and no man shutteth, and shutteth and no man openeth". This is one announcement of His ecclesiastical authority, it is for the "churches"; and the reference is to the words of the prophet (Isa. 22:22; Rev. 2:7; 1:18). The language is similar to the familiar passage concerning the Child born and Son given, "and the government shall be upon His shoulder", a kingdom increasing, administered from the throne of David, established "henceforth", that is from the time of His birth as God's gift, "even forever" (Isa. 9:6-7).

David the sweet psalmist of Israel apprehended that the covenant made with him was of spiritual character. In the language of his last words the Spirit enabled him to foresee and foretell that his own temporal house in the material form of an earthly kingdom would be superseded by that of His Son the Messiah, although it would not immediately "grow", or spring forth. In this he exults for it is "an everlasting covenant ordered in all things and sure", the realization of which "is all my salvation and all my desire." We must not presume to correct David's spiritualizing here by declaring that what he meant was the extension or facsimile of his own kingdom millennially re-established in Jerusalem. Everlastingness cannot be comprehended within a thousand years. Like Moses before him, David spiritualizes, or should we say, literalizes, his covenant-making God, calling Him "The Rock". thus anticipating the foundation upon which Christ the Messiah would invincibly build His church (2 Sam. 23).

The same Spirit inspired Peter on the day of Pentecost, itself an Old Testament festival with a Gospel fulfilment, to declare that David, being a prophet, predicted that Messiah, "the fruit of his loins", would be raised up "to sit upon his throne". And it is pointedly affirmed by Peter that David, "seeing this before"; that is, that Christ was to be raised up to sit upon his throne, "spake of the resurrection of Christ". "Therefore", declared Peter, He is thus "by the right hand of God exalt-ed". "For David", said Peter, "is not ascended into the heavens". Why the negative, save to make it clear that David himself was not to be re-enthroned, but "Christ should sit on his throne"? And so Peter quoted the words used by the Lord Jesus of Himself and first written by David: "Sit Thou on my right hand until I make Thy foes Thy foot-stool". The language seems especially to stress this matter. David, whose body awaits resurrection, did not write of himself, but he did write of the Occu-pant of his throne. He wrote of the resurrection of Messiah in order that He as Son of David should sit on that throne. This now has taken effect. "Therefore", said the apostle, "let the house of Israel know assuredly that God hath made that same Jesus, Whom ye have crucified, both Lord and Christ". They were to be assured with all certainty by these indisputable facts, by these fulfilled pre-dictions, sealed by the mighty and moving diffusion of the Holy Ghost, that David's Son and Lord was indeed the Messiah enthroned as David expected,

"God having sworn with an oath unto him". The heavenly was the reality, the earthly the pattern, of the throne as of the temple. David's announcement of this, spoken by the Spirit, David's last words confirming it which also the Spirit spake by him, being now accomplished, the enthroned Messiah exercised His prerogative in bestowing the promised Spirit upon His apostles and His church unto the world-wide proclamation of "the sure mercies of David" according to the "everlasting covenant" that not only David but all the redeemed of the Lord might find therein "all my salvation and all my desire" (1 Chr. 28:11-19; Acts 2:13; 2 Sam. 23).

David's joyful anticipation of this ultimate heavenly Messianic sovereignty is evident since he sweetly sang of it in his Psalms, and it is impressive how heaven rather than earth — Zion above rather than below — fulfilled his expectations. He celebrated no earthly throne or kingdom, but that which should be "built up to all generations", and established in "the very heavens" for Him of Whom it is said, "I will make Him My Firstborn, higher than the kings of the earth". Of His reign, David writes, "His throne will endure as the days of heaven", established "as the moon and as a faithful witness in heaven", for His are "the heavens and the earth, the world and its fulness". Such are the terms about David's throne when Messiah should occupy the reality, and he writes: "Blessed is the people that know the joyful sound: they shall walk, O Lord, in the light of Thy countenance".

On earth and in Jerusalem David's glory would "be made to cease and his throne cast to the ground", consequently the lament is made, "Lord, where are Thy former loving-kindnesses which Thou swarest unto David in Thy truth?" For the answer of peace direction is given to heaven, the covenant has not failed but is fulfilled in Christ, and so "Mercy shall be built up for ever: Thy faithfulness shalt Thou establish in the very heavens". Accordingly David celebrated the ascent to the throne of His Son and Lord, saying, "And the heavens shall praise Thy wonders, O Lord: Thy

faithfulness also in the congregation of the saints.
For who in the heaven can be compared unto the
Lord? who among the sons of the mighty can be
likened unto the Lord?" (Ps. 89: 5, 6. The psalm
in its detailed particulars is worthy of close
attention.)

Having ascended on high, the Lord Jesus as
majestic Head of the church revealed through the
Apostle John His administrative relation to the
churches on earth. Reference has already been
made to two important announcements thus made;
namely, His human descent from David, being his
"Offspring", and as to His Deity, David's "Root"
(which would correspond with "Lord"), and He is
invested with governmental authority over the
kingdom in that He possesses and operates
David's "key". It is important to note that the
Davidic Kingship of Christ is not here found in a
Jewish millennial context, but in His direction of
the policy of representative Christian churches. It
is in His use of "the key of David" that He set
before the church "an open door which no man
can shut". It is as the "Root and Offspring of
David" that He "testified these things in the
churches" (Rev. 3:7; 22:16).

The final promise or reward to believers in these
Apocalyptic church letters is the following: "To
him that overcometh will I grant to sit with Me
in My throne even as I also overcame, and am set
down with My Father in His throne" (Rev. 3:21).
A differentiation is frequently but wrongly made
by dispensationalists between the thrones, with the
gratuitous assumption that at His second coming
the Lord Jesus will vacate His Father's throne to
occupy "His Own throne". It is, of course, by this
interpolation of the possessive "own" that "My
Father's throne" is made to differ from "My
throne", and by supposition that His Own throne
is explained to be the re-establishment of the secu-
lar throne of David. Is there Biblical warrant for
this distinction? The additional pronoun is not in
the text. Yet it will be found that where the emphasis is necessary it is supplied in a number of
instances by the same apostle. These but serve to

support His oneness with the Father even as to
the throne (John 1:12; 4:41; 5:30; 6:38; 7:18;
8:50; 10:3, 4; 13:1; 17:5, 11). In the Apocalypse
the pronoun occurs in reference to the redeeming
blood (Rev. 1:5) and by its use Paul emphasized
its relation to Deity (Acts 20:18). The Man Christ
Jesus, having endured the cross and overcome on
earth, has received the highest reward of His
Father's recognition in heaven. His investiture was
given in inspired vision and record, and "by faith
we see Jesus crowned with glory and honour"
(Dan. 7; Rev. 5; Ps. 24; Heb. 2). Believers who
are by His grace also overcomers are encouraged
with a promise of similar reward which now it is
His prerogative to bestow. But this does not separate the thrones of Father and Son, it unites believers with the Son and the Father.

The Scriptures testify of this perfect equality,
this absolute oneness, of the Father and the Son:
"The Father hath committed all judgment unto the
Son. As My Father hath sent Me even so send I
you . . . All Mine are Thine and Thine are Mine
. . . His Own sheep, My sheep: no man is able to
pluck them out of My Father's hand . . . whatsoever things the Father doeth these also doeth the
Son likewise . . . As the Father hath life in Himself so hath He given to the Son to have life in
Himself . . . As the Father raiseth up the dead and
quickeneth them, even so the Son quickeneth whom
He will . . . He that hath seen Me hath seen the
Father . . . I and My Father are one . . . The Father
hath given all things into His hands . . . As Thou
Father art in Me and I in Thee, that they also may
be one in Us . . . All men should honour the Son
even as they honour the Father; he that honoureth
not the Son honoureth not the Father Who hath
sent Him . . . Glorify Thou Me with Thine Own
Self, with the glory which I had with Thee before
the world was".

"Unto the Son He saith, Thy throne, O God is
for ever and ever; a sceptre of righteousness is the
sceptre of Thy kingdom: Thou hast loved righteousness and hated iniquity; therefore God, even Thy
God, hath anointed Thee with the oil of gladness

above Thy fellows". These words are addressed to
Christ risen and ascended. They were penned by
David when he meditatively exulted in "the King",
his Son according to the flesh, Whose throne with
its majesty, power and glory is forever and ever,
and "Whose name would be remembered to all generations" and Who "the people should praise forever and ever". (Ps. 55; Heb. 1). "His kingdom" is
the "Father's kingdom", "the kingdom of Christ
and of God". "The glory of His Father" is "His
Own glory" (Matt. 13:41-43; Eph. 5:5; Matt. 16:27
with Luke 9:26).

The rewarding promise, therefore, cannot be construed to mean that the exalted Son is without a
throne of His own! The incentive is, "With Me".
The throne is one, and the thronal rewards are in
heaven as succeeding chapters show. There He is
enthroned as "the Root of David" Who also is the
Lamb (Rev. 5:5-6). Salvation is ascribed to God
"Who sitteth upon the throne and unto the Lamb"
(Rev. 7:10). Of that heavenly city and situation
it is written, "The Lord God almighty and the
Lamb are the temple of it, and the glory of God
did lighten it and the Lamb is the light thereof",
and "the water of life proceedeth out of the throne
of God and of the Lamb", for "the throne of God
and the Lamb shall be in it" (Rev. 21:22-23;
22:1-3). Therefore the whole universe ascribeth
"blessing and honour and glory and power unto
Him that sitteth upon the throne and unto the
Lamb for ever and ever" (Rev. 5:13).

So insistent is the Spirit of inspiration upon the
"eternal purpose which God purposed in Christ
Jesus", and therefore upon His appearing in "the
fulness of the time", that again and again during
the centuries and millenniums before His advent,
in the midst of narrative of current events which
concerned the immediate danger of deliverance of
the chosen people, and sometimes their continuance,
there abruptly appears a Messianic prophecy in
terms not superficially clear but leaving no doubt
as to Who is spoken of. All is important, but this is
of the utmost importance. Among many pearls
there is but One of great price. Pagan races, power-

ful enemies of God's people, though chastened for their transgressions, which Israel herself did not escape, are yet viewed in the light of Messianic mercy, for Christ is "the Desire of *all* nations"; of Assyria, Chaldea, Egypt, Ethiopia, Damascus, Moab, Edom, all the ends of the earth, for "in His name shall the Gentiles trust". An instance of this is the word, "And in mercy shall the throne be established: and he shall sit upon it in truth in the tabernacle of David, judging and seeking judgment, and hasting righteousness" (Isa. 16:5). Who else can the pronoun refer to but Messiah? The prophecy associates the throne with the tabernacle of David, and with the ministration of mercy, truth, judgment and righteousness, truly an evangelical anticipation, which directs us to the apostolic conference on this very matter.

As the apostles successfully proceeded upon their missionary vocation, problems arose among converts from Jewish orthodoxy and Gentile paganism (Acts 15). Certain Hebrew Christians from Judea "taught the brethren and said, Except ye be circumcised after the manner of Moses, ye cannot be saved". Similarly troubled were the churches in Galatia and elsewhere. The Judaizers received anathematizing condemnation from Paul since a different Gospel was thereby preached (Gal. 1). The error did not consist in supplanting Christ for Moses, but in supplementing the meritorious sufficiency of the grace of Christ by legal requirement. Paul proclaimed Christ a complete Saviour. There remains no place for the reimposition of the ceremonialism of Moses. At this conference Peter explained that the common salvation meant the abolition of difference and preferences with which, corroborating, James observed that "the words of the prophets *agreed*", and this received the approval of the apostles, the elders and the church.

This general prophetic confirmation that "the Gentiles should hear the word of the gospel and believe" James supported by a particular quotation (Amos 9:11). With the evangelizing of the nations then (and still) proceeding it was declared "the words of the prophets agree", and so also the specimen quotation from Amos. "Agree", that is, they speak together the same thing, they co-operate, they harmonize. "Agree" is the key word. The evidence is thereupon quoted: "After this I will return and will build again the tabernacle of David which is fallen down". The prophet introduced a time element, "in that day", which in the context is concurrent with Israel's scattering among the nations in the divine displeasure. This scattering would agree with that predicted by the Lord Jesus Himself, and the verse immediately preceding the prophecy describes the foolish and fatal attitude of multitudes of the people in the destruction of Jerusalem: "All the sinners of my people shall die by the sword, which say, The evil shall not overtake nor prevent us" (Amos 9:10; Luke 21). The sifting of Israel (v. 9) has been paraphrased thus: "I will cause the Israelites to be tossed about through all nations as corn is shaken about in a sieve, in such a way, however, that whilst the chaff and dust (all the sinners of my people) fall through (perish), all the solid grains (the elect) remain (are preserved). So, in the spiritual Israel, God gathers one convert here, another there, into His church: not the least is lost" (Jamieson, Fausset and Brown: Amos 9:9; Rom. 11:26).

The prophetic agreement with apostolic evangelizing is established, therefore, in purpose and time. James's "after this" cannot direct to a post-Christian age for this would involve disagreement between the prophetic and apostolic testimony. It corresponds to Amos's "in that day", that is to say, upon and during the sifting of Israel among the nations. This is precisely what was then beginning to take effect, and for this reason Amos is quoted as a specimen authority and explanation. Thus understanding, the conference arrived at a solution of the problem that had convened them. Amos names Edom with all the Gentiles, especially to mark the removal under the grace of the Gospel of the "difference", as Peter puts it, which hitherto had existed between Jacob and Esau (Edom) as well as generally between Jews and Gentiles. This wall of partition had now been done away in Christ.

The prophecy cited as being in agreement with the evangelizing of the nations was in this form: "I will build again the tabernacle of David". This by dispensationalists is construed as awaiting the millennial age, whereas the Jerusalem conference understood it as concerned with the present missionary age. To postpone to a coming time a prophecy declared by the apostles to be *the same thing* as the preaching of grace which at that very time occupied them, and on which they relied for support when some would outrage grace by imposing again the law, and in which case there could exist no such agreement as they declared to be the case, surely approaches the danger of wresting the Scriptures (2 Pet. 3:16). But again, literality would require the restoration of the very "tabernacle of David", and the tabernacle of David is not the same as the temple of Solomon. A distinction is made; the one superseded the other and they are not to be confused (Acts 7:46-47). David provided a temporary tabernacle to house the ark until the permanent temple should be erected for which he received the plan, and made considerable preparation. Is history to be repeated? And what of the ark of the covenant? (cf. Jer. 3:16).

By some the words are regarded as representing David's affairs in prosperity, "fallen down" expressing the low condition of the kingdom in Amos's time, and its restoration under Messiah. If so, this is itself a spiritualized interpretation and would seem to agree with the conclusion of the apostles. The word is appropriate to Christ, Who, becoming incarnate, "tabernacled amongst us" and was known as the "Son of David". Moreover, having expelled the commercialists from the temple, He said, "Destroy this temple" and it is explained that "He spake of the temple of His Body". He is both tabernacle and temple, indeed He is all. "Every whit uttereth His glory". The words of Amos and his fellow prophets find their spiritual complement now in the ministry of the Lord Jesus Christ and His church among all nations, with the establishing of Christian worship concerning which He made promise, saying, "there am I in the midst" (cf.

Ezek. 37:24-28). Again, therefore, it may be seen
that God meant what He said through the prophets,
whom the apostles invariably accepted as authoritative. But we must depend upon the apostles to
interpret for us the divine meaning. The presence
of God among His worshipping people is no longer
symbolized by the ark, nor is their worship located
in tabernacle or temple "made with hands", for
in such God "dwelleth not" (Acts 7:48; 17:24;
John 4:21-24). Accordingly, when the Lord of
glory in visions of the Apocalypse unveiled scenes
above where He is enthroned, and sent His angel
to "testify these things in the churches", we read,
"the *temple* of God opened in heaven, and there was
seen in His temple the *ark* of His testimony", and
again, "I looked, and behold, the *temple* of the
tabernacle of the *testimony* was opened in heaven".
All the literal structures provided in Israel on
earth were symbolic of spiritual realities in Christ
in heaven where He ministers "in the true tabernacle which the Lord pitched and not man" (Rev.
22:16; 11:19; 15:5; Heb. 8:2). In the Messiah's
heavenly glorification and mediatorship, sovereignty and rule, the types of Moses, David and Solomon
are all substantiated according to the Original, for
He is the Alpha and Omega, the First and the Last.

CANAAN AND HEAVEN:
TYPICAL AND TRUE

CHRIST became partaker with us of flesh and blood, by incarnation fulfilling the redeeming legal necessity, and so becoming our Kinsman. In this respect He was Abraham's promised Seed, and He so became that He might lay hold of Abraham's spiritual seed, the children, by destroying the Devil and delivering them whom he legally held in the bondage of sin and death (Heb. 2).

The children thus delivered became "partakers" of Christ", which meant they were "partakers of the heavenly calling". These are exhorted, therefore, and daily to exhort one another, to "hold fast the beginning of their confidence steadfast unto the end", a command which is directed against the ever-present possibility of unbelief (Heb. 3).

This daily exhorting is based upon the divine word to Israel through Moses and Joshua and David, "Today, if ye will hear His voice, harden not your hearts". Heart-hardening is expressed in unbelief, but partakership of Christ is entered upon and sustained through faith. This partakership of the heavenly calling, partakership of Christ, means entering into God's rest. To this our Lord may have referred when He said, "Come unto Me, and I will give you rest: learn of Me and ye shall find rest unto your souls", the historical background of which may have been the prophet's word to the unbelieving nation, "Stand ye in the ways and see, and ask for the old paths, where is the good way, and walk therein, and ye shall find rest for your souls. But they said, we will not walk therein" (Jer. 6:16).

From the beginning God had called attention to His rest, first in the Sabbath-rest at creation. This was not a rest from weariness in working, it was the rest of satisfaction with work well done. All was very good. Man had no part in that good work, and sin had not yet wrought its ruination. "Hast thou not known, hast thou not heard, that the everlasting God, the Lord, *the Creator* of the ends of the earth, fainteth not, neither is weary?" (Isa. 40:28). Notwithstanding the entrance of sin bringing the pronouncement of divine judgment upon creation, and indicating the holy displeasure of God, the Sabbath was continued in legislation and type, anticipating a new creation and a new satisfaction.

In His unfolding purpose, the Gospel, it is said, was preached in the literal yet typical Canaan rest, into which the generation of responsible Israelites, redeemed from Egypt, entered not because of unbelief. Yet, even those who did enter, the new generation with Caleb and Joshua, failed to realize God's perfect rest in Canaan, their land of rest. For it is explained that if Joshua had given them rest, God would not have spoken of another day. They had subdued so far their enemies, and had become settled in their inheritances, fulfilling the geographical boundaries originally promised, and Joshua testified, "there failed not aught of any good thing which the Lord had promised, all came to pass"; yet they had not entered into God's rest. Hence, "so long a time" after, the time between Joshua and David, again God spake, this time in David, saying, "To day, if ye will hear His voice, harden not your hearts" (Heb. 4).

Neither under Moses or Joshua or the Judges or Samuel or Saul did Israel attain unto God's rest. Not indeed under David, the king after God's own heart, who had subdued all his enemies round about, or Solomon, whose kingdom extended to the literal boundaries of the land promised to Abraham (cf.

Gen. 15:18; 2 Sam. 8:3; 1 Kings 4:21-24; 2 Chr. 7:8) and which reached such heights of glory that in the later historical accounts David is always the exemplary king, the standard by which successors are approved or disapproved; and in the prophetical Scriptures he is the ideal ruler whose very name, and not that of Solomon, is given to His greater Son, Messiah. Not even under David's regime, with Jerusalem all-glorious, with the ark of the covenant, symbol of the divine presence, at rest, Solomon succeeding with the temple exceeding magnifical as the house of His dwelling, did the people truly enter into God's rest. There remaineth, therefore, over and beyond, a rest for the people of God, God's rest. For that rest necessitated the new creation, with sin banished; the intended but far-exceeding complement of the original creation, in which He with His redeemed Church will find satisfaction forever.

We thus gather that God meant what He said when the report concerning the Canaan land of rest was brought by the two faithful messengers, Joshua and Caleb, but the people entered not in because of unbelief. He meant what He said when the new generation under Joshua possessed their possessions in the land promised them. He meant what He said to David speaking of Zion, "This is My rest forever, here will I dwell, for I have desired it". But He did not say what He meant. He meant the sabbath rest at creation, He meant the Canaan rest promised to Abraham and his seed, He meant the occupied land of rest under Joshua, reaching its apex of glory under David and Solomon. He meant these, but though actual and literal in themselves, He meant them to represent the heavenly rest, the rest into which our Lord Jesus has entered through conquest of our enemies and resurrection to the throne of His kingdom, His work finished and perfect, and surely pronounced "very good" in Heaven's welcome (Acts 3:21), the rest of satisfaction forever established. He meant that partakers of Christ, and therefore of the heavenly calling, should through faith enter into that rest of which the literal Canaan was a type. But the Scriptures do not say that He meant by His rest that the earthly Canaan would be millennially re-occupied under David again as the king. He meant that Hebrews as well as Gentiles through Gospel faith should now enter His rest, and thereafter in the presence of Christ their Redeemer would possess the land that is fairer than day. This is the hope of Israel, preached also unto the Gentiles, for her earthly inheritance was forfeited through unbelief and apostasy; they corrupted and defiled it and it faded away; but this is "incorruptible, undefiled and fadeth not away" being "reserved in heaven" (1 Pet. 1:3-5).

We have observed that Canaan was a type of God's heavenly rest. The people of old under Moses failed through unbelief to enter into the land of rest, but wandered in the wilderness where their bodies were laid to rest. Under Joshua the new generation, notwithstanding that they, unlike their fathers, did enter into the land, yet like them failed to apprehend the divine significance of Canaan and entered not into God's rest, so that to generation upon generation in the land the repeated remonstrance was given, "To day, if ye will hear His voice, harden not your hearts". That announcement still stands, and it is still true that "there remaineth a rest to the people of God." The exhortation, therefore, is still valid, "Let us therefore labour to enter into that rest, lest any man fall after the same example of unbelief". Unbelief in respect of Canaan, the earthly inheritance, is a warning with respect to God's rest, the heavenly inheritance. The indispensable principles of faith and unbelief apply to both. The Gospel is preached unto us as well as unto them, "but the word preached did not profit them, not being mixed with faith in them that heard it". Though Israel entered carnally upon the Canaan inheritance, the word of the prophet proved true: "If ye be willing and obedient ye shall eat the good of the land; but if ye refuse and rebel ye shall be devoured with the sword: for the mouth of the Lord hath spoken it" (Isa. 1:19-20). History verifies the admonition.

It is possible to gain the earthly and fail of the heavenly. It was possible to have gained both. And it is possible to fail of the earthly and gain the heavenly. It went "ill with Moses for Israel's sake", and he was not suffered to enter the land (Ps. 106: 32), yet later he "appeared in glory", and with Elijah, spake on the mount with the transfigured Son of God. They "spake of His decease (exodus) which He should accomplish at Jerusalem". That accomplishment was the payment and acceptance of the ransom price by which "He opened the kingdom of heaven to all believers". After the audience they returned to their heavenly rest. There, having gained the victory, the host of redeemed sing, not in a restored Canaan on earth but in heaven, "the song of Moses and of the Lamb" (Rev. 15). And attached to the heavenly city, the new Jerusalem "which is the mother of us all" (believers; Gal. 4), are the names of the twelve tribes of Israel and the twelve apostles of the Lamb. It is not that then Israel belongs to Jerusalem below and the Church to Jerusalem above, but all saved through the blood of the Lamb have a heavenly inheritance. Jerusalem below indeed "is in bondage with her children", and in the Book of the Revelation of Jesus Christ, the description remains unrelieved: "the great city which spiritually is called Sodom and Egypt, where also our Lord was crucified" (Rev. 11:8); whereas, of "that great city, the holy Jerusalem, descending out of heaven from God" it may be said, where also our Lord is glorified! (Rev. 21:10).

In an American Fundamentalist journal (Aug. '62) and with apparent approval in an English Prophetic magazine (March-Apr. '63) the following appeared: "God's promises to the three patriarchs require resurrection for their fulfilment. To Abraham, a mere sojourner in the chosen land, He said: 'All the land which thou seest, to thee will I give it, and to thy seed after thee forever' (Gen. 13: 15). Abraham must be raised from the dead to receive this inheritance. Similarly, God spoke to Isaac: 'Unto thee and to thy seed I will give all these countries' (Gen. 26:33); and to Jacob: 'The land whereon thou liest, to thee will I give it, and to thy seed' (Gen. 28:13). At the same time He promised to make the patriarchs a blessing to all the families of the earth. Not yet have these magnificent promises seen fulfilment: they await the resurrection".

The bodies of the patriarchs, together with all who share "the faith of their faithful father, Abraham" (Rom. 4), will in the resurrection be clothed with immortality, and receive their promised inheritance in Christ, even as now in the intermediate state their spirits are consciously at rest with Christ. In resurrection they bear "the image of the heavenly" and not again "the earthly" (1 Cor. 15). The obvious literalistic character of this statement would seem to refer to the earthly Canaan millennially restored, in which case it is proposed that Abraham, Isaac and Jacob will receive a temporal, carnal and mortal inheritance while they themselves will be gloriously fitted for an eternal, spiritual and immortal state. Some have stated, and consistency would require it, that even David, personally, since "David" is named, is to sit again upon his throne in Jerusalem in resurrected form! "Flesh and blood cannot inherit the kingdom of God, neither doth corruption inherit incorruption". Would not the reverse also be true? When confronted with this problem the answer is given, "We know as yet but in part"! and "with God all things are possible"! We are reminded of the boys in Sunday School, reading how David, walking on the roof of his house, saw Bathsheba. One of the boys looking up through the window at the steep roofs of the houses without, enquired how the king could walk on the roof of his house! The teacher, on this point as ignorant as his scholar, stifled the inquiry with, "Don't grumble at the Bible"! Meanwhile the teacher in an adjoining class overheard the conversation. Leaning towards his fellow-teacher he whispered: "The answer to the difficulty is, 'With men it is impossible, but with God all things are possible' "!

The correction of the concluding assumption is already given by Paul who makes it clear that when God said, "In thee and in thy Seed shall all families of the earth be blessed" He was not referring to the patriarchs or their natural progeny in a resurrected state, but to the Lord Jesus Christ, and that is the reason he used the singular: "He saith not, and to seeds, as of many; but as of one" (Gal. 3). Again, the same Scripture states that the time of the blessing of all nations is now through the Gospel, and not in a future age through the Jews.

Of the patriarchs we read that they "died in faith". They had embraced the promises seen afar off, and being persuaded, "they confessed that they were strangers and pilgrims *in the earth*". Thus confessing they "declared plainly that they sought a better country, that is, an heavenly". If they had been mindful of an earthly country, they could have returned. It is even said that they "sojourned in the *land of promise* as in a *strange* country." The patriarchs therefore, did not find, and did not expect to find their rest in the earthly Canaan. They apprehended the meaning of the divine promises more accurately than their modern literalist interpreters (Heb. 11). "The God of glory" appeared unto and called Abram, and the material inheritance of which God said, "I will show thee", to be an "everlasting possession" sealed by an "everlasting covenant" they received as the "shadow of good things to come" and "better things", for "they looked for a city which hath foundations whose Builder and Maker is God". The patriarchal progeny did possess the land, and God meant what He said, but what He truly meant only the men of faith apprehended. This is in perfect accord with the divine manner in which the revealing of God's purpose and will was made known to the Old Testament people.

Canaan, as the proffered rest to strangers and pilgrims in the wilderness, is typical of heaven. The theme has been expressed in some of our loved Christian hymns. It is also thought that from another point of view Canaan's occupation and experience is representative of the believer's progress in the Christian life in conflict and victory, the flesh and the Spirit, the old nature carnal, earthly, and the new nature, spiritual, heavenly. In this sense it is true that believers do now enter into rest, for they take upon them the yoke of Christ; it is also true that "there remaineth a rest to the people of God".

"Perfect submission, *all is at rest,*
I in my Saviour am happy and blest;
Watching and waiting, looking above,
Filled with His goodness, lost in His love."

THE HOPE AND SALVATION
OF ISRAEL

THE HOPE of Israel which Paul preached was not exclusively the hope of the Jews; it was not even the hope which that nation cherished. It was no more Israel's hope distinctively than the God of Israel was Israel's God and not the God of the whole earth, or the Messiah of Israel was Israel's Messiah and not the "Desire of all nations", or the commonwealth of Israel was wealth for Israel alone, for in Christ Gentiles partake of the same. Jehovah, Who is God alone and claims the attention of the whole earth, was revealed through Israel; the hope of mankind was communicated through the Scriptures committed to Israel. In this she had an "advantage" but no monopoly (Rom. 3:2). The hope is announced in the Gospel (Col. 1:5). The apostle described it as "the hope of resurrection of the dead" (Acts 23:6), "hope toward God" agreeable to "all things that are written in the law and in the prophets". This, he said, the Jews themselves allowed, "that there shall be a resurrection of the dead, both of the just and unjust" (Acts 24:14-15). The Jews, charging Paul with heresy in preaching "the hope of Israel", were unable to sustain any charge against him, "except it be for this one voice . . . touching the resurrection of the dead I am called in question" (Acts 24:21).

As before one tribunal after another he was allowed opportunity to bear witness, this one thing he stressed, that Israel's hope is realized through faith in a risen Messiah Who died on the cross for sins and thereafter entered into His glory. "Now I stand and am judged for the hope of the promise made unto our fathers: unto which promise our twelve tribes, instantly serving God day and night, hope to come. For which hope's sake I am accused of the Jews. Why should it be thought a thing incredible with you, that God should raise the dead?" It is the resurrection of Christ which is fundamentally in question, his enemies themselves being witness, for said Festus, "they brought none accusation of such things as I supposed, but on one, Jesus, which was dead, Whom Paul affirmed to be alive" (Acts 25:18-19; 26:6-8). In defending his ministry and his hope of everlasting life through Jesus Christ, Whom he had seen in risen glory and by Whom he had been "arrested" when as unbelieving as the Jews who now accused him, he averred that he declared "none other things than those which the prophets and Moses did say should come, that Christ should suffer and that He should be the first that should rise from the dead, and should show light unto the people, and to the Gentiles". "For these causes", he protested, "the Jews went about to kill me". Against this threat he was fortified by the assurance that God would deliver him from the hostility of the Jews and the Gentiles to whom, being appointed the apostle to the Gentiles, he was sent "to open their eyes, and to turn them from darkness to light, and from the power of Satan unto God, that they may receive forgiveness of sins, and inheritance among them which are sanctified" (Acts 26:17-18). This is the hope which Paul preached to Jews and Gentiles alike.

Saul of Tarsus in his blind prejudice had done "many things contrary to the name of Jesus of Nazareth" including his persecution of Jewish believers, for he himself had held the false hope of a Jewish nationalism, but upon his conversion they heard "that he which persecuted us in the past now preacheth the faith which once he destroyed" (Acts 26:9; Gal. 1:23). Never deviating from his hopeful preaching but obtaining help of God to continue, he pressed on, and when for the last time (as far as record is given) as the Lord's prisoner he addressed the official representatives of the Jewish nation, he declared, "for the hope of Israel I am bound with this chain". At the same time he uttered against them in denouncing their unbelief the condemnatory words of Isaiah, leaving them in their state of judicial blindness, and added, "Be it known therefore unto you, that the salvation of God is sent unto the Gentiles, and that they will hear it" (Acts 28:25-28). Unless Scripture be wrested of its meaning what can be the sense of these words but that the hope of salvation was the same as he had preached to the Jews? At Antioch earlier a similar situation had occurred: the Jews having rejected his preaching, "the Gentiles besought that *these words* might be preached unto them", which in response Paul was eager to do (Acts 13:42-48). The hope of Israel which Paul preached, he had himself embraced at his conversion, and the same vision and deliverance from Satan and forgiveness, the same salvation and inheritance in Christ, he desired for his kinsmen according to the flesh and for the Gentiles to whom he was sent. If repetition denotes emphasis or if silence is eloquent, no justification whatsoever can be gleaned from this testimony of Paul for construing the "hope of Israel" as other than "the salvation which is in Christ Jesus with eternal glory" (2 Tim. 2:10). Never does Paul hold out to the Jews the "hope" of a future national millennial rehabilitation to be introduced at the Second Advent of Christ. the realization of a national hope contingent upon national repentance. Paul knew nothing of such nationalism. Had the apostle thus interpreted "the hope of Israel" as do dispensationalists today, had he encouraged them in such a prospect, they surely would have welcomed him as the herald of their material and temporal deliverance, even as some did the Lord Jesus Himself when He miraculously provided for their carnal satisfaction and by force they would have made Him their king but He purposely avoided them (John 6:15) ! Deceived by such aspirations, they rejected Paul as they rejected his

Lord for the same reason, and as predicted they would welcome false Messiahs as, indeed, they have done (John 5:43; Matt. 24:23-24). "If ye believe not that I am He", spake the Lord Jesus to the Jews of His time, "ye shall die in your sins, and whither I go ye cannot come".

A hypothetical case is sometimes argued that had the Jews nationally accepted the Lord Jesus Christ, He would have then fulfilled to them their national hope at His First Advent. It is also suggested that at Pentecost Peter again offered to them the kingdom conditioned upon their official repentance, and later, it is said, Paul repeated this before he turned to the Gentiles. There is not a whit of evidence supporting this, but if speculation is indulged in as to what would have occurred had the nation welcomed the Messiah when "He came unto His own", it might be answered that in such case the people would have individually held relation to the Saviour in the same manner as did those of their nation who received Him and entered upon discipleship. And had the number of His Hebrew followers been thus augmented, had all the rulers believed on Him, had the whole people received Him gladly, it might still be asked, in view of the population of the world, "What are they amongst so many?" It is decreed that He is to have the nations for His inheritance and the uttermost part of the earth for His possession, which is to be the ultimate achievement of His evangelical commission (Ps. 2:8; Acts 1:8).

Peter was the apostle to the circumcision though he ministered also to the Gentiles; Paul to the uncircumsion, though he also ministered to the Jews. What had Peter to say to dispersed Jewish believers for their encouragement and comfort? He announced a "living hope", living because, as Paul also testified, it was founded upon the death and resurrection of Jesus Christ; the hope he expounded as "an inheritance incorruptible, and undefiled. and that fadeth not away, reserved in heaven", just, as we have already observed, as Paul preached, boldly withstanding his Jewish accusers, "enemies of the cross of Christ who mind earthly things" (Phil.

3:19). By the oblation of His cross Christ opened the door to heavenly things. The hope announced by Peter, therefore, was the reverse of the earthly inheritance of Canaan, which because of the nation's apostasy became corrupted and defiled and faded away from their possession. Is not this "living hope" so described in contrast with the earthly hope which had perished? James also addressed his epistle to "the twelve tribes", even as Paul had spoken of that "to which our twelve tribes hope to come". These tribes must have been viewed representatively for in their totality they were not qualified by grace to be described in the terms which James employs. They were, therefore, the firstfruits, part of that "remnant according to the election of grace"; some had been gathered to Christ out of all the tribes of Israel, and unto the end more must be gathered in. They are called "firstfruits" (Jas. 1:18). Were they the Pentecostal firstfruits? The names of the twelve tribes of the children of Israel and the twelve apostles of the Lamb are inscribed upon the heavenly Jerusalem (Rev. 21:12-14). And what of the sealed number in each tribe (Rev. 7)? James assured these tribes that being rich in faith they are "heirs of the kingdom which God hath promised to them that love Him" (Jas. 2:5). They were also chosen of God, "the election of grace"; they were racially members of the scattered nation (1 Pet. 1:1), but there is no reference to them as even representative members of a returning nation to an earthly inheritance. As when the seed of Abraham are mentioned these are believers in Christ (Gal. 3:29), and Israel the remnant elect within the nation (Rom. 11:5), and the Jews, those inwardly renewed by the Spirit (Rom. 2:28-29), and circumcision, that which is of the heart (Rom. 2:29; Phil. 3:3), so the twelve tribes are those members of the tribes chosen of God to inherit the heavenly Canaan. Not in this world is their hope, for "whosoever will be a friend of the world is the enemy of God" (Jas. 4:4). These, as the Hebrews addressed in the epistle bearing that name, had a "hope set before them as the anchor of the soul for us both sure and steadfast, and entereth into that within the veil, whither our Forerunner is entered, even Jesus" (Heb. 6:19-20). The only hope of the Hebrews is the goal of heavenly glory where Christ is crowned. And this also is the hope of chosen believers out of all nations.

Such New Testament unfolding sets out what God meant when He "established a testimony in Jacob and appointed a law in Israel, that they might set their hope in God" (Ps. 78:7; cf. 1 Pet. 1:21). It is clear, therefore, that God meant what He said in announcing at sundry times and in divers manners the hope of Israel, but that He said what He meant by this hope in "the word of the truth of the gospel" which directs to "the hope laid up in heaven" (Col. 1:5). For when all differences between Jews and Gentiles were done away in Christ, when Gentiles who before were strangers and aliens, having no hope, remained no longer outcasts but were constituted "fellow-citizens with the saints", it was written, "there is one body and one Spirit, even as ye are called in *one hope* of your calling, one Lord, one faith, one baptism, one God and Father of all, Who is above all, and through all, and in you all" (Eph. 4:4-6). The singularity and uniqueness which qualifies the three Persons of the Godhead applies also to faith of salvation, the baptism of confession and the hope of eternal blessedness.

The salvation of Israel, according to the premillennial presentation of the Second Coming of Christ, is to be of national scope and is interpreted as including, together with spiritual blessing, political and governmental status with authoritarian superiority over the nations of the earth, under Messiah enthroned in Palestine's Jerusalem; the twelve tribes of Israel being resettled in their former inheritance, a temple rebuilt, with ceremonial service re-established; feasts and sacerdotal worship reinstituted; a reinstitution of the old covenant as under Moses and David but revived in new covenant estate under Messiah.

There is not a single passage in the New Testament which authorizes this expectation. Old Testament passages are usually relied upon, and the futuristic and literal sense given them takes no account of the symbolism in which the terms are couched.

It is insisted, however, that Paul's closing words in his treatment of Israel's case in relation to the Gentiles and the Gospel in Romans chapters 9 to 11 justify this interpretation.

It is accepted as a sound rule in Biblical exegesis that where a sense may be doubtful or neutral other references to the same subject, particularly in the context, may decide the issue. "In the mouth of two or three witnesses every word shall be established" is a rule applicable. What, then, did Paul mean when he used the word, "Salvation"? The answer would determine, for example, what God meant when in old time through His prophets He gave such promise as "Israel shall be saved in the Lord with an everlasting salvation; ye shall not be ashamed nor confounded world without end" (Isa. 45:17). What, then, is to be understood by Israel's salvation? That God meant what He said in this gracious assurance and that it altogether out-measures any millennial limitation is patent even in the prophet's own terms: what God meant is explained in this Gospel exposition by Paul.

Although a "Hebrew of the Hebrews", being commissioned "apostle to the Gentiles" he here addressed them (Rom. 11:13), and he deemed it needful to caution them against the tendency to conceit lest they should consider the Jews to be totally cast off by God and they themselves now favoured in preference. Rather, he explained the Jews forfeited their priority through unbelief. and faith alone is standing ground for Jew and Gentile alike (Rom. 11:20). His reaction is expressed in genuine emotion for the well-being of his kinsman according to the flesh — concern, indeed, not for revival of their nationhood or material establishment in Canaan, but for their spiritual and eternal salvation in Christ, in which he himself now rejoiced through mercy exceeding abundant, being a "pattern" to subsequent believers (1 Tim. 1:16). He repeats the non-distinguishing statement of an earlier chapter: "there is no difference between the

Jew and the Greek" (Rom. 3:22; 10:12). He affirms that personal faith is indispensable. He uses the figure of an olive tree. To believe is to be graffed in. Unbelief occasioned Israel's being broken off, and "if — expressing the contingency — they abide not still in unbelief they shall be graffed in, for God is able to graff them in again". But not so ingraffed to exist as a separate entity, a distinct olive tree all their own, thus re-erecting barriers broken down (Eph. 2), but into that same olive tree into which Gentile believers are already ingraffed in place of Jewish branches broken off. So that believing Jews are ingraffed to and with Gentiles.

The apostle's first use of the term salvation is in an Old Testament quotation (Isaiah 10:22; Rom. 9:27). The prophecy here of Israel's "return" cannot be regarded as an earthly resettlement in the land after captivity or scattering among the nations, for in the apostle's substitution by the Spirit for "return" the word "saved" which he repeatedly uses in a spiritual sense, he supplies the meaning of what God said through the prophet; that is, when God said they should "return" He meant they should be "saved". The "consumption decreed" is the "short work" as stated by Paul, by which not Israel totally or nationally, but selectively, even "a remnant only" is intended: "a remnant shall return (be saved) even the remnant of Jacob, unto the mighty God" (Isa. 10:21). These are spoken of as "the escaped of the house of Jacob" who "shall stay upon the Lord, the holy One of Israel". And the time stated, "in that day", is also settled for us here as this day of Gospel grace, of Christ's building His church, one body of saved Jews and Gentiles: otherwise illustrated as one olive tree.

Paul's next reference is the unveiling of his heart's desire for Israel; namely, "that they may be saved" (10:1). He thereupon proceeds to explain what he means by salvation, even justifying righteousness through faith in Christ Jesus Who died and rose again; that is, the Gospel which he says is the object or end of the law, in contrast with the legal righteousness which Moses described. At the same time Paul shows that what God said through Moses concerning the nearness of the saving means was intended to direct to the "word of faith" and "the righteousness which is of faith" (Deut. 30). Salvation, he says is not contingent upon any further work of Christ from below or from above, significantly not even upon His coming down again from heaven. Salvation is not contingent on His Second Coming, rather this saving word is "in thy mouth and in thy heart". The confession of faith in a crucified and risen Saviour is salvation; and this is the proclamation to all without distinction, for "whosoever shall call upon the name of the Lord shall be saved". The verse is a quotation (Joel 2:32). The preceding verses give promise of the Spirit's outpouring as Peter affirmed at Pentecost: "this is that which was spoken by the prophet Joel" concluding with the same words here used by Paul. We have, therefore, this twofold witness that God meant what He said through the Hebrew prophet: "It shall come to pass that whosoever shall call upon the name of the Lord shall be delivered, for in Mount Zion and in Jerusalem shall be deliverance as the Lord hath said, and in the remnant whom the Lord shall call". And now through the apostles' preaching he showed what God meant by the Pentecostal ingathering of Jews and thenceforward the Gentiles also, for "their sound went into all the earth, and their words unto the ends of the world" (Rom. 10:18). Salvation according to Paul, fulfilling his heart's desire and prayer for Israel, is evangelical and spiritual; he says nothing of its being millennial and national; and is found through believing the "report" of the Gospel as set out in Isa. 53, for "faith cometh by hearing and hearing by the word of God". This is Paul's inspired interpretation of what God had said concerning salvation for Israel in Moses and the Prophets.

In the next reference, Paul avers that the same "salvation is come unto the Gentiles" upon Israel's not seeking it in the way of faith. Notwithstanding this apparent discouragement in respect of the Jews, however, Paul being the apostle to the Gentiles did so magnify his office as to provoke Jews to jealousy and thus, "save some of them" (11:14), the burden of salvation with Paul being always spiritual and urgent. It is the "remnant according to the election of grace" which he always has in view, for "the election hath obtained it, while the rest were blinded". And he quotes Isaiah and David as confirming this permanent judgment (Rom. 11:7-10). Finally, as if to give the sum of his argument, Paul says, "And so all Israel shall be saved". Unless therefore, some clear distinction be made, salvation must here be understood in the same sense as in the exposition of the case throughout. "So all Israel shall be saved". Saved through God sending them preachers of His Gospel that they may hear the Word by which faith cometh, believing, and calling upon the name of the Lord, as their prophet Isaiah and Joel had promised, as Peter preached at Pentecost and Paul here reaffirms with confidence.

This then is how the apostle viewed the salvation of his brethren, which his heart desired and for which he prayed. And these are the means he depended upon to that end. And now is the time when their salvation must be accomplished, for while Jesus their Messiah was once crucified, He is now "exalted a Prince and a Saviour for to give repentance to Israel and forgiveness of sins" (Acts 5:31).

ISRAEL AND "ISRAEL"

ISRAELITES were a highly favoured race, their crowning glory being that of them, "as concerning the flesh the Messiah came, Who is over all, God blessed for ever" (Rom. 9:5). Thus does the apostle trace to their goal God-given benefits to Israel. Messiah, however, did not come *for* Israel or **exclusively** *to* Israel, they have no monopoly or claim above others. He chose to come *of* Israel. That was to their "advantage", as was also the commitment to them of the divine oracles written to expound Him (Rom. 3:1). He could have come of any other race had God so willed it. He belongs to no one race, He is "the Desire of all nations" and "all nations shall call Him blessed". He is not the second Jacob: He is "the second Man." He is not the last Jew, or the flower of that race; He is "the last Adam" and "the Lord from heaven". Blessings announced to Israel are here not because Christ came of Israel, but because He comes to Israel in the Gospel as He comes to all mankind: "He came and preached peace to them that are afar off and to them that are nigh" (Eph. 2:17). He benefits those who receive Him whatever their race (John 1:12). The Hebrew director of a Jewish Christian Mission declared in a public meeting that Christ had a Jewish body, that it was a Jewish body they nailed to the cross, and in which He rose and ascended; and with a Jewish body He will come the second time—

literal boasting in the flesh indeed! Here is another claim from a Jewish Mission magazine: "Had Jesus been a native of any other nation He would have become a limited Saviour, benefitting chiefly the people among whom He was born. As a Greek He might have been expected to propagate beauty and learning; as a Roman, strategy, power and strength. But as a Jew, He became the universal Saviour, for the Jewish nation had been chosen to spread the knowledge of God throughout the whole wide world. Therefore Jesus could be no other than a Jew". The truth, of course, is that the promise of universal salvation was made to Abraham and his Seed, and Abraham was not a Jew; "and that Seed is Christ". Moreover, the Jews utterly failed to spread the knowledge of the true God; they merited the judgment of God in that they corrupted such knowledge as had been committed to them by divine revelation, and even imported pagan idolatry into their own land. It was entirely due to the divine purpose and preservation that the nation continued until Messiah had come as promised. For God's choice no reason is found; human or national merit does not exist; all lies within His Own undisclosed sovereign decree. And we may justly assume that had God been pleased to choose any other people, He could have determined and accomplished the same result. "The purpose of God" stands "according to election" and does not depend on human efficiency. "No flesh shall glory in His sight; he that glorieth, let him glory in the Lord". "For of Him, and through Him, and to Him are all things, to Whom be glory for ever." Because the incarnate Saviour came of the Jews they are not on that account the more entitled to Him than the rest of mankind, nor because He did not come of Gentiles are they thereby denied His gracious visitation.

Israel's blessings are vicarious. "Not for your sakes but for My Holy Name's sake" is the repeated reminder in the prophets; and to all the blessed it is written, "Your sins are forgiven for His Name's sake." The name is not the personal name, save that such name is chosen because of truth intended by it; the name stands for His reputation, His character, His achievements. It is indeed "a good name rather to be chosen than great riches". Hence He will glorify His great and holy name. (Compare the significant event recorded in Exodus 33:18-23 and its implementation in 34:1-8, where the proclamation of the name of the Lord is given in His covenanted mercy). May not the very name "Israel" be of this distinctive order? The apostle seems to reason that this is the case. Not all Jews who claim descent from Jacob have right to Jacob's divinely changed name, though they generally make use of it. "They are not all Israel who are of Israel". Israel, therefore, as Paul explained divine selection by this differentiation, does not include the entire people who bear the name racially. They are not Israel because of racial descent from Jacob, for a carnal claim is not entertained at all. Those only of a character determined other than by descent, race or nationhood, are Israel. "Behold", directed our Lord to Nathaniel, "an Israelite indeed, in whom is no guile" (no Jacob?). He was representatively or typically a true Israelite for he confessed Jesus to be the Son of God; all, therefore, to whom it is given to do that must be akin to Nathaniel (John 1:47-49; 20:31). And notably thereupon our Lord advised Nathaniel, the true Israelite, of the spiritual intention of Jacob's ladder: "From this time forth ye shall see heaven open, and the angels of God ascending and descending upon the Son of Man" (John 1:51; Gen. 28:12). "Truly, God is good to Israel" (Ps. 73), and who are "Israel", asked Mr. David Baron, who we profitably heard expound this psalm? "Even such as are of a cleansed heart". The Bible explains itself if we will notice how it interprets and applies its own chosen terms. Wrote John Flavel the Puritan, "If Abraham's faith be not in your hearts, it will be no advantage that Abraham's blood runs in your veins".

The Bible being written for spiritual purposes, it does not appear amiss to read, "they are not all Israel who are of Israel". Nor would it be amiss if we also read, "they are not all Jews who are of the Jews", but how incongruous it would be to say, "They are not all Arabs who are of the Arabs", or "they are not all English who are of the English". Today a resettled people has assumed the title and applies it also to their country or state, but obviously the Israel first mentioned in this text is a specialized Israel, the Israel to which the word of promise proved effectual, and to whom the salvation which is in Christ Jesus appertained, the election of grace. Here is explained what God meant when He said "Israel". These in reality Paul reasoned are the only Israel entitled so to be designated, and eventually this will be established when all distinctions and rivalries are done away in Christ. It is made clear as Paul calls in evidence the consistent ways of God from the beginning that the only entitlement to the name "Israel" is from spiritual relationship to Jesus Christ. By elimination the apostle establishes this, and whatever his own emotions towards his kinsmen according to the flesh, he adoringly welcomes the unchallengeable will and purpose of his sovereign Lord (Rom. 11:33-36).

The seed of Abraham, though including Ishmael and his children by Keturah, is electively and spiritually restricted to Isaac, for the children of the promise, that is, of spiritual birth and not according to the flesh by natural descent, are the children of God. These only are Israel in the divine estimation. Again, although Jacob and Esau were sons of Isaac, Jacob and not Esau was chosen, the decisive decree being made of sovereign grace before their birth. To Jacob, to the exclusion of Esau, the name was revealed. Arising from this divine selection and rejection Paul quotes Moses concerning the compassionate and hardening will of God, and instances His control of Pharaoh's actions, and the potter's choice of vessels unto honour and dishonour, of wrath unto destruction or of mercy unto glory. And here Paul explains the embrace of the merciful will of God, effectual through the Spirit's call in the Gospel: "even US"—glad he is to be associated with saved Gentiles in the prospect of Glory—"whom He hath called, not of the Jews only but also of the Gentiles", which conclusion is the fulfilment of the words of Israel's prophet (Hosea 2:23; Rom. 9:24-26). These all and together, he quotes, shall be called "the children of the living God". He keeps, therefore, to the principle and unfolding of his text: "they are not all Israel who are of Israel", that the children of the promise are the children of God and counted for the seed (Rom. 9:8). Jews and Gentiles together, saved by grace, are the called of God, called as were Abraham and Isaac and Jacob, "vessels of mercy afore prepared unto glory".

The word "called" is inseparable from foreknowledge and election and predestination, and as with the ordered human means employed unto the sinner's response: sent, preach, hear, believe, call (Rom. 10:13-15), so with the ordered divine cause affecting God's purpose: foreknown, predestinated, called, justified, glorified (Rom. 8:29-30). Thus the question, "Hath God cast away His people?" is emphatically answered by this qualification, "God hath not cast away His people *which He foreknew*" (Rom. 11:1-2). From personal evidence, Paul is himself witness. From historic evidence the reserved of Elijah's day are cited, and as to the entire Christian dispensation, "even so at this present time there is a remnant according to the election of grace" (Rom. 9:27; 11:5, 7, 28). This election, like the selection of the fathers, Abraham, Isaac and Jacob, to the exclusion of the non-elect, comprises the children of the promise, the children of God, and therefore, the spiritual Israel, the Israel whom God really meant when He gave His promises to Israel. They are the spiritual Israel, as distinguished from carnal Israel. They are Israel, the remnant, the election of grace, to be distinguished from Israel "the rest", the children of the flesh. The means designed to discover "the elect" from "the rest", Paul reasons and that in which he himself was engaged, that he "might save some of them", is the preaching of the Gospel. Salvation is of grace, and while Israel hath not obtained it, "the election hath obtained it and the rest were blinded" (Rom. 11:7). We see that Israel is here again divided, "the election" and "the rest". The elect are those "on whom He will have mercy", the rest those "whom He hardeneth" (Rom. 9:18). Isaiah is quoted in support, and David, for this hardened condition or state of blindness is the fulfilment of predicted judgment, words of severity indeed which convey the sense that the hardened state is irremediable (Rom. 11:8-10; Isa. 29:10; Ps. 69:22-28).

From this examination it seems clear that in Paul's analysis there are two Israels, and as the same noun is used so are the same pronouns used of both sections. The qualifications must determine which Israel is meant. That spiritual Israel is the church is not to be so lightly refuted as the editor of a Hebrew Christian magazine appeared to think could be done substituting the word "Church" for "Israel" throughout this passage (Rom. 11:33-36). This dismissal of a revelation of the inscrutable ways of God rather exposed the superficiality of the writer. It is not true that the name "Israel" as here used rigidly means the literal racial Israel, otherwise, Jews, as distinguished from the church. It is true that "Israel" is here used for the remnant, the elect, the called, the saved, incorporated in the church. It is also true that the church is composed not of saved Jews *or* Gentiles, as when some wrongly speak of the Jewish Church and the Gentile Church, but of saved Jews together with Gentiles, one body, and that these are "the Israel of God", "even US", writes Paul in this very context, "whom He hath called, not of the Jews only, but also of the Gentiles". Distinguishing grace unto salvation is of God, and of God alone, and if our criticizing spirits question and rebel, the answer is written: "Nay but, O man, who art thou that repliest against God", that disputeth with God? "Is there unrighteousness with God?" (Rom. 9:14, 20). There are those who "judge themselves unworthy of eternal life", they put the Gospel from them (Acts 13:46). Yet in the divine mercy it remains written, "God is able to graff them in again, if they abide not still in unbelief".

Attention may briefly be drawn to a somewhat similar distinguishing passage in the earlier part of the epistle (Rom. 2:28-29), the merely outward Jew, the natural, the racial, is not a Jew as God regards the title; nor is circumcision "outward in the flesh" since it was intended of God to signify

spiritual truth. Thus it would seem Paul thinks of
the Jew as one of pure descent and association on
the return from the captivity when the title first appeared, as representing spiritual emancipation
through faith in the Lord Jesus Christ. Hence its
general use is corrected, and its specialized intent
is noted, probably to rebuke "the Jews" for their
pride and boast. The apostle himself "a Hebrew of
the Hebrews" and "a Jew", counted all his gains
but loss for the excellency of Christ, and he claimed
"we are the circumcision, which worship God in
the spirit, and rejoice in Christ Jesus, *and have no
confidence in the flesh*" (Phil. 3:3). The qualification is altogether spiritual; there is no racial distinction. Christ Jesus is ALL. "They are not all
Israel who are of Israel", is Paul's first and governing principle in this treatise of God's purposes
for Israel directed especially to the Gentiles (11:
13). He never departs from it. His final assurance,
therefore, "All Israel shall be saved", must be so
understood. Not the race or "the rest", but the
election and the remnant.

We append some comments upon this important
matter: (Romans 9)

"The apostle now approaches . . . the rejection of the Jews and the calling of the
Gentiles. That God had so determined is the point
about to be established. The apostle does this by
showing, in the first place, that God is perfectly
free thus to act (6-24), and in the second, that He
had declared in the prophets that such was His
intention (25-33). The promises by which He had
bound Himself were not made to the natural descendants of Abraham as such, but to his spiritual
seed. The Word of God had not failed for not all
the natural descendants of the patriarch are the
true people of God, to whom alone the promises
properly belong, 'for they which are the children
of the flesh, those are *not* the children of God'. As
Isaac was born in virtue of a special divine inter-
position, so now, the real children of God are born,
not after the flesh, *but by His special grace*" (Dr.
Charles Hodge).

"The Jews might object that if they were cast

off and rejected, then God is unfaithful and His promises are ineffectual. This Paul answers by making a distinction among Israelites. Some are Israelites only in respect of their carnal descent, others are children of the promise. The nation stood in relation to God in which no other nation was ever placed, but only a part of them enjoyed a spiritual relation. Children by lineal descent means such as are not distinguished by a more excellent privilege than their being offspring by blood. Children of the promise are those who are peculiarly marked out and sealed by their heavenly Father. *These only are counted for the seed*" (Robert Haldane).

"The common election of the Israelitish nation does not prevent the Sovereign of infinite holiness from choosing for Himself, according to His secret counsel, whatever portion of that people He is determined to save. When Paul says they are not all Israel who are of Israel . . . he includes all the descendants of Abraham, the father of believers, under one member of the sentence, and points out by the other, those only who are true and genuine sons of the friend of God, and not a degenerate race" (John Calvin).

"They who are of Israel denote all the members of that nation. By the words, are not all Israel, Paul signalises *among* the nation a true Israel, that elect people, that holy remnant, which is constantly spoken of in the Old Testament, and to which alone the decree of election refers, so that rejection may apply to the mass without compromising the election of the true Israel . . . Could even Isaac and his race, though proceeding from Abraham, and that through the intervention of a divine factor, be regarded without any other condition as real children of God? Evidently not, for if the faith of Abraham ceased to belong to them, they became a purely carnal seed" (Dr. F. Godet).

"FULNESS" MEANS TOTALITY AND FINALITY

"UNTIL the fulness of the Gentiles be come in" (Rom. 11:25). The sentence anticipates the realization of an objective, the salvation of Gentiles to the full extent of the purpose of God in Christ, expressed in the words of the great commission that "repentance and remission of sins should be preached in His name among all nations beginning from Jerusalem" (Luke 24). It is associated with the "mystery" or secret which had been hidden but is now revealed. In this respect it corresponds to the same apostle's revelation in the Epistle to the Ephesians. How many generations or millenniums this operation would cover is not stated. It accords with words of Paul to conclude this Epistle: God, he says, "is of power to establish you, according to my gospel and the preaching of Jesus Christ, according to the revelation of the mystery which was kept secret since the world began, but now is made manifest, and by the Scriptures of the prophets, according to the commandment of the everlasting God, made known to all nations for the obedience of faith" (Rom. 16:25-26). He thus describes the incoming of the fulness of the Gentiles. This is also announced as the "outtaking" from among the nations a people for His name called the remnant or residue (Amos 9:12; Acts 15:14). God, therefore, through the Gospel will continue from generation to generation to "take out" a people until the fulness,

99

that is, the totality of this selection shall have "come in".

As the divine purpose does not contemplate the salvation of Gentiles universally but selectively and this selection will constitute their "fulness", so also it is not declared to be God's purpose to save the entire nation of the Jews but from them also the "fulness"; namely, the remnant according to "the election of grace" (Rom. 11:5, 11, 12). Hence we have the parallel sentence, "blindness in part is happened unto Israel". It is a solemn judgment to which we must submit, beholding "the goodness and severity of God." It conforms to the argument of elimination with which Paul began (ch. 9), for God "hath mercy on whom He will have mercy, and whom He will He hardeneth" (that is, blindeth 9:19). Hardening is set in opposition to showing mercy. Yet there is no unrighteousness with God (9:14).

In neither case does "fulness" mean the entirety of Jews or Gentiles as such, but the total sum of the divinely chosen among them. Fulness would preclude any supplementation or addition, any subsequent incoming of Gentiles or ingrafting of Jews. There is no dispensational qualification. Completeness and perfectness and totality are reached. The measure is full. It is an impressive fact that the apostle in this case uses the adverb "so" indicating the manner; that is, *how* "all Israel shall be saved", and not *when*, announcing the time. The construction of the sentence would require that we understand Israel's entire salvation will be accomplished in the manner described, and *not after* the fulness of the Gentiles shall have come in. It will be brought about during the same process of Gentile incoming. The "blindness" is but "in part"; that is, the judgment rests upon part of the nation but not all, agreeable to the apostle's earlier words, "the election hath obtained it and the rest were blinded"; "He hath mercy on whom He will, and whom He will, He hardeneth".

It is, therefore, proposed by some that "all Israel" here mentioned is the incorporation of believing Jews and Gentiles, in agreement with the same

apostle's further revelation of the mystery in his
Ephesian epistle. This is Biblical consistency (cf.
also Rom. 9:24-25). The incoming of Jew and Gentile "fulness" is concurrent: "And so all Israel—
the fulness of the Jews and the fulness of the Gentiles—shall be saved". This would agree with the
apostle's words where he addressed Gentiles in particular (11:12-13). It would seem that the saving
of both Jews and Gentiles, according to Paul's
reasoning here, is accomplished through the Gospel
in this present time. Their "fall" refers to the entire
nation; their "fulness" to the election or remnant
within that nation (11:12). It was so with mankind: The Fall was without exception, the fulness
is without distinction. In this manner Isaiah predicted the same truth: his pronouncement of judicial blindness is quoted a number of times in the
New Testament (see Isa. 6:9-10). "And yet (even
after the entire desolation) in it shall be a tithe,
and (even this tenth) shall return and be for a consuming (shall again be consumed but not utterly)
for like the terebinth and like the oak (the two
most common forest trees of Palestine) which in
falling (or when felled) have substance (or vitality)
in them, so a holy seed shall be the substance (vital
principle) of it (the tenth or remnant which seemed
itself to be destroyed) — Dr. A. J. Alexander,
Princeton.

Elsewhere in our study reference has been made
to the parable used here by Paul of the olive tree.
Gentile branches are through faith graffed in;
Jewish branches were through unbelief broken off.
Yet even the broken-off branches God is able to
graff in again—the language is that of possibility,
it does not aver the actuality. By such operation,
however, it is to be noted, they would be joined with
and to Gentiles already ingraffed. This can be only
on the indispensable principle that salvation is by
grace through faith; "if they abide not still in unbelief" expresses uncertainty and a contingency. It
is not prediction. In the parable, therefore, the
apostle regards the salvation of Jews and Gentiles
as a joint undertaking in the great evangelizing
purpose of God, simultaneously accomplished, and

resulting in their partaking together of the life and nourishment of the olive tree. Or, as in the Ephesian epistle and employing another figure, together they are "fellowmembers of the same body". For if beforetime, the apostle reminds them, the Gentiles were "aliens from the commonwealth of Israel and strangers from the covenants of promise", and now in Christ Jesus they are "no longer strangers and foreigners but fellow-citizens with the saints", they must have citizenship in the commonwealth of Israel, with entitlement to bear that name (Eph. 2:12-19). "Ye were aliens from the commonwealth of Israel (in the time of the prophets), but now ye are members of the true Israel, built upon the foundation of the New Testament apostles and Old Testament Prophets, Jesus Christ Himself the chief cornerstone" (Jamieson, Fausset and Brown). Those, therefore, who regard "all Israel" as inclusive of all believing Jews and Gentiles have good reason for considering they are on Scriptural ground.

Another view is that "all Israel" refers strictly to members of the Jewish race, "them that are my flesh" as Paul puts it. Even so, whether this passage can even inferentially be construed as a promise of national salvation contingent upon and subsequent to full Gentile evangelization is open to question. Shall blindness now judicially visited then be superseded by vision, or shall God's hardening be exchanged for God's mercy? If so, how are we to view the divine Will (Rom. 9:15-18)? Now is their day of salvation. The words simply announce that the spiritual state of part of the race of Israel remains unrelieved; there is no promise of illumination. How simple for Paul, had he cherished a Jewish national rehabilitation in Palestine for a millennium with his consuming desire for his people's salvation if such were his meaning, to have written: Blindness in part is happened unto Israel, but this will continue only until the fulness of the Gentiles be come in, and then God will remove the blindness, and the whole nation shall be saved! This indeed is the dispensational view, but is not that of the inspired apostle.

This sense of the passage is supported, it is said, by the word "until" which has been given the force of a time limit beyond which blindness is not to continue, but the opposite condition; that is, salvation for the nation until then judicially blinded will be given effect. This intention is not necessarily conveyed by the word "until". It would appear that where "until" carries a time limit beyond which there will be a reversal of condition, this is stated as in the word, "I will not drink of the vine until I drink it new with you in My Father's kingdom." But "Sit Thou on My right hand until I make Thy foes Thy footstool" need not imply that the Lord Jesus will vacate that "right hand" when this is accomplished; rather it is the assurance that His enemies shall never dethrone Him; eventually all will be subdued at His feet and He will be acclaimed, as indeed He is, supreme Victor. David did not vacate his throne when he had subdued all his enemies, on the contrary he was firmly and indisputably established thereupon. "Jerusalem shall be trodden down of the Gentiles until the times of the Gentiles be fulfilled" is no promise of Israel's ascendancy thereupon, but a confirmation of judgment upon her because as previously stated, "she knew not the time of her visitation" and "the things which belong to thy peace are now hid from thine eyes" (Luke 19:41-44; 21:24). In the procedure of the beginning Jewish opportunity preceded that of the Gentile, but is never said to follow it. "Ye shall not see Me henceforth until ye shall say, Blessed is He that cometh in the name of the Lord" is wrongly said to be a prediction; it is rather a prescription, of which as the context illuminates, an example was given as the Lord entered the city (Matt. 21:9) and of which the rulers made complaint. Therefore, He said, "Until *ye* acknowledge my Messiahship as they have done, ye shall not see me." This is exactly the order of the original prophecy fulfilled in our Lord's resurrection and thereafter as He Himself declared and later His apostles afterwards (cf. Ps. 118:22-26 with Matt. 22:42 and Acts 4:11, following upon Peter's address to the Jews in Acts 3 where he made this condition so clear).

When Isaiah enquired how long the predicted judicial hardening should continue and was told "Until the cities be wasted . . . and utterly desolate" (Isa. 6:11-13), there was no promise of future national restoration but the preservation of a remnant called "the holy seed"; and this is precisely the reasoning of Paul in Romans 9 to 11.

Examination of the occurrences of the word "until" elsewhere confirms this use of it. "Until I die I will not remove my integrity from me", said Job (Job 27:5). Did he mean his integrity would be removed after his death? "Samuel came to see Saul no more until his death" (1 Sam. 15:35): does this mean the prophet resumed his visits after Saul's death? Apostate Israel would be hardened until her utter desolation (Isa. 6:11): does this mean the hardening would be relieved when the desolation became established? "This iniquity shall not be purged until ye die" (Isa. 22:14). Would the iniquity be purged after death? "He will not fail nor forsake thee until thou hast finished all the work" (1 Chron. 28:20): must Solomon expect to be forsaken when the work was finished? "They knew not until the flood came and took them all away" (Matt. 24:39): were they enlightened after that judgment? "For until the law sin was in the world" (Rom. 5:13): was sin no longer in the world after the law came? "Judge nothing before the time until the Lord come" (1 Cor. 4:5). May Christians then supplant the judgeship of the Lord? The word "until" emphasizes the continuance of the action or state described and not the reversal of conditions at the terminus.

The accommodation of the word "until" to support the sense of "when" for "so" and import the idea of time in place of manner is said to accord with the quotation which follows, with the reference to covenant benefits. The formula which it introduces, however, is not as is usual with a prediction, "And it shall come to pass" but "as it is written". The words quoted from Isaiah do not therefore necessarily imply futurity; that is, an event following the second coming of Christ. They were of predictive character when Isaiah wrote, but now may be regarded as historically fulfilled in the event of Messiah's first advent and recognized by the apostle with "as it is written", as in the case of many other quotations thus introduced. Dr. A. J. Alexander in his commentary on Isaiah gives it thus. " 'Then shall come for Zion a Redeemer and for the converts from transgression in Jacob'. The original construction necessarily suggests the idea of succession and dependence. 'For' is 'as to or respect to'. So in this place it simply means nothing more than that the advent of the great Deliverer has respect to Zion, without deciding what particular respect, whether local, temporal or any other nature altogether". Thus the prophet's "The Redeemer shall come" may be understood as Paul's recognition of fulfilment, and he is enheartened with respect to Israel's salvation because of it.

The turning away of her ungodliness is precisely Peter's announcement of present blessing "to turn away every one of you from his iniquities" (Acts 3:26) and with Paul's own preaching at Antioch (Acts 13:38-39). It would agree also with the corresponding mention of Sion by Paul (Rom. 9:33) and by Peter (1 Pet. 2:6).

Again in this context Paul is confident of "the election" who are "beloved for the fathers' sakes", but not of that "part" to which "blindness is happened", and this confirms his earlier distinction that "the election hath obtained it, and the rest were blinded" (Rom. 11:7). Does he now reverse this at the end and mean, "those blinded have now obtained"? In this wisdom of God he perceives the reciprocal ministry of Jews to Gentiles and in turn of Gentiles to Jews; that is to say, by reason of the unbelief of the Jews, "we turn", said Paul "to the Gentiles" (Acts 13:46; cf. Rom. 11:14) ; thus "they obtained mercy". And now, having obtained mercy, saved Gentiles minister to the Jews "that through your (Gentile) mercy, they also may obtain mercy". This has been exactly the divine prescription for the evangelization of the nations, and it has been proceeded upon, the history of missions being witness. It is thus seen that "God hath concluded them all (Jews and Gentiles) in unbelief that He might have mercy upon all" (Rom. 11:28-32). "The gifts and calling of God", therefore, "are without repentance" (Rom. 11:29), and the promise advanced at the beginning of his treatise is consistently followed to the end, that there is a distinction between Israel and "Israel", and, therefore, it is "not as though the word of God hath taken none effect" (Rom. 9:6) for "so all Israel shall be saved".

A dozen or so occurrences of "fulness" make it beyond question that whatever the subject, this qualifying word attributes to it the sense of completeness or repleteness and totality; the meaning given being, to finish, to accomplish, to satisfy; that which fills out to the uttermost. Nothing, therefore, of the nature of the fulness specified can be lacking: there is no surplus and no supplement; no subtraction and no addition.

Fulness of deity dwells in the incarnate Son: totality of Godhead is His: and the church is filled full (complete) in Him Who is her Head (Col. 1:19; 2:9, 10).

Grace in its fulness is resident in Christ: out from this fulness we receive; there is no other reservoir (John 1:14, 16).

Fulness of blessing is in the Gospel. There is no supplementary source (Rom. 15:29).

Time's fulness, introduced with Christ's first advent, concludes with His second advent: then Eternity (Gal. 4:4; Eph. 1:10).

To be filled unto all the fulness of God would appear to be the limitless limit in the surpassing knowledge of the love of Christ (Eph. 3:19).

The church is "the fulness of Him Who filleth all in all". His "body" is not lacking or maimed. It is as "a perfect man". At His coming it will be presented a glorious church, not having spot or wrinkle or any such thing, but holy and without blemish. The church is composed of the redeemed of all nations, denationalized and united as being "all one in Christ Jesus" (Eph. 1:23; 4:13; Gal. 3:28; Eph. 5:27).

The fulness of Jews and Gentiles expresses the totality of the redeemed simultaneously brought in through the Gospel in this "day of salvation". There

can be nothing lacking in, or added to, this fulness
(Rom. 11:12; 11:25; 2 Cor. 6:2; cf. Isa. 49:1-12).

But the dispensational assertion is represented
thus: "The millennium will be the great harvest-
time of the earth when millions of unconverted souls
will be gathered into the garners of God". Again,
"The millennial earth will still be essentially the
same as that in which we now dwell; inhabited by
men in unredeemed bodies liable to sickness and
death; men, who even when sanctified by grace, will
have still to say as believers do now, that in their
flesh dwelleth no good thing". Again: "The millennial earth will be visited and reigned over by Christ
and the risen saints who themselves will dwell in
heavenly places not made with hands" (B. W. N.).

There is "one body" writes the apostle, even as
there is "one Lord". As the redeemed constituting
the body of Christ in its fulness permits of no addition, and one Lord permits of no rival, so the
fulness of the one body allows of no later millennial
contribution. She is described as the "one new man"
or one new mankind or race.

Salvation is by grace, "and if by grace it is no
more of works: otherwise grace is no more grace;
but if it be of works, then it is no more of grace,
otherwise work is no more work". In like manner
it may be said that if fulness be capable of supplementation or addition, then fulness is no more
fulness.

As the world of space and time draws towards
its end it may be the good pleasure of God to in-
gather through the Gospel, and in spite of such
persecution of the church as she is warned to expect and as symbolically prophesied (Rev. 20:8, 9
etc.) multitudes both of Jews and Gentiles, thus
attaining the fulness intended. And so, if the fall
and diminishing and casting away of the Jews at
the beginning meant the salvation of the
Gentiles and the riches and reconciling of the
world; how much more their fulness and the receiving of them will be—not "still to dwell in unredeemed bodies, liable to sickness and death" as
quoted above, but—"life from the dead"; as resurrection and new creation and eternal life in the
ages to come.

GOD DOES NOT WALK
BACKWARDS

ISRAEL'S priesthood and its services, the old covenant ministry within the economy of the chosen nation, was discontinued with the cessation of their national status, being rendered obsolete by the achievements of Christ in the fulness of time Who, in virtue of His fulfilling and final sacrifice, ministers on high as the great High Priest after the order of Melchizedek, the Mediator of the new cov enant, the minister of the true tabernacle which the Lord pitched and not man (Heb. 8:2). To this ministry He is "consecrated for evermore" (Heb. 7:28). When He, the Lamb of God, bore away the sin of the world, being "foreordained before the foundation of the world but manifest in these last times" (1 Pet. 1:20); when He cried on the cross "It is finished", the abolition of the old by an act of God was demonstrated in the rending of the temple vail from the top to the bottom. The old order was both appointed and annulled by God. "He taketh away the first that He might establish the second", and those who happily apprehend this may apply the language of the patriarch and say, "The Lord gave and the Lord hath taken away, blessed be the name of the Lord". In general the New Testament bears witness to this, and in particular it is the whole content of the Epistle to the Hebrews in its exposition. "Let us go on" is the word of the Lord here, "but if any man draw back, My soul

109

shall have no pleasure in him" (Heb. 6:1; 10:38).

His Own resurrection attested the finished work of Christ, and being now alive for evermore and in indisputable command of all events, He watched over His word to perform it, and fulfilled His Own prediction confirming Daniel's prophecy, of the entire destruction of the temple itself, there "not being left one stone upon another" of which maybe, the rending of the vail was intended to be the harbinger. Its services, therefore, were discontinued, the people were scattered among the nations, and the judgmentary transference previously announced was affected; namely, "the kingdom of God shall be taken from you and given to a nation bringing forth the fruits thereof" (Matt. 21:43; 1 Pet. 2:9; Heb. 12:28). This kingdom, then, was transferred to the Church, of whom also the words originally spoken by Moses to Israel upon their redemption from Egypt, were henceforth descriptive: "Ye are a chosen generation, a royal priesthood, a holy nation, a peculiar people". They were also "living stones" builded upon Christ the Rock foundation, "a spiritual house, the temple of the living God" (1 Pet. 2:5-10; Ex. 19:5-6). When the kingdom was in possession of unfruitful Israel, the new fruitful nation had no constitutional establishment. Following the rending of the vail, however, sign of His having "consecrated for us a new and living way by which we come to God", "the middle wall of partition" between Jews and Gentiles was broken down, never to be re-erected. In fact Paul averred that to build again the things destroyed would be transgression, and the "things" he referred to were these very impositions of the old covenant (Gal. 1:18).

The sacrifices of the old covenant were esteemed to be necessary to "the patterns" (Heb. 9:13-23). They were altogether unsuitable and ineffective for new covenant purposes, they "could never take away sins"; the new covenant sacrifice alone and forever did that (Heb. 10:12). By and because of this the Lord Jesus abolished the old and established the new, and "He sat down", the work finished and satisfaction made, not in Jerusalem where He was delivered up to crucifixion, but on the right hand of God where He is glorified. His was the excelling sacrifice, related to "the heavenly things themselves". The patterns had no more place since the realities were permanent. He looks forward, not back. He condones no such apostasy as the reintroduction on earth of old covenant sacrifice and priestly service. Exalted in heaven, His expectation is that His enemies shall be made His footstool. These enemies will be subjugated during and by means of His enthronement above, for "He must reign till He hath put all enemies under His feet". The last is death itself, at His second coming. "Then cometh the end" (1 Cor. 15:25). Until then the justifying and regenerative benefits of the new covenant Gospel which by His death on Calvary He "caused to prevail" (Dan. 9:27) are proclaimed by its ministers, a far more excellent ministry for the apostolic preachers of His grace than the administration of condemnation under Moses' law. "For the letter (the old covenant) killeth, but the spirit (the new covenant) giveth life". The former is "done away" in Christ (2 Cor. 3). The two are mutually exclusive. The old was appointed as "a figure for the time then present" and "until the time of reformation", for "the way into the holiest of all was not yet made manifest while as the first tabernacle was yet standing" for in spite of ceremonial sacrificing year after year sins "remained untaken away". Completely and forever the "blood of the new covenant shed for many for the remission of sins" atoned "for the transgressions that were under the first covenant"; that is to say, the second remedied the defectiveness and ineffectiveness of the first. Now, therefore, "the way is made manifest" for "He hath consecrated for us a new and living way by which we come to God" and believers have "boldness to enter into the holiest by the blood of Jesus". New covenant worshippers freely and reverently engage in spiritual service and they are bidden so do "so much the more as (they) see the day approaching" (Heb. 8:9-10; 10:25). "The day" is that of the second coming of Christ, "for yet a little while and He that shall come will come and will not tarry".

This is worship which God seeks, introduced by our Lord's sacrificial ministry, and is in spirit and in truth (in a true spiritual manner, John 4:23). Is such to give place, when Christ comes again, to a reintroduction of the "beggarly elements", the "shadows", the "patterns", "the figures of the true"? So it is taught by those who treat Ezekiel's prophecy as a setting forth with literal intention of a future earthly millennial age. It is reasonable, therefore, in the light of new covenant finalities, to examine whether the ceremonial given by the prophet of the exile, the temple, the city, etc. may not have been intended symbolically to foreview the "heavenly things" spoken of in the Hebrews epistle, the temple which is His church and the new Jerusalem which is above. Particulars are given of sacrificial offerings instituted by Moses, and if they were typical of Christ's one offering, as we know they were, why not also Ezekiel's? The prophets served as did Moses under the old covenant economy, but they looked forward, as also did Moses, to Christ and the new covenant. Animal sacrifices belong to the old covenant, to that only, and not to the new, and it is the new, the everlasting covenant which Ezekiel foresees.

It is proposed in explanation, however, that the reinstitution in Israel's restored economy will look back commemoratively as under Moses it looked forward anticipatively. This would be a contradiction of their historical temporary character and of their abolition in Christ. Memorials are erected in the absence of those commemorated, but in the coming age it is said, He will be present: He will have come to earth the second time; He will be in their midst; He will sit upon David's throne in Jerusalem! If this is to be, wherefore memorials? The Christian institution of The Lord's Supper is a memorial only "until He come", when it will cease to be observed for His redeemed will be forever with the Lord. But if remembrance, a recalling the past, is intended, what are we specifically instructed that such sacrifices for sin and trespass commemorate? Not the one sacrifice of Christ which forever put them away, not the new covenant which says, "their sins and their iniquities will I remember no more", but *sins remaining*. Otherwise, "would they not cease to be offered?" Animal sacrifices are not said either themselves to take away sins or to *memorialize* another sacrifice which did; rather "in them a remembrance is again made of sins". In Ezekiel's context David is spoken of as the king, the prince, the one shepherd to be set over the people, "even My servant David" (Ezek. 34:23-24; 37:24) but he is named in association with the "everlasting covenant" with which the old sacrifices have nothing to do. Is it not recognized that "David" here spoken of is not the historical king of Israel, but the Messiah? Other parts of the prophecy, therefore, should be viewed in this same spiritualized manner.

Essential to the ritual of animal sacrifices is the sacerdotal priesthood, and the prophet's visions of instruction included this also. In the present Christian age Old Testament ordinances are done away, and believers are constituted a royal and holy priesthood to offer up spiritual sacrifices acceptable to God through Jesus Christ, Who. by the obedience of His life and the oblation of His death forever finished the work. Moreover, it is stated that participants in the first resurrection shall be priests of God and of Christ (Rev. 1:6; 20:6). Strong words of denunciation are written in the New Testament concerning the reimposition of the rites and ceremonies of the Law, and a "drawing back" from the faith of Christ unto these is said to be "unto perdition". Can it be that a return to such ordinances in the millennium will no longer be anathematized but approved?

It must be borne in mind also that Ezekiel's prophecy, as also those of Haggai and Zechariah, had in view the return from the Babylonian captivity, the restoration of the temple and city and the repossession of the land. The returned and new builders were encouraged by glorious visions of God. Hence, it has been pointed out that the dimensions given are prodigious. "Ezekiel's temple is delineated larger than all the earthly Jerusalem and his Jerusalem larger than all the land of Canaan"

(Fairbairn). A comment by Jamieson, Fausset and Brown confirms this: "The Septuagint substitutes cubits for reeds to escape the immense compass given to the whole. Fairbairn rightly supports the English Version which agrees with the Hebrew"... the "accommodation was indulged in to surmount what appeared to be a literal difficulty". Moreover, as some particulars are identical with the New Testament description of the heavenly Jerusalem, it may be understood that while God meant what He said, and the temple and city and nation were re-established after the exile, He did not say what He fully meant until New Testament writers were inspired by the same Spirit of Christ to set Him forth in spiritual and heavenly and eternal realities.

The Mosaic legislation was written in plainness of speech, and consisted in terms of divine command requiring legal obedience. The people, therefore, could understand thus far what God said, and they responded, "All that the Lord hath said we will do and be obedient". On the other hand, Ezekiel's is couched in highly symbolical and figurative language. In consideration of this allowance is made for some elasticity of interpretation. But however Moses is read there is no doubt of the terms: "What is written in the law, how readest thou?" asked our Lord. "All these have I kept from my youth"; "This do and thou shalt live". Contrariwise, who save the divinely initiated would attempt dogmatically to interpret Ezekiel's enigmatic visions? The spiritual meaning of God's ordinances under Moses is given in the New Testament. Should not the explanation of Ezekiel's prophetic ceremonialism be sought in the same evangelical truth? The argument for spiritualized fulfilment, in which God says what He means, is weighty indeed.

Equally the divine message came to Zechariah in figurative visions; we could expect, therefore, that fulfilment of a spiritual character is intended. There is no doubt, for example, that "the Branch" is the designation of Messiah (Zech. 3:8; 6:12; cf. Isa. 4:2; 11-1; Jer. 33:15). Joshua and his fellows are spoken of as "men wondered at" or "for a sign", and it may therefore be assumed that the restorative work they were engaged on, upon return from captivity in which Zechariah and his colleague Haggai encouraged them (Ezra 5:1-2), forecast the greater work to be wrought by Messiah. "I will bring forth My Servant the Branch: behold the Man Whose name is the Branch". It is to Christ, then, that attention is called, and this is added: "He shall build the temple of the Lord, even He shall build the temple of the Lord, and He shall bear the glory and shall sit and rule upon His throne". Literalists insist that the meaning of this prophecy is that a millennial temple in Jerusalem is envisaged, with a throne upon which Messiah shall rule as King-Priest. This would at once appear to conflict with the New Testament in that "if He were on earth He should not be a priest, seeing there are priests that offer gifts according to the law", which, if Ezekiel be taken literally, is again to be the case! "But now hath He obtained a more excellent ministry". Is He then to abandon the "more excellent ministry" for an inferior? Ezekiel, if thus taken literally, provides for the re-introduction on earth of the system of Levitical priesthood (e.g. Ezek. 43:19). Messiah's kingly priesthood "after the order of Melchizedek" (and not after Aaron) He exercises on the throne of the majesty in heaven. This is also the throne of grace, for He is both King of righteousness and King of peace. Zechariah's words, therefore, were the foreshadowing of His heavenly mediatorship. He is the one Mediator between God and man, Himself Man, which accords with the words "Behold the Man Whose name is the Branch", and was recognized by another Zechariah illuminated by the Holy Spirit, at His incarnation (Luke 1:78, translated Dayspring); and the temple He would build, as He said, is none other than His church, so spoken of by the apostles (Matt. 16:18; Eph. 2:20). It is significantly stated by the prophet that the ministry of the King-Priest would be peace: "the counsel of peace shall be between them both", which words, although they may refer to the joint ministry of King and Priest, have their fulfilment as the accomplishment of His cross, by which He there "made peace" and "came and preached peace to them that are far off and to them that are nigh"; Jew and Gentile who through faith in Him "both have access by one Spirit unto the Father". That God meant what He said was verified in the restoration which Zechariah encouraged by his prophesying, but that his language had a greater and more spiritual meaning was reserved for revelation later when Christ, having offered Himself without spot unto God, took His seat triumphantly on high, Head of His church, Priest forever after the order of Melchizedek.

"God does not walk backwards" was the comment of Dr. T. T. Shields to some visiting preachers who had ventilated their dispensational views after the above pattern. How appropriately that sentence sums up the judgement of the New Covenant Gospel! In Christ the shadows of the law are all fulfilled, and now withdraw.

ELIJAH AND JOHN
THE BAPTIST

THE closing word in the Old Testament is: "Behold, I send you Elijah the prophet before the coming of the great and dreadful day of the Lord: And he shall turn (or convert) the hearts of the fathers to (or with) the children, and the heart of the children with the fathers, lest I come and smite the earth with a curse" (Mal. 3:5-6). The rulers of the Jews regarded this prophecy quite literally, and, indeed, our Lord being questioned thereupon, confirmed that God meant what He said, that *"Elias verily* cometh first and restoreth all things" and He added, "But I say unto you that Elias is *indeed* come, and they have done unto him whatsoever they listed, as it is written of him". If it be insisted that God meant what He said literally, that is personally, what is to be understood by our Lord's "verily" and "indeed"? He further explained "how it is written of the Son of Man that He must suffer many things and be set at nought" (Mark 9:11-13). The prophecy, our Lord observed, was fulfilled in the ministry of His forerunner, John the Baptist, in which God said what He meant. "God is His Own interpreter and He will make it plain". And if the Jews, looking upon the outward appearance, would find some marks of identity, the similarity of the way of life of both these prophets may not have been accidental and may be worthy of our own consideration (2 Kings 1:8; Mark 1:6).

117

It is generally recognized that the evangelical section of Isaiah's prophecy begins with chapter 40. The book itself has been called "the fifth gospel". The announcement of "comfort" for Jerusalem is in the gospel; the law was the minister of condemnation. Zion and Jerusalem are used to represent the people and not the place, as also the kingdom is the nation and not the territory (Isa. 52:1, 2; Exod. 19:6; Rev. 1:6; Matt. 23:37; Gal. 4:25 etc.). This is the voice of comfort to the people. The terms of the message are that "her warfare is accomplished and her iniquity pardoned". Warfare is not here the conflict she had been engaged in with surrounding enemies; and a corresponding evangelical announcement uses the literal overthrow of her first physical enemies as representing the obliteration of her sins, a spiritual deliverance (Micah 7:19). Thus the spiritualization of Moses is found in the Prophets; the principle does not await New Testament illumination. "Warfare" is her ceremonial service, the routine of her sacerdotal functions, applied here "more expressly to the old dispensation as a period of restriction and restraint" (Alexander). To "perform the service of the tabernacle" is given in the margin, "war the warfare" (Num. 4:23, 30, 35, 39, 43, 47; 8:24-25). It had to do with the typical conquest of sin. Perhaps, the apostle's injunction to Timothy respecting his ministry concerning Christ's conquest and our redemption had this background in view (1 Tim. 1:18).

It is clear that the prophet's comforting announcement was predictive of the accomplishment of Mosaic typical ceremonialism, and therefore, Jerusalem is bidden hear the "Voice" which introduces the Messiah, in Whom all types and shadows disappeared and the weary warfare ceased; warfare over the long centuries, continuous offerings for sin, and sin as continuously reasserting its condemnatory verdict, still holding the dominion, the people captive to its thraldom and power. The "Voice" is that of John the Baptist, forerunner to the Saviour (John 1:23). "The word of the Lord came unto John" as he commenced his ministry, "preaching the baptism of repentance for the remission of sins" which is said to have been "as it is written in the book of the words of Isaiah the prophet" (Luke 3:2-6). The prophecy is fully quoted as follows: "The voice of one crying in the wilderness, Prepare ye the way of the Lord, make His paths straight. Every valley shall be filled and every mountain and hill shall be brought low; and the crooked shall be made straight, and the rough ways shall be made smooth; and all flesh shall see the salvation of God". A levelling process, the removing of obstruction, is indicated by preparing the way, which is illustrated in the picturesque language. It cannot be said that any such physical consequences attended John's ministry, and therefore, the words must have received, as they were intended to receive, a spiritual fulfilment; that is to say, although Isaiah predicted John the Baptist's message in terms affecting paths and valleys and mountains and hills and rough and crooked places, and of these being appropriately levelled or elevated, made straight or plain, he meant the moral and spiritual overturning and uprooting effects following the "Voice" of divine authority which "prepared the way of the Lord", repentance and reformation of life, the bringing forth of fruits worthy of such. It was also given to John to introduce the Saviour Himself, as well as to prepare His way, and His designation as "the Lamb of God Who beareth away the sin of the world" was precisely in conformity with Isaiah's comforting gospel, that with the putting away of sin by the sacrifice of the true Lamb, ceremonial "warfare" would cease and sins be abundantly pardoned. Could there be a clearer example of literal prediction fulfilled in spiritualization?

There appears to be no ground here for regarding the spiritual ministry of the Baptist as an *application* of a literal prophecy, as though the physical changes spoken of await Christ's second advent with the reappearance of Elijah the prophet in preparation for that event. To what purpose, in that case, does Luke quote this particular verse as implemented in John's ministry? Moreover, when John proceeded to warn the self-righteous Jews in terms of severity: "O generation of vipers, who hath warned you to flee from the wrath to come?" he indicated no later mercy, no intimation of the physical fulfilment of Isaiah's words at a time yet ahead. His only admonition concerned "the wrath to come", and not of glory to be revealed. Indeed, Luke by the Spirit interprets Isaiah's words, "the glory of the Lord shall be revealed, and all flesh shall see it together" (that is, alike or equally), as "all flesh shall see the salvation of God"; that is to say, in preparing the way of the Lord every obstruction would be removed so as to reveal to the whole world God's great salvation in Him Whose name is the Saviour (Luke 3:6; Isa. 40:5).

Two predictions preparatory to the advent of Messiah are given in the final book of the Old Testament, each having the like introduction: "Behold I will send My messenger, and he shall prepare the way before Me"; "Behold I will send you Elijah the prophet before the coming of the great and notable day of the Lord" (Mal. 3:1; 4:5). The evangelist in opening his gospel identified both the "messenger" of Malachi and the "Voice" of Isaiah with John the Baptist (Mark 1:2-3). It is further recorded that the angel's announcement to his father concerning John the Baptist was that "he shall go before Him in the spirit and power of Elias, to turn the hearts of the fathers to the children, and the disobedient to the wisdom of the just: to make ready a people prepared for the Lord". This is indeed the very ministry to which Elijah is commissioned, and here it is said to be that of John the Baptist (Mal. 4:5-6; Luke 1:16, 17). What other logical and scriptural conclusion may be arrived at, therefore, than that "the Lord's messenger" and Elijah to come are one and the same person, John the Baptist? Moreover, the angel appeared to take a sentence from the prophecy concerning the messenger and attach it to the message touching Elijah: "he shall prepare the way before Me"; that is, John the Baptist, and "to make ready a people prepared for the Lord". of Elijah (cf. Mal. 3:1 with Luke 1:17). Indeed, if the historical David when spoken of predictively is Messiah, why should not the historical Elijah, reintroduced in prophecy, be John the Baptist?

John, when enquired of by the Jews about his office, did not himself claim to be Elijah. Nor, indeed, was he the "Elijah" to "restore all things" after *their* pattern, any more than Jesus was the kind of Messiah they expected. Later, however, it was confirmed by the Lord Himself that the promise that Elijah would appear before Messiah's coming was implemented in John's ministry (John 1:21; Matt. 11:13, 14; Mark 9:11-13; Luke 17:10-13). The scribes expected Elias to come first and the Lord acknowledged their correctness, and of John He said, "This is Elias which was for to come". It has been pointed out that the Lord included a kind of qualification, saying, "If ye will receive it". This, however, does not negative His positive assertion that John did fulfil the prophecy. He did not say or mean, "If you do not receive him in John the Baptist you will have another opportunity later on of receiving Elias in person". The despising by them of Elias-John did not determine that John was not Elias, even as the rejection by the Jews of Messiah-Jesus did not refute the claim of Jesus to be the Messiah. "Shall their unbelief make the faithfulness of God without effect? God forbid . . . Let God be true and every man a liar". The serious consequences of their unbelief would react neither upon John nor Jesus but upon themselves. If they did not receive His forerunner and the Messiah Himself their own condemnation was alone to be expected. John's testimony made this clear. And our Lord said, "If ye believe not that I am He ye shall die in your sins, and whither I go there ye cannot come". Those who did receive Him following the direction of His forerunner would benefit greatly accordingly. Being turned from their iniquity they would receive remission of sins. In the humiliating and exalting ministry of John the Baptist, therefore, is to be observed God's meaning when through Isaiah He spoke in material terms of the removing of obstructions, of levelling, humiliating and exalting, thus converting the hearts of parents and children into the way of the Lord. The great and

notable day of the Lord, it would seem, received
its inception at His incarnation, "when He cometh
into the world" introducing "the fulness of time",
and will extend unto His coming the second time
"to judge the living and the dead at His appearing
and His Kingdom". "Lest", the prophet said, "I
come and smite the earth with a curse". He came
Himself to bear the curse; He comes to wear the
crown.

Our Lord's enquiry as to the general opinion of
His Own identity brought the answer in the first
place, John the Baptist (risen from the dead) and
Elijah (whom the scribes said would precede the
Messiah). Thus men seemed to associate these two
Old Testament prophets (Matt. 16:14; 14:2). The
occasion of His identifying Elijah with John the
Baptist was that of His Own transfiguration, a foreview of "His power and coming" (Matt. 17:1-13;
2 Pet. 1:16). Here Moses with Elijah appeared in
glory and spake of His decease which He should
accomplish at Jerusalem; accomplished, and therefore, vindicated in resurrection: the privileged
apostles being charged not to declare the vision
until after His resurrection. Hence they questioned
one with another "what the rising from the dead
should mean" (Mark 9:10).

The association of Moses with Elijah is significant, for the closing verses in the Old Testament
unite the two thus: "Remember ye the law of My
servant Moses, with the statutes and judgments",
and "Behold I will send you Elijah the prophet
before the coming of the great and dreadful day
of the Lord". Moses, therefore, representing the
law, and Elijah, representing the prophets, discuss
with the Lord Jesus His fulfilment of all that is
Messianically written in the law and prophets when
the deed of judgment with mercy "finished the work
which God gave Him to do". His testimony had
been that He came "not to be ministered unto, but
to minister, and to give His life a ransom for
many". In person John the Baptist came in the
power and spirit of Elijah, as a voice crying in the
wilderness, to prepare the way of Messiah, thus
introducing His years of public service. Elijah in

person appeared with Moses in glory, at the end of that ministry, and spake of His exodus which He would perform fully in death and resurrection. Then there came the voice from the excellent glory, "This is My beloved Son in Whom I am well pleased, hear ye Him." John said, "He must increase and I must decrease". Elijah and Moses also withdraw, and Christ alone remains to be heard and believed unto everlasting life.

Dispensationalists who hold in part a literalistic and futuristic view of the Apocalypse identify "My two witnesses" (Rev. 11:3) as Moses and Elijah, to reappear in mortal condition for three-and-a-half years in Jerusalem, martyred and resurrected after three-and-a-half days. Such would be the literal understanding, perhaps also taking a day for a year. The context shows that Jerusalem is then apostate, "spiritually called Sodom and Egypt" and identified as that city by the directive, "where also our Lord was crucified". Here, surely, the text itself introduces spiritualization. The evidence supporting the "witnesses" as Moses and Elijah is the similarity of their miraculous powers to those exercised by the historical persons. But must the repetition of signs determine the reappearance of the instruments originally associated with them? May not God likewise operate through others?

The churches of the Apocalypse were admonished because one was charged, "thou sufferest that woman Jezebel . . . to seduce My servants" (Rev. 2:20) and another, "thou hast there them that hold the doctrine of Balaam" (2:14). But this is not understood as indicating the reappearance of Ahab's Jezebel and Balak's Balaam in the churches. Similarly, the fact that the Man of Sin is called "the son of perdition" (2 Thes. 2) and Judas the betrayer is himself so called, does not necessarily imply, as some fancifully hold, that the Man of Sin will be Judas reincarnated (John 17:12) ! Judging by the similarity of His mighty works, Herod even mistakenly thought Jesus to be John the Baptist risen from the dead.

However the two witnesses are interpreted, surely the words of the Lord Jesus Christ concerning Elijah are decisive and final. "Verily Elias cometh

first" for God means what He says, "but I say unto
you that Elias is indeed come"; thus God says what
He means. The Elijah prophecy, according to the
Lord Jesus Christ, is not merely applied to John
the Baptist; it was fulfilled in the Forerunner and on
the mount where Elijah appeared and the Voice
said, "This is My beloved Son, hear ye Him". Testimony given by Him through the Spirit from heaven
in no way conflicts with truth spoken by Him in
person on earth (John 16:12-13; Rev. 22:16).

A KINGDOM WHICH CANNOT BE MOVED

Dispensational theorists can be superficially attractive. The ministry of the Lord Jesus Christ is arranged for Him by them into three successive sections under His titles and offices of prophet, priest and king. The prophet section is said to extend from Bethlehem to Calvary; the priest section from Calvary to the Second Coming, whereupon becoming king He will set up the kingdom! Scripture readily will show how erroneous is this dividing of the word of truth, and of Christ of Whose offices it can be said these three are one (cf. Heb. 1:1; 7:1-3; Zech. 6:13; Acts 3). He exercises His prophetic ministry while He is priest, and His priestly ministry the while being prophet, and He is now and forever king, His "kingdom still increasing, a kingdom without end".

Contrary to theories of dispensationalists e.g. Scofield Bible, the kingdom of God and the kingdom of heaven are one and the same kingdom. A comparison of the occurrences in the Gospels will suffice to determine this, unless the Scripture be wrested from its plain teaching. Even the pagan emperor learned that "the heavens do rule", and he testified of God and of His kingdom that "He doeth according to His will in the army of heaven, and among the inhabitants of the earth; and none can stay His hand, or say unto Him, What doest Thou?"

126

(Dan. 4). The selfsame subject may merit manifold qualifying terms.

Those favoured believers who "waited for the kingdom of God" identified it with the coming of Messiah, His birth, life, death, resurrection (e.g. Mark 15:43; cf. Luke 2:25, 38). Certain privileged apostles were promised a sight of the kingdom before death, the reference being to the transfiguration scene, the kingdom associated with Christ's glory (Luke 9:27; 1 Thess. 2:12; 2 Peter 1:16, 17).

"My kingdom is not of this world," said our Lord to His judge; it would be from heaven. Thus, parabolically, He spoke in another place, of leaving the world "to receive for Himself a kingdom and to return". The kingdom, therefore, would not be secured by His servants' fight as in this world but is His by sovereign right (John 18:36; Luke 19:12). The Jews thought "that the kingdom of God should immediately appear"; that is, blaze up and come into sight. Such was their idea of a Messianic kingdom to be set up on earth, from Jerusalem. But Christ's kingdom is ruled from heaven where He received it upon His ascension to glory (cf. Matt. 28:18; authority is a word denoting government, sovereignty, kingdom). Upon His return He would administer reward or loss to His subjects.

Again, He said, "the kingdom of God cometh not with observation"; that is, with outward show (mg.), with pomp and ceremony as that of an earthly potentate. "The kingdom of God", He added, "is within you" perhaps, among you. It was not something displayed externally to be as here or there. So far from establishing a kingdom of that shape, He said, "The days will come when ye shall desire to see one of the days of the Son of Man, and ye shall not see it". He had come in mercy, to seek and to save; His second coming, as the lightning, would be in judgment (Luke 17).

The kingdom is one, "the kingdom of Christ and of God", even as its throne is "the throne of God and the Lamb", as also its temple and illumination. For "all Thine are Mine and Mine are Thine". Equality is His with God the Father in dignity, power and glory. Addressing His disciples in parables, and describing believers as "the children of the kingdom", He spoke of it as "His kingdom" and "the kingdom of their Father". Their theories require dispensationalists to divide this kingdom into two, placing the millennium between (the reference is to 1 Cor. 15:24). The emphatic *"then, at that time"*, is ignored. At His coming "He will purge out of His kingdom all things that offend", and then, *at that time*, "shall the righteous shine forth as the sun in the kingdom of their Father" (Eph. 5:5; Rev. 21; John 5; Matt. 13; cf. also Matt. 26:29 and Luke 22:16 where the Kingdom of God is "the Kingdom of my Father"). These parables are illustrative of the progress of the kingdom between the first and second advents of Christ. Thus we read generally of the kingdom and also the kingdom of heaven, the kingdom of God, Christ's kingdom and His Father's kingdom. It is not to be introduced or set up or established at His second coming. It might be more accurate to say that the kingdom will then be cleansed and completed and consummated for its eternal establishment, incorporating the new earth as well as heaven. Within the kingdom thus viewed there are now reality and imitation. The righteous are "the children of the kingdom", contrasted with others previously so called who are "cast out" (Matt. 8:12) and who are probably spoken of here in their true relationship as "the children of the wicked one". At His coming the solemn and eternal judgment shall take place. The kingdom is the sphere of Christian profession, real and unreal, as wide as the world reached by the gospel (Matt. 13:38).

Prior to Christ's advent, Israel as the people of God constituted the kingdom, but then also the remnant is distinguished from the rest, for "they are not all Israel who are of Israel". In Israel the kingdom was conditionally and typically represented. This was initially declared by Moses upon their redemption from Egypt when about to receive the divine law (Ex. 19:3-6). In the New Testament these privileges are transferred to the Church, which includes the elect of Israel, the new nation, in the covenant of grace (Tit. 2:14; 1 Pet. 2:9-10). "Moses was king in Jeshrun" (Deut. 33:4; 32:15), but the typical foreshadowings of the kingdom of Christ awaited the reigns of David and Solomon.

Israel's apostasy and seventy years' captivity, from which the chosen remnant returned for the one paramount reason that by divine election, Messiah should come of Israel, through the tribe of Judah, was followed by the introduction of the times of the Gentiles. Nebuchadnezzar dreamed of a great image symbolizing four successive empires to fill history until God's "fulness of time" should commence with the birth of Christ at Bethlehem (Gal. 4). Daniel interpreted the dream, and all accordingly came to pass. The dream concluded with a stone cut out of the mountain without hands and itself becoming a great mountain filling the whole earth. This is Messiah's kingdom which would supersede the fourth kingdom of the image, the disruption and destruction of which are predicted.

Dispensationalists postpone this kingdom to the second coming of Christ, and some expect a revival of Rome's ten kingdoms, though the Scripture does not state that these toes represent kingdoms. The stone smites the image on the feet. The original ten kingdoms are, of course, history. However this may be, the figure of the stone and its action befits the first rather than the second advent. Christ consistently is the stone or rock. "A stone cut out without hands" would signify the smallness of the miraculous beginning. "Becoming a great mountain" indicates an advancing process, in which all the earlier kingdoms, Babylon, Medo-Persia, Greece, Rome, would be broken and consumed. The gradual advancement of the kingdom is suggested in these words, and would agree with the idea of "increase" (Isa. 9:6), and growth (Isa. 11:1, 10; cf. Rom. 15:12, where the prophet's "in that day" the apostle understands to be the present evangelization of the nations; when Christ risen shall "rest" in His glory as He now does), and our Lord's parables of the kingdom (Matt. 13:31-33). The Stone-kingdom "shall never be destroyed" — attempts would be made to destroy it; "it shall not be left to other people" — enemies would seek to gain possession; (as in the case of the four kingdoms of the image); "it shall stand forever"; that is, eternally. Our Lord described His Church and Kingdom as the same institution; founded upon Himself, the Rock, and "the gates of hell shall not prevail against it" (Matt. 16:18-19; 18:17-18).

> Crowns and thrones may perish,
>   Kingdoms rise and wane;
> But the Church of Jesus
>   Constant shall remain;
> Gates of hell can never
>   'Gainst that Church prevail:
> We have Christ's Own promise,
>   And that cannot fail.

God would set up His kingdom "in the days of these kings"; that is, the four named. Bethlehem's advent (at the time predicted: Luke 2:1) agrees with the word "a stone cut out without hands" (cf. Micah 5:2; Zec. 9:9-10), and its becoming a great mountain and filling the whole earth is co-extensive with the gospel preached unto "the uttermost part of the earth" according to His instruction for this is to be the extent of His kingdom (Acts 1:8; Ps. 2:8. cf. Acts 4:25-26). Daniel, perceiving that the end of the 70 years' captivity was imminent, directed his intercessory prayer accordingly, whereupon heaven's messenger gave to him precisely the number of years unto the appearing of Messiah the Prince, and His death on Calvary, by which types and prophecies would be fulfilled, salvation by grace provided being confirmed by the new and everlasting covenant of His kingdom (Dan. 9:2-3, 24-27).

This is the kingdom of which Daniel was given a vision with further particulars (Dan. 7). The description of the investiture of the Son of Man answers to that of the Apocalypse (Rev. 1-2, 5), where the ascended Lord is seen by John as Head of His churches on earth during His absence in heaven. The emphasis seems to be upon "the saints of the high places" (Dan. 7:18, 22, 25, 27; Eph. 1:3, 20; 2:6; 3:10; 6:12). Their identification with the Lord Jesus Christ in suffering and in glory, is indicated in these Scriptures. And upon the destruction of all His and their enemies, they are to reign with Him in the "everlasting kingdom". It is to be noted that their first mention is in connection with the four successive kingdoms, and particularly the last, Rome. That is the time-element here (Dan. 7:17-18). The several references to the saints of the most high or heavenly places not only ensure that they reign with Christ but also envisage their suffering with Him, as, indeed, the gospel promises. "Through much tribulation we must enter the kingdom of God." They share with Christ in His rejection and reward. The dream and vision cover the experiences of the Church throughout their pilgrim course and terminate with their reigning with Christ in the everlasting kingdom.

In view of the fact that the advent of Christ meant the intrusion of His kingdom upon the world, being contemporaneous with the disruption of the fourth kingdom, that of Rome, which history witnesses was the case, the fortunes of the saints upon earth may be here signified in their main features, for they "wrestle against spiritual wickedness in high places". For Christ's investiture upon His ascending on high gave Him reigning administrative power until He shall have gathered together into one all things in Himself which are in heaven and which are on earth, even in Him (Eph. 1:10).

In view of His imminent return to heaven, the Lord Jesus instructed His apostles concerning the kingdom of God. Being Jews, and not yet having received the Spirit of illumination for Whom they waited, they cherished the Judaistic idea of an earthly kingdom to be established under their Messiah. Therefore, they asked, "Wilt Thou at this time restore again the kingdom to Israel?" (Acts 1:3-7). Following the Pentecostal enduement with enthusiasm they preached the name of the Lord Jesus, believers being baptized, the outward sign of their having entered the kingdom of God through repentance and faith. For this they suffered, and were exhorted that "through much tribulation we must enter the kingdom". With Jews in the synagogues they disputed and persuaded concerning the kingdom, as Paul also did in his own hired house where they waited upon him. It was no restoration of the kingdom to Israel they proclaimed, otherwise there were no disputation or need of persuasion; no rejection of their message whereupon they turned to the Gentiles (Acts 1:12; 14:22; 28:28)!

It would be wrong to assume, as some do, that the non-committal reply of the Lord to their enquiry: "It is not for you to know the times or the seasons which the Father hath put in His own power", was His acknowledgement that the kingdom would be so restored at sometime if not "at this time". At no place in the Scriptures does it say that God will give back to the Jews this Kingdom in the future. He released them from their national and confined as well as false conception by charging them with a larger duty and privilege, and the promise of spiritual empowerment which would solve all their problems. By the Holy Spirit the things of Christ would be revealed which they were "not able to bear" hitherto, and it was to their advantage that He would depart and the Spirit would come (John 14-16).

A passage of parallel construction appears in the preceding chapter (John 21). Peter, having been informed of his infirmity and death, enquired as to the future of John, to which the Lord replied "If I will that he tarry till I come, what is that to thee, follow thou Me". The false conclusion drawn from this was that John would remain alive until the Lord's return, while Peter would die, whereas all was qualified by the important, "If I will". Similarly in the question about a restored kingdom to Israel, it is wrongly assumed that our Lord's referring all to His Father's authority was tantamount to an affirmative reply, the precise time only being unkown. In the one case emphasis is placed upon the Father's authority; in the other upon the Saviour's will. The conclusion about Israel's kingdom is as speculative as was the saying about John's longevity. Moreover, our Lord said, "It is not for you to know"; yet dispensationalists "know" so much that they presume to inform us of the whole order of events to the setting up of the alleged kingdom!

Instead, the gospel was to be carried to the uttermost part of the earth, and our Lord had already declared the result: "They shall come from the east and from the west, and from the north and from the south, and shall sit down in the kingdom of God. They shall sit down with Abraham, Isaac and Jacob in the kingdom of heaven: but the children of the kingdom shall be cast out into outer darkness" (Matt. 8:11; Luke 13:28). In repeating His promise to the patriarchs, wherein the gospel was then preached by Scripture foresight (Gal. 3:8), this universal scope is mentioned in similar terms: "And thy seed shall be as the dust of the earth, and thou shalt break forth to the west and to the east, and to the north and to the south: and in thee and thy Seed shall all the families of the earth be blessed" (Gen. 28:14).

In His sermon on the mount, regarded as the laws of the kingdom, the Lord gave the prescription: "Seek ye first the kingdom of God and His righteousness, and all these things shall be added unto you". "These things" summed up the temporalities of life which were the concern in general of the nations, the affairs of this life. The disciples of the Lord Jesus were not to be anxious for today or the morrow, for current needs or future supplies. "Your heavenly Father knoweth that ye have need" and therefore, "they shall be added".

Their prior occupation, therefore, should be with His kingdom and righteousness, not concerned so much with the temporal but spiritual, not this life but the life eternal, not the rule of men but the righteousness of God. The apostle, formerly imbued with the idea of a temporal kingdom for his nation, but now spiritually enlightened, commented: "The kindom of God is not meat and drink, but righteousness and peace and joy in the Holy Ghost" a kingdom not in any way of carnal character, but wholly of spiritual quality and eternal (Rom.

14:17).

Only by a new creation, a spiritual birth, a birth from above — for "Jerusalem which is above is free, and is the mother of us all" (Gal. 4:26) — do sinners enter the kingdom of God in reality, and it is the Father's good pleasure to give the kingdom to the little flock of Christ's disciples (Luke 12:32). Even "the drunkards and harlots go into the kingdom of God before you", He rebukingly said to the rulers of the Jews—sinners whom He came to save and in His merits to make "fit for the kingdom".

He plainly announced the transference of the kingdom from the Jews to the Church. The husbandman whose vineyard fruits they confiscated must have reminded them of the prophet's parable of similar mercy and judgment (Matt. 21; Isa. 5; Ps. 80). The sending of His Son, however, saying "they will reverence My Son", was the divine ultimatum, for this He did "last of all", patience and forebearance and opportunity being exhausted. "This is the heir", they said, "come, let us kill Him and let us seize on His inheritance". They were their own judges and pronounced their own verdict: "He will miserably destroy those wicked men and let out His vineyard to others". The vineyard represented the kingdom. Reminding them of their prophesied rejection of Him, He said: "Therefore, the kingdom of God shall be taken from you, and given to a nation bringing forth the fruits thereof". The new nation is the Church (1 Pet. 2:9). Israel had been put in trust with God's kingdom, they were accountable to Him for it, but they failed to render to Him the fruits. Therefore, the kingdom would be taken from them, taken up and carried away from them, and entrusted to others. The expression is of transference but not of restoration later to the earlier trustees (cf. Tregelles on Dan. 2. p. 7).

The petition, "Thy kingdom come" in what is generally known as the Lord's prayer, is understood by many to indicate the spread of Christianity unto world conversion, or the achievement of the ecumenical aspiration, the world church. By others it is interpreted as a millennial establishment upon His second coming. The interpretative words which follow, however, are not satisfied by either of these conceptions. The following words from a volume of family prayers arranged by the late Dr. Joseph Parker deserve quotation here: "Almighty God, Thou art King over all; Thou rulest as Thou wilt, yet Thou dost not tell us why Thou dost so rule. But work Thou in us the miracle of patience so that we patiently and lovingly may await the issue, not saying one word until we hear from the heavens as from the cross, 'It is finished'. The tempter means to spoil Thy work and kill our faith, but we believe he is under Thy power, and Thou wilt at last crush every foe of purity and righteousness, love and justice, and then Thy universe will be as Thy heaven. Enable us to rest in this truth and to build our life upon it. Pity us with the love of Thy cross, with the compassion of Thine Own propitiatory blood, and give us to know that where sin abounds grace does much more abound, an infinite sea rolling over some sunken pebble".

"Thy will be done on earth as it is in heaven". That is our Lord's exposition of "Thy kingdom come". "Thy universe shall be as Thy heaven". There the divine will which is good and acceptable and perfect, is sovereign, supreme, unopposed, all-pervading, and affords unsullied happiness. Words fail to express how the will of God is done in heaven. But that is the divinely-inspired prayer of His church for the earth; it is God's promise and her prospect. A universe, heaven and earth, the eternal kingdom of righteousness. This is vastly different from a world christianized by the union of churches and faiths; different also from the improved though still imperfect conditions envisaged in an earthly millennium thereafter to be destroyed. This is the everlasting kingdom of the new earth and heavens for which the apostles looked and the church expected (2 Pet. 3). "Wherefore, we, receiving a kingdom which cannot be moved, let us have grace whereby we may serve God acceptably with reverence and godly fear: for our God is a consuming fire" (Heb. 12: 25-29).

GAPS AND GUESSES

CHRONOLOGICAL gaps appear to be necessary to dispensational guesses. Parentheses of time or subject are proposed in psalms, types and prophecies even when the diction of Scripture is without abruptness, and connected. Some introduce them early. The divine revelation, it is conjectured, begins with a gap. Between the events recorded in the first and second verses in the Bible, a gap of unmeasured and unrevealed length is introduced. The first verse, it is said, refers to an "original creation" overtaken in judgment, while the second verse records the beginning of a new creation, that of the present heavens and earth. This alleged "disruption of the world" it is claimed, is an event "forming a great dividing line in the dispensations of the ages". In support of this word, "foundation" (e.g. Eph. 1:3) is given as overthrow, whereas its plain meaning, to throw or cast down, is exactly what is done in laying a foundation, and the Authorized Version is correct.

The original earth is supposed to have been inhabited by a pre-Adamic race of which today we have no cognizance, or by Lucifer, son of the morning, and his angels. The fall of Satan is said to have taken place during this pre-historic period, and "disease was rife long before man appeared, and was not directly attributable to Adam's sin", and "ages before Adam's sin had appeared in this planet", and "every living thing had been swept to death". In order to force the gap theory to fit the prophet's revelation of Lucifer (Ezekiel 28), it is suggested ,that the planets were affected in the judgment spoken of, and "the light of the sun had been completely withdrawn" . . . The "prince of this world", it is said, "was set in an Edenic Garden", and that wherein Adam was placed is spoken of as "the later Eden". It is, however, acknowledged that "of the character of that original scene we are given no details in Scripture". Dating speculation includes "eight million years ago", and it is remarked that "no reputable scientist would accept" the Biblical chronology. Indeed, it is acknowledged that this theory which "refers the first creative act to the dateless past, gives scope for all the geologic ages". We are instructed to "avoid", not to accommodate "the oppositions of science falsely so called, which some professing have erred concerning the faith" (1 Tim. 6:20-21). The New Testament attribution of sin, disease and death in their origin to Adam, "the first man", and to the one Edenic tragedy and not a double and repeated paradisaical disaster, should suffice for believers. (Our references are to *The Scofield Bible, The Companion Bible* and *The Harvester* where the editor writes on the subject in which he seems to rely much on Pember, and pagan mythology; but the error, of course is widely disseminated). The other side is well presented by theologians worthy to be considered.

The theory we have referred to is supported by an erroneous sense gratuitously given to the words, "And the earth was without form and void", the verb is said to have the force of "became", suggesting some kind of destructive overthrow. In fact, the phrase actually states the beginning of a creative process detailed in chapters 1 and 2, of which the first verse is titular comprehending the entire undertaking, so that appropriately we have at the end of the six days' work and with the seventh day's rest, *"Thus* the heavens and the earth were finished, and all the host of them". The verb carries

the meaning "came to be" or "came into existence"
and its recurrence supports this sense. "And God
said, Let there be light and there was light"; that
is, light came to be, or came into existence. Thus
also did the earth come into existence "without
form and void"; but it did not remain so, for "the
Spirit of God moved". The witness of the prophets
is called to support this gap theory. The reverse is
the case. In opposition to its remaining a formless
void, God "formed it to be inhabited", and this was
precisely the case when pronounced as "finished".
It remained not "empty" for God intended that it
should be suitably occupied by creatures He intended to place on the earth and in the heavens, the
highest of whom was Man, "in His own image and
likeness". He perfectly prepared the house for habitation before He introduced the occupants, and
then He pronounced all "very good". (See additional comments upon this subject in our earlier
chapter IV).

The doctrine of the new creation, repairing
Adam's fall, is also subjected to dispensational
gaps. We have, for instance, the familiar Messianic
prophecy: "Unto us a child is born" (Isa. 9), fulfilled at Bethlehem; and "unto us a son is given",
fulfilled on Calvary (cf. John 3:16), but thereupon
a gap of (so far) nearly two millenniums is proposed in the dispensational theory before the fulfilment of the next prophetic sentence, "and the
government shall be upon His shoulder". That is
supposed to await the earthly millennium. It is,
however, made clear by the preaching of Peter and
Paul (Acts 2:13) that upon God's raising up His
Son Jesus He invested Him with governmental
authority to occupy, as promised, the throne above,
of which the throne of David was intended to be
the type and pattern below. Thus, as Son of David,
Jesus was raised from the dead and ascended to
the right hand of power, "for David is not ascended", that is, to sit upon his throne; the "everlasting
covenant" announced to David was implemented by
his risen Son, through the Gospel, while He Himself in heavenly glory gives effect to the administration of the kingdom which David's prefigured, "a

kingdom still increasing, a kingdom without end". His meritorious titles, "Wonderful, Counsellor, the Mighty God, the everlasting Father, the Prince of Peace", describe the characters and offices He so perfectly befits. There is no gap in the consecutiveness of fulfilment if we accept the principle that God means what He says and says what He means, and what He means is conveyed in the wealth of the glorious Gospel of the blessed God, the everlasting Gospel, for all peoples and not merely of millennial duration for Jewish aggrandisement.

The theory is that upon the Lord's coming the second time (some say secretly, others with publicity) He will institute upon the earth a millennial reign of peace and prosperity. Varied are the amenities of this alleged reign. Not one among the many references to His second coming in the New Testament makes mention of any such consequence. Salvation for His redeemed elect and judgment upon apostate enemies are the two alternatives. Brief in general are the references, but a passage which deals at some length with the situation is found in 2 Peter, chapter 3. To this we give some attention because here again the difficulty in the dispensationalist theory is overcome by introducing a gap.

The Coming of the Lord introduces the day of the Lord which is also the day of God and the day of judgment and perdition of ungodly men, till when the heavens and earth which are now are reserved unto fire. The promise of His coming, at which unbelievers scoff, involves also the promise of the new heavens and new earth, and this is the prospect for which believers look, and unto which day they hasten. There is no interval of a time period between these events, the Coming, the Day of the Lord, the Day of God, the Day of Judgment and the New Heavens and new Earth, though there may be a succession; no reign of Christ on the earth for a thousand years is said to intervene. The reference to a day and a thousand years (doubtless an adaptation from Psalm 90) in God's accountancy explains, not a post-coming millennium, but a precoming apparent delay in the arrival of the day of

the Lord. As God accounts a thousand years as a
day, believers are to account His longsuffering as
the day of salvation, the obvious meaning being
that with the fulfilment of His promised coming
the salvation opportunity will finish and judgment
will fall. The reasoning of the apostle is clear and
plain.

There is no conflict with this statement in the
New Testament, not even in the millennial chapter
except the earthly dispensational view be insisted
upon, then the difficulty arises and some subterfuge
must try to overcome it. The sense of apparent
delay, suggested by the assurance that the Lord is
not slack concerning His coming but is longsuffering to usward, appears to agree with the Scripture
which declares the Creator and Redeemer will determine "that there shall be *delay* no longer" but
the kingship shall be that of our Lord and His
Christ, and He shall reign, with the result: "And
the nations were angry, and Thy wrath is come,
and the time of the dead that they should be judged,
and that Thou shouldest give reward unto Thy
servants the prophets, and to the saints, and to
them that fear Thy name small and great, and
shouldest destroy them that destroy the earth"
(Rev. 10, 11). The language of the millennial
chapter accords with this, as does also the earlier
chapter which introduces it (Rev. 20:6). No words
of such compass could more fitly describe the general judgment, and it is timed with the second
coming at the last trump (1 Cor. 15).

In order to accommodate the millennium in
Peter's passage, which he does not envisage, dispensationalists appear to have two theories. One
is that the millennium itself will be a protracted
day of judgment, a gap of 1000 years between the
Coming and that final Day. We quote: "Where the
judgment is mentioned without any qualifying words
it usually means the judgment which Christ is coming to execute at His second advent, and which
begins when He is revealed from heaven in flaming
fire, and continues through the millennium to the
arraignment of the great white throne at the end
of the millennium" (*Watching and Waiting* maga-

zine). Against this suggested protracted period of judgment, God's judicial act following long patience and admonition is abrupt and executed with dispatch. Examples in Biblical history seem to support this, as do the warnings of our Lord, and forewarnings about the suddenness of His coming (*cf.* Luke 17:30; I Thess. 5:2). Judgment is His "strange work". He delighteth in mercy, hence His extended longsuffering in the present time, and seeming delay in His coming, by scoffers taken advantage of unto challenging the veracity of His promise. "For He will finish the work and cut it short in righteousness, because a short work will the Lord make upon the earth". Such is His work of judgment (Isa. 28; Rom. 9; *cf.* Psa. 37, 73).

Again, it is said that while Peter does not mention the duration of the Day of the Lord, other Scriptures state it to be "definitely a thousand years" (Benjamin W. Newton), and upon this assumption it is surmised that the Day will "at its commencement be a day of judgment" (as Peter avers), but its progress "will be for a season stayed" (of which Peter is silent), the reason for this being the making place for the millennium. This beginning of judgment, it is said, will be but "a pledge and example of the great concluding dissolution of all things, but longsuffering will not at that time make a complete end, and the millennium harvest will be the result". This obviously is contrary to the Apostle's reasoning that divine longsuffering precedes but does not follow the second coming of the Lord. Thus a gap is proposed, a millennial gap, of arrested judgment. The attempt is made to support this by an elastic emphasis upon the words "in which" (v. 10), and "wherein", given as "in consequence of which" (v. 12). The judgment which Peter says will coincide with Christ's Coming is postponed to the end of a 1000 years, yet the fact of that postponed judgment is in consequence of that millennium. Strange indeed if *in consequence of* a blessed reign of peace and prosperity, a golden age, such terrific judgment should fall; illogical cause and effect! Moreover, it is obvious, and needs no such adjustment, that the solemn language portends judgment by reason of the *arrival* (coming) of the Lord, and does not allow for an interim millennium. And again, if the Scripture of Revelation 20 gives the Day of the Lord as "definitely a thousand years", the judgment does not occur within that 1000 years at all, for when it is finished, "a little season" of universal apostasy erupts, and it is in consequence of that, and not of the millennial Day of the Lord, that the judgment falls. And so far as the theory we criticize being "in accord with the rest of Scripture" the reverse is the case. Neither Peter nor John says anything of a pre-millennial Coming, but a pre-judgment Coming. And these two apostles in agreement have Paul also as witness "in all his epistles to these very things" (2 Pet. 3:16).

The words are: "The Lord is not slack concerning His promise" — the promise of His coming and with it the new creation (vv. 4, 13); "but is longsuffering to usward" — that is, in this present time of Gospel preaching and acceptance; "not willing that any should perish" — in the judgment accompanying His Coming; "but that all should come to repentance" — in this time of His clemency and longsuffering; "for the day of the Lord will come as a thief in the night in the which" — not a millennium on earth with Jewish national sovereignty, and a harvest in conversions among the Gentiles, but "the heavens shall pass away with a great noise . . . the earth also and the works that are therein shall be burnt up".

The Day will bring everlasting salvation to all generations of Christ's redeemed, called and chosen and faithful, then risen, raptured and glorified. But it will not introduce a second chance to either Jews or Gentiles, to despisers of the longsuffering of God, or a saving opportunity to further generations upon the ruined earth. It will be not a millennium of a sinful world's renovation followed by its final conflagration, but of convulsions in the heavens and the cremation of the earth, superseded by the creation of "all things new", a universe in which righteousness alone will abide, where "we shall see His face, and never, never sin, but from the rivers of His grace drink endless pleasures in".

It has been remarked in these articles that the two main reasons given for the election and preservation of the nation of Israel were, to them were committed the Scriptures, and of them, as concerning the flesh, the Messiah should come (Rom. 3:2; 9:5). Therefore, through all their vicissitudes God watched over them "for His name's sake" and "to fulfil His word". The remnant's return from exile is an example of this. About the time of expiry God gave to Daniel an inspired chronological forecast, verifying His word in the fulfilment of the first and final objective of His eternal purpose; namely, the sending of His Own Son as Redeemer. The forecast came as a revelation to Daniel in response to his intercession and confession on behalf of his people. The prayer was incited by his recognition and estimation, based on Jeremiah's prophecy, that the seventy years' captivity to Babylon had run their course (Dan. 9:1-3). Prediction to Daniel was prayer-matter. Was he encouraged by Ezekiel's prophetic ministry (Ezek. 36, 37)? Daniel counted upon the faithfulness of God to terminate the captivity without interruption or delay beyond the stated time. His final word of intercessory appeal was: "O Lord, hear; O Lord, forgive; O Lord, *hearken and do: defer not,* for Thine Own sake, O my God" (v. 19).

Thereupon Gabriel "swiftly" relieved the prophet's anxiety with an answer of peace, a promise of rehabilitation as the prophets had forecast, and especially that which was the burden of all prophecy, the appearing of the promised Messiah. Brief reference is made to the temporal restoration invoked, for evidently the coming of Christ and the spiritual benefits of the redemption He would accomplish are the chief concern. These were enumerated at the commencement of Gabriel's announcement, and could be the achievement only of Christ by His fulfilling obedience and oblation upon the cross (v. 24; see also the evangelical prophets of the period, Ezekiel, Haggai, Zechariah, Malachi). "I am now come forth to give thee skill and understanding", said Gabriel, "therefore, understand and consider" (vv. 22, 23). Jeremiah's seventy years now ended are superseded by Gabriel's seventy sevens of years, or 490 years. It is here that dispensationalists interpolate a gap of indeterminable length. Surely, as history had now confirmed the accuracy of Jeremiah's consecutive and gapless 70 years, Daniel would "understand" that history would also verify in due time the accuracy of Gabriel's consecutive and gapless 490 years! Had Jeremiah's 70 years permitted of or covered a break in continuity of undefined length, how then could the God-fearing prophet have understood the number of the years, and if the possibility of a gaping chronological doubt could have been entertained, since the time element was so crucial, how could Daniel have directed his prayer with any confidence? This connection which Daniel himself records between the 70 years then expiring and the 490 thereupon to begin cannot be ignored in any sound interpretation of the prophecy.

Moreover, no gap existed between the end of the 70 years and the beginning of the 490, for God had predictively named Cyrus as His servant unto the return of the remnant and the rebuilding of city and temple: "thus saith the Lord that confirmeth the word of His servant and performeth the counsel of His messengers, that saith to Jerusalem, thou shalt be inhabited . . . that saith of Cyrus, He is My shepherd and shall perform all My pleasure, even saying to Jerusalem, thou shalt be built, and to the temple, thy foundation shall be laid" . . . "I have raised him up in righteousness and I will direct all his ways; he shall build My city, he shall let go all My captives" (Isa. 44, 45; 2 Chron. 36; Ezra 1). Independent of the Biblical record, Josephus in his *Antiquities of the Jews* (first century A.D.) records the decree of Cyrus, commencing thus: "King Cyrus to Sisinnes and Sathrabuzanes, sendeth greeting. I have given leave to as many of the Jews that dwell in my country as please, to return to their own country, and to rebuild their city, and to build the temple of God at Jerusalem". Inventors of the gap theory gratuitously name

Artaxerxes as the starting point, against the inspired assertion in these Scriptures naming Cyrus. The state of the city which burdened Nehemiah was due to the walls and gates having been shattered by local enemies in the forecast "troublous times" when the work proceeded and was suspended.

There is no need for conjecture about the commencing date, for reliability may be placed upon the Scripture of Truth, and as the 70 years' captivity were predicted by Jeremiah, so God has spoken through Isaiah in respect to the 490 years, in that He has named Cyrus as His anointed servant in initiating the fulfilment. It has been chronologically shown that from Cyrus to Christ satisfied the period named "unto Messiah the Prince", and reaches the beginning of His public ministry, "when Jesus himself began to be about thirty years of age", being baptized of John and significantly marked out as the Christ the Son of God, being "made manifest to Israel", and as Peter declared in His review, "how God anointed (Messiah) Jesus of Nazareth with the Holy Ghost and with power, Who went about doing good". Indeed, He Himself had opened His ministry by opening and reading the roll and reading: "The Spirit of the Lord is upon Me because He hath anointed Me to preach the gospel" etc. adding, "this day is this scripture fulfilled in your ears" (John 1; Luke 4; Acts 10; Isa. 61).

The first seven sevens (49 years) of this period are separately mentioned because, as explained, they would be occupied in the restoration "even in troublous times", which is borne out by the history. The explanation, however, does not immediately follow the time allotted because the prevaling objective is the coming of Christ and His redeeming mission, and the return from captivity was governed by this. Added to the "seven sevens" (49 years) threfore, are "three score and two sevens" (434 years, making 483). It is recognized that these are continuous and admit of no gap, reaching to the time of the manifiestation of Messiah the Prince, "after" which He is "cut off". This leaves one seven (7 years) to complete the 70 sevens (490 years). According to the futurist theory, this remaining period of 7 years is postponed indefinitely. If, we may enquire, the first two divided periods "follow on directly" (which is admitted), what ground is there for the speculation that the remaining seven years do not follow on directly upon the 483 years? By this dispensational postponement these seven years are transferred from relation to Christ to Antichrist, from the Messiah to His great enemy. Moreover, the theory involves a gap of four times the length of the complete prophetic unit of 490 years for thereby these final seven years are still to come! We submit that while there are within this statement references to relevant events touching the enemies of Israel and of their Messiah, and His judgments upon them for their rejection of Him, in the destruction of Jerusalem under the Romans, these are not within the coverage of the 490 years. The prediction is a measure of continuous time, concluding with the crucifixion of Christ and its consequences and requires no invention of a gap to complete it.

"After the three score and two weeks shall Messiah be cut off and shall have nothing": no recognition or reception by the people of and to whom He came (John 1:11). "After" places the crucifixion within the "one week" remaining, the last of the 70, completing the 490 years. This remaining "seven" indicates how long "after". The pronoun, "He" refers to the Messiah, Who is the Subject of the entire numerical prediction. Following "Messiah shall be cut off" a forewarning is given quite relevantly of the judgment to be visited upon the Christ-rejecting nation, which Christ Himself confirmed, fulfilled in the destruction of the holy city and temple by the events of A.D. 70 (Matt. 24, Luke 21). Further details of the crucifixion and its significance are now given, for the cutting off of Messiah was not only the deed of "wicked hands" but according to "the determinate counsel and foreknowledge of God" (Acts 2:23). "After" His appearing and rejection and by His being "cut off", and in the "one seven"

remaining, He would "cause to prevail a covenant
with many". This covenant, unlike its predecessor
which was broken and dissolved, He would *cause
to prevail* (see Jer. 31:31-34 with Heb. 8:8-12).
By the same deed, that is, His being crucified, the
old covenant was done away: "He taketh away the
first that He may establish the second"; He "offered
one sacrifice for sins forever" and "there remaineth
no more sacrifice for sins" (2 Cor. 3; Heb. 10). Of
this He spake at the last supper: "the new covenant in My blood shed for many for the remission
of sins", "the blood of the everlasting covenant" on
account of which He was raised from the dead, and
in virtue of which the God of peace will "make you
perfect"; that is the "many", the remnant, His redeemed selected from Jews and Gentiles, "a people
for His name" (see the references to the "many":
Isa. 53:8-11; Matt. 20:28; 26:28; Rom. 5:15; and
cf. Isa. 42:6; 55:3; Mal. 3:1, etc.). Thus the covenant shall "prevail" everlastingly. The passage
does not affirm that a seven years' covenant will
be made by Antichrist and that it will be
broken halfway through, which is the futuristic
interpretation. ascribing it to Antichrist. No word
is written about making and breaking a covenant.
It does not say that the covenant will permit the
Jew's sacrificial worship to be reinstituted in a
temple to be rebuilt for seven years, nor that causing the sacrifice and oblation to cease will be breaking the covenant. Rather it is explained that "in
the midst of the week" that would be, three-and-
half years after His manifestation, now a matter
of historic accuracy and by His being "cut off",
"He would cause the sacrifice and the oblation to
cease". This He did, that by His perfect and final
sacrifice the new covenant should prevail.

The judgment visited in A.D. 70 spoken of above
(v. 26) is now again described, but whereas the
first reference was to the instruments, "the people
of the prince that shall come"; namely, the Roman
armies (Luke 21:20), here it is Messiah Himself
Who sovereignly gives effect to His own word. The
words are: "*He* shall cause to prevail a covenant";
"*He* shall cause the sacrifice to cease"; and "with

the abominable armies *He* shall make it desolate". Christ risen and glorified, having all authority in heaven and in earth, He directed the events of A.D. 70, of which He gave warning, quoting Daniel and brought about the "consummation" and the "end". This was His final word about the Jewish nation: "When ye shall see Jerusalem compassed with armies . . . these be the days of vengeance that all things written may be fulfilled . . . and they shall be led away captive into all nations: and Jerusalem shall be trodden down of the Gentiles until the times of the Gentiles be fulfilled". Paul also doubtless referred to this when he wrote: "for the wrath is come upon them to the uttermost". The uttermost; that was the unparalleled and unrepeatable tribulation (Matt. 24:21; 1 Thess. 2:15-16). Christ's being "cut off" or crucified and Jerusalem's destruction with all that it involved, were as cause and effect. Hence He ascended to the right hand of power and watched over His word to perform it, having said: "heaven and earth shall pass away, but My word shall not pass away" (Matt. 21:41; 22:7; Luke 23:28-30; *cf.* Rev. 6:15).

We may observe that the proposed dispensational severance of the last seven years from the total unit and its deferment is no more warranted than would have been the dividing in similar manner of Jeremiah's seventy years. Neither is the ascription of the pronoun, "He", to Antichrist with the conjecture of a future seven years' covenant to be broken in the midst. This would involve the reintroduction of Mosaic typical sacerdotalism which Christ the Reality did away and fulfilled and superseded, reversion to which the New Testament regards as Hebrew apostasy (Gal. 1; Heb. 6). It would also involve divine recognition of a system now abolished but reintroduced at the instigation of Antichrist, which is not only unworthy of God the holy One, but would outrage His own evangelical principles, and the doctrine of Gospel grace. Scripture and reason teach otherwise, and it is wiser to build upon Biblical and historical accuracy than resort to the speculative gaps and guesses of modern dispensationalism.

When Gabriel approached Daniel in answer to his supplication, he first of all because of their paramount importance, announced a sequence of evangelical benefits which only the Messiah could achieve. He named them thus: "to finish the transgression and to make an end of sins, and to make reconciliation for iniquity, and to bring in everlasting righteousness, and to seal up the vision and prophecy, and to anoint the most holy". It could not be more abundantly clear from the New Testament that these were effected by the obedience of Christ unto death of the cross. He only so completely and finally dealt with transgression and sins, and iniquity (Ps. 32). He only made reconciliation or atonement now preachéd in the Gospel (2 Cor. 5; Heb. 2:17). He only brought in everlasting righteousness, imputed to sinners through faith (Rom. 5). He sealed up vision by Himself being the last, and exceeding all previous prophets, and fulfilling "all that was written" (Acts 5; Heb. 1). And He anointed the most holy, in that He consecrated for us the new and living way, affording "the many" access to the holiest of all by His own blood (Heb. 10). Believers, both Jew and Gentile, the wall of partition being broken down by His cross, both being given "access by one Spirit unto the Father", the Old Testament does not require for its realization the reproduction of the old order. "The Old is by the New revealed". As with the Levitical and other typical anticipations, so the predictive terminology in which God spake is to be understood in the terms of the Gospel which interprets what He means.

THE MILLENNIAL
ADMINISTRATION OF THE
ASCENDED MESSIAH

BY EMPHASIS upon earthly and temporal benefits of a millennial age dispensationalists tend to minimize the immeasurable attainments and glories of Christ's supreme redeeming victory by His cross. It is because He became obedient unto death, a penal and capital punishment vicariously endured of His own volition, that universal dominion is already meritoriously given to Him. Because He made Himself of no reputation, how vast is His reputation now! (Phil. 2). To usward who believe is the power which God wrought in Christ when He raised Him from the dead and set Him at His own right hand in the heavenlies, "far above all principality and power and might and dominion, and every name that is named not only in this world, but also in that which is to come" (Eph. 1). There is no language, millennial or otherwise, which is so prodigiously and worthily written of the Lord Jesus Christ as in this Gospel. The celebration of His Calvary conquest is made in heaven from whence He, in His exercise of universal authority (Matt. 28) directs His Church and her activities on the earth (Rev. 2, 3), the Holy Spirit, bestowed as promised, being His effectual empowerment.

Truly it may often appear that the Church has lost her vision and resorts to warfare with carnal weapons. But no transference of privilege or power to an earthly carnal age, said yet to come, — as

when, for example, it is remarked that "this and
that are not for the Church now but for the age to
come, the Church is not now reigning with Christ,
that is reserved for the millennium" — should be as
an excuse or escapement respecting the resources
obtained by and in Christ for His people in this
present time (Eph. 3:20). The sweep of language
in this doxology could scarcely be greater in any
context: the glory is God's in Christ, the context
is the Church, not the Jew; and not for a future
age on earth but unto all ages, and not for a thousand years, but world without end. And all is entirely due to the Gospel which expounds and pro-
claims the achievements of the Lord Jesus by His
sufferings unto death. Any proposed interlude before
He enjoys "the glories that follow" is eclipsed altogether (1 Pet. 1:11; Luke 24:26).

The millennial phraseology (Rev. 20) is in har-
mony with the entire Apocalypse communicated by
the Lord Jesus Christ to the churches (Rev. 22:16),
not literally intended but "signified", and therefore
symbolical and figurative (Rev. 1:1). What does
this millennial language signify (Rev. 20. 1-6)? We
have remarked that Christ's victories are spiritual,
celebrated in heaven, with their effect in the calling
of the Church, composed of redeemed sinners in all
the earth and from among all nations. Heaven and
not earth is the scene of the millennium. The references to the earth concern the arrested deceiving of
the nations and the martyrdom of the faithful, now
seen in heavenly rest and glory. "Flesh and blood"
the natural form of earthly existence, "cannot inherit the kingdom of God". In resurrection with
what body do they come? "It is raised a spiritual
body". If, therefore, the first resurrection is of the
body, it is nevertheless of spiritual and not material
substance, suited not to earthly conditions but to
heavenly. "The first man is of the earth, earthy;
the second Man is the Lord from heaven. As is the
earthy such are they also that are earthy: and as
is the heavenly, such are they also that are heavenly.
And as we have borne the image of the earthy, we
shall also bear the image of the heavenly" (1 Cor.
15). The reign of Christ and His saints, being

heavenly and spiritual, is not on earth, and the earthly figure of a thousand years, therefore, need not be understood as in a world of earthly, literal, temporal terms of limitation as pertain to a fallen creation (cf. Gen. 5). The revelation of Jesus Christ, by symbolic and figurative diction and numerals "He sent and *signified* by His angel" (Rev. 1:1).

In conformity with the general character, therefore, the numerals may be considered in a figurative and representative, and not a fixedly rigid manner. The churches are representative of the whole, yet but seven are addressed. The one hundred and forty-four thousand may be an earthly contrast with heaven's innumerable multitude. Ten thousand times ten thousand and thousands of thousands describe the uncountable worshippers of the Lamb. The dimensions of the New Jerusalem and its wall are not taken literally, a city fifteen hundred miles broad, long and high, and a wall of three hundred feet. Moreover, it is the bride, the Lamb's wife. It would appear to be the manner of Scripture to make contrasts in measurements of time to illustrate that where sin abounded grace doth superabound. We read in the Apocalypse of 1260 days, 42 months, time, times and dividing of time, a short time, a little season, all in relation to evil and set against 1000 years, everlasting, and forever and ever, in respect of God's rule. Again we read of "a little wrath" and "everlasting kindness"; "a small moment" and "great mercies": "light affliction for a moment" and "eternal weight of glory"; "sufferings of the present time not worthy to be compared with the glory to be revealed"; "a little while, how little, and He shall come and not tarry". Yet how prolonged has been that "little"! "I became dead and behold I am alive forevermore". "If we suffer we shall reign with Him"; "As sin hath reigned unto death, so grace shall reign through righteousness unto eternal life". A thousand years are with God as a day and a day as a thousand years. We suggest there is good ground for considering whether the repeated "thousand years" might not figuratively signify a period of far more extending duration (Rev. 20). The Devil bound for a thousand years: released for a little season; the Saviour's immeasurable victory: the Devil's ignominious defeat! In like manner, the terms describing the succession of temporal kingdoms, whether represented by Image or Beasts present an enheartening disparity when set against, as they are, the everlasting kingdom of Christ. For but a limited season "War" is made against the saints of the heavenly places even to "wear them out", notwithstanding they shall "possess the kingdom forever, even forever and ever" for "the kingdom and the greatness of the kingdom under the whole heaven shall be given to the people of the saints of the Most High" — not for a mere millennium for it is added — "Whose kingdom is an everlasting kingdom, and all dominions shall serve and obey Him" (Daniel).

Regarding the thousand years of Revelation 20 as the literal duration of an earthly reign of Christ instituted from the time of His second advent, dispensationalism fits into this framework a self-selected substance from the Old Testament. This is done in some instances without respecting the testimony of history in the course of which it may be observed fulfilment has taken place. This millennial reign, we are told, will implement the covenant the Lord made with Abraham as to his seed possessing the land (Gen. 15 etc.). This, however, is not for a mere thousand years, but, if figures are to be taken thus literally, "His covenant" with Abraham, Isaac, Jacob and Israel, is "the word which He commanded to a thousand generations", which, taking a generation to be approximately forty years, would be forty thousand years, or forty millenniums. The next word calls it "an everlasting covenant" and then Canaan is named. We may be told, of course, that this expression, "a thousand generations" is not intended to be taken literally. But why should these forty millenniums be interpreted in a different manner to the substance of the covenant, and why should not they be as literal as the one millennium of the New Testament? It is evident that numerals so used in Scripture, whether in Old or New Testament, are not to be taken precisely, but express the enduring intention of God's covenant of **Grace,** which is also described in terms of everlastingness (Ps. 105:8-11; Gen. 17:7-8; Jer. 32:39-40).

The Angel seen to descend from heaven and imprison the Devil is surely the Lord Himself, for even Michael the archangel had said, "the Lord rebuke thee, Satan" (Jude), and the risen Lord alone holds the keys of death and of hell (Rev. 1:18; 9:1; 22:16, where the star is the symbol). In the Old Testament the angel of the covenant represents the Lord Jesus and the Apocalypse is replete with Old Testament allusions. The Evil One is fully described as he has been known throughout revealed history, "the old serpent" tracing that history back to Eden where it was said of the woman that her "Seed", referring to the first advent of Christ (Gal. 4), would bruise the serpent's head. Here in the casting down of Satan is the symbolized event. The bruising of the Saviour's heel, a temporary wounding, was no less than the bruising of the serpent's head, a fatal blow.

Satan is cast into the abyss from which there may and will be release, but only at the bidding of the reigning Lord (*cf.* ch. 9). By this casting down of Satan is intended the restraining and controlling of his movement and activity as symbolized in the great chain, "great" signifying magnitude or measure. When did the Lord Jesus thus deal with the Devil? Must we speculate about a future millennium on earth, for which such binding takes effect, rather than rely upon Scripture testimony whose terms undoubtedly determine this event? Moreover, the Devil must not be considered alone: his emissaries share with him. During His earthly ministry demons cast out of the unfortunate possessed fearfully asked the Lord, "Art Thou come to torment us before the time?" Even then restraint was placed upon them by Him, and although He granted their request, their destination was the abyss (Luke 8:31).

"Now", He said, referring to His being "lifted up from the earth signifying what death He should die", "now shall the prince of this world be cast out", and this He described as the world's judgment or crisis. For then and by this deed, said He, "I will draw all men unto Me". This accomplishment of world-wide redemption by His cross cannot be separated from His restraining of the Devil in his enthralling deceiving of the nations; and not only those of the privileged nation, the Jews who already had the testimony of God, but the Greeks representing all Gentile nations, would thus be drawn unto Him; all classes and conditions of men, released captives of Satan, that is the range of "I will draw *all* men unto Me". If by Christ's cross Satan was "cast out", where was he cast? The same Lord Who announced the event on earth symbolized the answer from heaven, and the same evangelist records both (John 12; Rev. 20). Now, therefore, Satan's powers over mankind are curtailed, and sinners for whom Christ died are transported out of the authority of darkness into the kingdom of God's dear Son (Col. 1). It may with reason be emphasized that not to the lifting up of the Saviour in preaching is this universal result attributed, but by His Own victorious conquest with the Devil are sinners liberated. The Gospel is the proclamation of the great deed. Was it in anticipation of this conquest of His cross that the Lord said to His apostles upon their reporting the success of their interim mission, "I beheld Satan fall like lightning from heaven", the devils then made subject unto them through His name being their anticipation of the "greater things" He would do through them upon His ascension (Luke 10:18; John 14:12)? "Rather rejoice", He added, "that your names are written in heaven", for being thus written they would share His throne. For the universal effectiveness of the preaching of the cross the Holy Spirit's enduement and presence were essential. This the Lord Jesus promised upon His ascension; He had also made promise before His death, in which connection He said: "When He is come He will convince the world of judgment because *the prince of this world is judged*".

By the death of His cross the Lord Jesus "overcame the wicked one" even to the extent of paralyzing his activities, bringing to naught or making useless, which is another way of expressing the curbing of his powers by the great chain. This was effected by His first advent and is not related to the second (Heb. 2:14-15; Col. 2:15). It were surprising, indeed, if this tremendous event, and the language used to describe it—of Christ's victory on Calvary in His rout of the enemy; paralyzing the Devil, spoiling principalities and powers, with the public spectacle of His triumph—did not signify a mighty restraint thereby put upon Satan, with all the blessed consequences of His reign, He having ascended to heaven's throne, in the good news effectually prevailing among the nations. To this end He "came down from heaven"; it does not await a second coming. And again, it was with a view to saving His redeemed from the very fear of death, for they who are thus blessed in Him "shall not be hurt of the second death". "For this purpose was the Son of God manifested that He might destroy the works of the devil" (I John 3:8). He unbinds or loosens from the Devil's work by binding and restraining the Devil himself. Thus, according to His own parable the Son of God, the Stronger than the strong, bound the strong man in order to destroy his palace and despoil his goods, which again accords with the millennial Scripture.

"Consider the spread of Christ's kingdom. So surely as the face of our Saviour was marred when He suffered for us, so surely shall He "sprinkle many nations". By which we understand, first that the doctrines of the Gospel are to fall in a copious shower over all lands. Jesus shall by His speech which drops as the dew and descends as the rain, sprinkle not the Jews only but the Gentile nations everywhere. Thy brethren abhorred Thee, O Immanuel! They despised Thee, O Man of Nazareth! But all lands shall hear of Thee, and feel Thee coming down like showers upon the mown grass. The dusky tribes afar off, and the dwellers in the land of the setting sun shall hear Thy doctrine, and shall drink it in as the fleece of wool sucks up dew. Thou shalt sprinkle many nations with Thy gracious word. Dr. Kitto explains the passage by an Oriental custom. He says that kings when they invited their subjects to great festivals would employ persons to sprinkle with perfume all who arrived as they passed the palace gate. Jesus invites men of all nations to come to the Gospel feast, and as they enter He casts on them the sweet perfumes of His love and grace so that they are fragrant before the Lord. There were no perfumes for Thee, Lord Jesus, upon Calvary. Vinegar and gall were all they could offer Thee, but now since Thou has gone to heaven, Thou dost provide perfumes for multitudes of the sons of men, and nations, north, south, east and west, are refreshed with the delicious showers of fragrance which through the Gospel falls upon them, and not the common people only but also over their leaders and rulers: "the kings shall shut their mouths at Him".

"How shall this come to pass? Will there be a new machinery? 'It pleases God by the foolishness of preaching to save them that believe.' To conceive that our Lord will end the present mode of warfare as though it were admitted that evil could not be conquered by the use of His instrumentality is to my mind to do Him great dishonour. If the Devil can persuade you that Christ is going to give up the war, or is going to fight it out on another line, you will soon grow idle. It looks a task too gigantic, but the bare arm of the Lord, only think of that: His sleeve rolled up, omnipotence itself made bare, what cannot that accomplish? Stand back, devils, when God's bare arm comes into the fight you will all run like dogs, for you know your Master. Do not be downhearted and dispirited, do not run to new schemes and fancies and interpretations of prophecy. Go and preach Christ Jesus unto all the nations. Go and spread abroad the Saviour's blessed name, for He is the world's only hope, and His cross is the banner of our victory." *(Sermon by Charles Haddon Spurgeon on Isaiah 52:14-15; culled from The Gospel Witness).*

The triumph of Christ by His cross, resurrection and ascension, thereby rescuing innumerable multitudes of sinners of all nations, peoples and tongues from the thraldom of Satan and his kingdom of darkness, translating them into His own kingdom, commencing with His own mission but especially charged upon His apostles and the Church, and still operating and extending unto the uttermost part of the earth, witnesses to the utter defeat and restraining of the Devil, especially when comparison is made with the state of gross spiritual darkness which covered the peoples in the generations B.C. (Isa. 9:1-2 with Matt. 4:14-16). The one exception was chosen Israel, peculiarly called and protected for purposes of divine grace, otherwise she also would have been involved in the universal plight, proof of which is not wanting when the Lord hid His face from her. Events may yet demonstrate that the developing and unifying uprising of nations against Christ and His Church, the upsurging of ancient paganisms and atheistic political antagonisms, the apostasy of Christendom and of Israeli, Babylonianism spiritually and politically revived, will identify the "little season" of Satan's beguiling the nations yet again, his final attempt to deceive before he is doomed forever. Compare the effect of the Devil's restraint and release. At the end deception will be total and final, which is far different from his limited and arrested activity during this Gospel age when multitudes are converted from among all the nations. Now, from the four quarters of the earth or the uttermost part, the number of the evangelized is as the sand of the sea. But afterwards in the "little season" the prevailing deception is so described (Rev. 20:8; 5:9; 7:9; Gen. 22:17; Rom. 4:13-17; Luke 13:29).

Under divine restriction the Evil One is permitted to "walk about like a roaring lion seeking whom he may devour", which is a very restricted operation: "Going about seeking whom he may" is very different language from the unrestricted, "he shall go out to deceive the nations which are in the four corners of the earth" (1 Pet. 5:8; Rev. 20:8). Now he may be restricted in the faith and put to flight. He transformeth himself into an angel of light that if it were possible he might deceive the very elect, but the intention of that advice is the assurance of its impossibility. "Satan hath desired to have thee that he may sift thee as wheat, but I have prayed for thee that thy faith fail not" is the strengthening word of our great High Priest, not alone to Peter but to all His own, for by His intercession He will save them to the uttermost. Equipped in the whole armour of God the militant Church may stand against, withstand, and then stand in victory, for she is not ignorant of his devices and wiles, although her fortitude may be fiercely assailed. Doubtless, the Son of God in the interests of His saints, often says, "Get thee behind me, Satan", and it may be the covering angels still refer him to the Captain of our salvation, saying, "the Lord rebuke thee, Satan". At the opening of His public ministry the prince of this world would have had the Son of God cast down from His holy purpose of vicarious obedient service (Matt. 4), but at the end the position was reversed, and in view of His obedience unto the death of the cross, He said, "Now shall the prince of this world be cast out." Hallelujah!

Thrones were seen to be occupied, though the occupants are not described. Attention is drawn in particular to the "souls" of the martyrs. It is written of the Lord Jesus in fulfilment of an Old Testament anticipation, that "when He ascended on high He led captivity captive and gave gifts unto men" (namely, His Church on earth), and it is reasoned, "Now that He ascended, what is it but that He also first descended into the lower parts of the earth?" The margin gives, He led "a multitude of captives". Were these from the region called "the lower parts of the earth"? Were these released captives the "souls" of His redeemed, the saints of old, those already referred to, delivered through the death of their Redeemer, which rendered ineffective the Devil's power, by which they had been "all their lifetime subject to bondage" (Eph. 4; Ps. 68; Heb. 2)? These were joined in the generations then (and perhaps still to come) by myriads of believers until the thousand years are finished, "the spirits of justified men made perfect", for they finally are perfected in completeness and not in part (Heb. 11:40; 12:23).

Let saints below in concert sing with those to
glory gone;
For all the servants of our King in earth and
heaven are one.
One family, we dwell in Him, one Church above,
beneath;
Though now divided by the stream, the narrow
stream of death.
One army of the living God, to His command
we bow;
Part of the host has crossed the flood, and part
are crossing now.
This moment to their endless home there pass
some spirits blest;
And we are to the margin come and wait our
call to rest.

The "souls" now seen to live and reign were
before seen in imprecatory prayer (Rev. 6). There
they were given white robes, righteous robes of
victory, though they rest for a little season till their
number should be completed. Would this answer
to the same "little season" in our millennial chapter?
Why white robes if not to reign with Christ, and
is not this their rest, and will not judgment be
visited after the little season of Satan's release?
"What are these which are arrayed in white robes,
and whence came they" (Rev. 7:13)? Paul,
of "departing to be with Christ" commented
"which is far better", so that *bodily* resurrection
is not essential to being "with Christ". This state
is to be "at home with the Lord", and these are
the "blessed dead who die in the Lord" (Phil. 1:23;
2 Cor. 5:8; Rev. 14:13).

"They lived"; the "souls of them" whose bodies
were slain, lived. Scripture differentiates between
soul and body, and also between the souls of those
who have died and souls as persons still in the
body. "Fear not them which kill the body but are
not able to kill the soul". "Souls of them", therefore,
refers to the disembodied state, for this expression
cannot describe souls as persons in the body before
or after resurrection (cf. Gen. 12:5; Acts 27:37).
The vision, therefore, would serve as a comforting
revelation to others likewise to suffer as announced

to the "souls" in chapter 6. "They lived". They had
lived on earth, but although their lives were cut
short enforcedly by the enemy death, for Christ's
name sake, yet they lived with Christ in heaven.
Dying Stephen saw the heavens opened, the glory
of God, and the Lord Jesus at His right hand, and
he prayed: "Lord Jesus, receive my spirit", and
"devout men carried his body to burial" (Acts 7).
"The rest of the dead" implies that these "souls"
also were regarded as among the dead. But, contrary
to "the rest", they "lived"; that is the victorious
revelation. These blest "souls" lived though they
were not now in the body. As Bunyan's Christian
sang of Faithful after his martyrdom:

Well, Faithful, thou hast faithfully protest
Unto thy Lord with Whom thou shalt be blest;
When faithless ones with all their vain delights,
Are crying out under their hellish plights,
Sing, Faithful, sing and let thy name survive,
For though they killed thee, *thou art yet alive.*

"But the rest of the dead lived not until . . ." The
time-pointer, "until" does not necessarily insure
that "the rest" will likewise "live" when the
thousand years shall have expired. "Until" may
carry the force of finality and fixity as shown in
instances of the use of the word in a previous chapter (XII). "Until", therefore, may emphatically express, and by way of intended contrast, that
throughout the period symbolized by the thousand
years while the souls of the dead in Christ are blest,
these remain unblest. If it be insisted, as it is by
some, that "lived" must have the same meaning in
both instances, and that "the rest" shall also "live"
after the thousand years, the answer is that even
literalists must acknowledge that this cannot be
the case, for if the first resurrection be of the body,
it is a spiritual and glorified body with which they
come (1 Cor. 15), and it cannot be that "the rest",
being unbelievers, shall so live. Hence the verb 'to
live' in these two cases by this argument must bear
different meanings; otherwise "lived not until" may
be construed to imply universalism. Whereas if,
as we suggest, this phrase has the force of finality,
as in its use elsewhere, the meaning is that "the

rest" shall not live at all. They remain "the dead"
(v. 12).

"This is the first resurrection" refers to those
who "lived" and "reigned with Christ". What is
meant by the first resurrection? It is not to be confused with the apostle's word, "the dead in Christ
shall rise first" (1 Thess. 4). "First" is not there
used of a prior resurrection to be followed by a
later one, but that the dead rise first and afterwards
are translated together with those who are alive
and remain unto the coming of the Lord. Thus the
context explains, "we shall not precede them that
sleep"; actually those who sleep in Jesus shall have
priority, and all shall be then glorified together.
Resurrection first and then rapture. The first resurrection may be in opposition to the first death.
Spiritual death ensued upon Adam's disobedience,
and through his sin the whole race shared with
their head. "Through one man's disobedience many
were constituted sinners". "And so death passed
upon all men for that all had sinned". The quickening power of Christ is the only remedy, and this
is the gracious effect of the One Man's obedience
through which many are constituted righteous
(Rom. 5). "For as the Father raiseth up the dead
and quickeneth them, even so the Son quickeneth
whom He will". In His exercise of this prerogative
He spoke of resurrections spiritual and physical,
but He did not speak of two physical resurrections
separated by a millennial period. The spiritual, according to the words of the Lord Jesus Christ, is
the first resurrection, and is characteristic, as the
apostle stated, of the Gospel age, "You hath He
quickened who were dead in trespasses and sins"
(Eph. 2; Col. 2). "For if by one man's offence
death reigned by one, they which receive abundance
of grace and of the gift of righteousness shall reign
in life by one, Jesus Christ". The assertion of His
power both spiritually and physically to quicken
from the dead is plainly spoken by our Lord and
in the order intended, and again heard and written
by the same apostle of the Apocalypse. "Verily,
verily, I say unto you, the hour is coming *and now
is,* when the dead shall hear the voice of the Son

of God, and they that hear shall live". This is the spiritual and first resurrection. Bodily resurrection awaits the day of judgment, of which in contrast He continued to say, "Marvel not at this, for the hour is coming in the which all that are in the graves shall hear His voice, and shall come forth: they that have done good unto the resurrection of life, and they that have done evil unto the resurrection of damnation".

"They lived" is set in opposition to "the rest of the dead". With hearing and believing His word, everlasting life is given, with the promise that all such "shall not come into condemnation but have passed out of death into life". Physically they may die, but life is imperishably still theirs, and here (in Rev. 6 and 20) is a vision of the state of the blessed dead who die in the Lord, who die in faith (John 5; Heb. 11; Rev. 14). Judged after the flesh by outward appearance, no difference is perceptible (as Solomon and the Psalmist observed, Eccl. 3; Ps. 49). The righteous dieth even as the wicked; believers and unbelievers are called "the dead", as to the body. But the souls of the blessed dead are with Christ, for where He is there shall they be also. Every generation of them, from the first martyr Abel to the last victim of the final Antichrist, throughout the whole period of Christ's mediatorial reign in heaven, the while He directs His Gospel among all nations on the earth, to the outcalling of sinners redeemed, though death claims them alike with unbelievers, yet unlike unbelievers they are at rest, they live, they reign with Christ. "He that believeth on Me, though he were dead yet shall he live, and whosoever liveth and believeth on Me shall never die" (John 11). In life they reign with Christ and are comforted, while "the rest" remain condemned and in remorse.

"They lived not until"—that is, throughout the millennium of the saints' blessedness, and then, when the thousand years of the Lord's reigning Gospel administration are finished, and following the subsequent "little season" of the defeated Devil's final insurrection, the dead shall be raised unto judgment. But they still are "the dead"; it is

not said that "the rest" then "lived". Rather the
living are recorded in the book of life, from which
the rest are omitted. And this is the determining
evidence: for there shall be "a resurrection of the
dead", not two but one, "both of the just and unjust" (Acts 24), "the hour" then having come
affecting "all in the graves" who shall come forth
unto life or damnation.

Two inestimable favours are theirs who have
part in the first resurrection, one negative and
one positive. They are blessed and holy: "blessed"
for they shall escape the second death (so John 5:
24). Elsewhere this is ascribed not to participation
in physical resurrection, but to faith, to overcoming
which accompanies spiritual life in Christ (Rev.
2:11; 3:21; 21:8; 1 John 5:5). "This is the first
resurrection" (v. 5) is set against "This is the
second death" v. 14). To partake of the first is to
escape the second. They are "holy" for they shall
be priests of God and of Christ. This also is not
due to prior bodily resurrection, but to the redeeming love of Christ, not awaiting a future dispensation but already enjoyed in the priesthood of all
believers (Rev. 1:4; Heb. 13:15; 1 Pet. 2:9).

"The little season" which is to follow this prolonged age of Gospel triumph, triumph even for the
noble army of martyrs, is to be marked by a further
deceiving of the nations by an unrestrained Devil;
the final apostasy consummating all apostasies, to
be abruptly ended at Christ's second coming in
power and great glory, and in flaming fire taking
vengeance in the day of judgment and perdition of
ungodly men; deceived by that wicked one "whom
the Lord shall consume with the spirit of His mouth,
and shall destroy with the brightness of His coming" (2 Thess. 1, 2). How well does prophecy agree!
Paul writes of the *restraint* placed upon the Evil
One energizing the Man of Sin and developing
apostasy; of the *deceivableness* of unrighteousness
in those who perish through belief of the lie, and
of their *strong delusion*. Such particulars accord
with John's revelation of post-millennial deception,
with the removal of restraint during the "little
season". Why put asunder by a thousand years (e.g.

2 Thess. 2 and Rev. 20) that which God has joined together? These should not be separated, that "in the mouth of two or three witnesses every word may be established."

The Scripture is unified and consistent. It purposely supplies varied aspects of one event. It is acknowledged that the visions of the Apocalypse are thus intended. Their fulfilment will partake of all the contributing particulars. This is true of the Second Advent. Compare, for example, on the basis of Rev. 20:7-11, which fixed the time as postmillennial, the following relative passages which contain references to the same event and obviously take place at the same time; that is in the one final fulfilment (Rev. 6:9-17; 10:6-7; 11:15-18; 16:14-16; 19:11-20): the great day of His wrath, the wrath of Almighty God, the wrath of the Lamb, the arraignment of small and great, the resurrection and judgment of the dead, the mystery of God finished, the rewarding of the saints, deception and defeat of the antichristian nations, the dissolution of the heavens and earth, etc. Therefore, the logical conclusion would be that the "seventh trumpet" is postmillennial, and so must be the Coming, if this event, as dispensationalists aver, takes place then. Is Christ to come twice with consuming fire? Does "time no longer" mean another thousand years? Is the Day of God and the Judgment, which here is general, (and cf. John 5:29), and the visitation of His wrath to commence, be arrested for a thousand years and then finished? Are the heavens and earth to flee away twice? A Pre-millennial coming? Yes, if the Coming is the First Advent. A Post-Millennial Coming? Yes, if the Coming is the Second Advent.

The view represented here is not novel, and dispensationalism is not ancient. Here is a comment from Dr. J. H. Todd from a lecture before the University of Dublin in 1838: "Very many commentators have supposed that the binding of Satan took place at our Lord's incarnation, or at least was the consequence of His crucifixion and the preaching of salvation in His name. And that the 'thousand years' during which the enemy of man is bound denotes the whole period from the foundation of the Church to the time of the end; the loosing of Satan for 'a little season' being co-incident with the reign of the Man of Sin, which is to be succeeded by the great day of judgment".

PROPHECY AND THE
ISRAELI STATE

THE PROVISION OF A HOME in Palestine for Jews, wrongly called at the time, "the original owners", and the establishment since of the State of Israeli, is heralded as, or in the way of, the fulfilment of Biblical prediction. Indeed, the announcement by the British government in 1917 is referred to as markedly occasioning divine favour. "From that moment", affirms a Hebrew-Christian magazine "victory was given to Britain and her allies". The inference is that victory was vicariously rewarded, and contrariwise, but for the Balfour Declaration Britain would have suffered defeat! If this premise is sound, we may conjure why God suffered us the more severe chastening of a repeated world war, since the humanitarian kindness of our country to the Jews has not changed. Governmental justice and benevolence are required of God among all nations. "Oxfam" (the Oxford Committee for Famine Relief) for instance, might equally receive His recognition, or relief afforded to the million Arab refugees made homeless through the Jews' homemaking.

The Jews are no longer God's chosen people in the sense in which they were from the call of Abram to the coming of Christ. He has His chosen among them as He has among all nations, and these will believe on the Lord Jesus Christ and be saved. "There is no difference between the Jew and the Gentile, for all have sinned and come short of the glory of God; and the same Lord over all is rich unto all that call upon Him." As to the rest who remain in unbelief there is nothing but "a certain fearful looking for of judgment and fiery indignation". Such are the final verdicts of Holy Scripture, and there is no exception to, or reversal of the principles for either Jew or Gentile, individual or national (Rom. 3:22; 10:12; Heb. 10:27; note the immediate Jewish contexts of these and relative Scriptures).

Dispensationalists have sometimes protested that believers are not to look for "signs" but for the Saviour. Now, however, we hear signs freely spoken of in respect of a possible imminent coming, among them and chiefly, the Jewish resettlement in Palestine. The question merits serious examination of the Scriptures, whether God is operatively in this event as He Who, having made promise, is now by His providential direction performing His Word? If it be so that Jews of the seed of Jacob have returned to Palestine, that is not necessarily fulfilling prophecy. What ostensibly may be regarded as the will and action of God could in reality prove to be the reverse. Nations and individuals alike may insist upon their own way, and find support in the Bible, and even prosper, and call it God's way, and yet be mistaken. The apostle makes it clear that it is their return to the Lord, that is, in receiving the Gospel of Christ, rather than returning to the land, which is esteemed and required, and in his quotation he substitutes "saved" for the prophet's "return". And it is invariably the remnant that is in view and not the nation. "Isaiah also crieth, though the number of the children of Israel be as the sand of the sea, a remnant shall be saved" (cf. Isa. 10:21-22; Rom. 9:27).

Kings, prophets, priests and people have claimed God on their side to the unveiling of their ignorance of God's will and insistence on their own will. Superficial judgment has often produced mistaken conclusions. The Palestinian settlement may have no special prophetic significance. "The Lord seeth not as man seeth; man looketh upon the outward appearance, but the Lord looketh upon the heart." David was a man of God's own heart or choice, and not the people's, otherwise he never would have been enthroned. Moses smote the rock and the waters flowed forth. His later repeated action gave similar results, but not of God. Judgment by appearances, that is, by getting the desired results, was no proof of divine approval. God designed to supply the thirst-quenching waters through speaking, but Moses got them again through striking. There is always a solemnly spiritual reason for a divine instruction. A superficial people might judge the event to be of God, but their satisfaction was carnal, and Moses suffered on their account (Ex. 17; Num. 20, etc.) "My ways are not yours", saith the Lord. So it may be with Zionism today.

A prophet might accompany his prophesyings with the promise of signs, and the signs appear, yet not what the eye seeth but what God speaketh is the test of His will. "An evil and adulterous generation seeketh after a sign." "The Jews require a sign," and Christians would appear to supply them using "the returning nation" as itself a sign! The Lord Jesus had no confidence in sign-believers (Deut. 13; John 2). David's plan to build a house for the Lord had the approval of the prophet, but both were mistaken. David's purpose to restore the ark from its lodging to the tabernacle of rest he had prepared was an excellent proposal. It gained the unanimous assent of priests and Levites, princes and people. What could suit the operation better than a brand new conveyance, in modern terms, "the best for God", "my utmost for His highest"! But in thus copying the way of the world fatality befell the undertaking. No such calamity marked the ark's earlier removal on "a new cart" which the Philistines made for it, which now David appeared to imitate. David meditated, consulted God's Word, learned his lesson and commented, "the Lord our God made a breach upon us because we sought Him not after the due order". And thereupon, doing God's work in God's way, he was favoured with good success. God is not with any people only as they are with Him (1 Chron. 13-15). Israel suffered because she copied other nations; when in favour with God she avoided their ways. Today, from every angle of view the Israeli State keeps abreast of the nations of the world

as one of them. This may not be God's doing, nor marvellous in our eyes, though pre-millennial changes in
Palestine are hailed as though fulfilling prophecy already.

Pre-exilic prophecies are no longer outstanding. They
were fulfilled as recorded in Israel's national restoration
on the expiry of Jeremiah's predicted seventy years' captivity, while the spiritual and evangelical characteristics
of those promises intentionally looked forward to Messiah's advent and redemption through the Gospel. So
they were released, not for their own sake, but for
Christ's sake, Who was to come. And this was the real
end and object of that historical return to the land, unto
which, it will be found, the humbling and penitent and
sanctifying conditions stated in Moses and the prophets
led them, for "He is faithful that promised". Inter-
spersed with the temporal particulars in the prophets
are Messianic promise and assurance which the New
Testament observes implemented in Bethlehem and
Galilee and Calvary, and Heavenly Glory; in the dispensation of the Spirit, the building of the Church, and
the eternal state of redemptive blessedness. The material
forms employed were those of the people appropriate to
their circumstances and times, but the objective was
spiritual and heavenly. Jews, unenlightened of the
Spirit, are no safer guides to the meaning of the Scriptures, not even those which concern their own nation,
than the unregenerate Gentile. Jews and their rulers,
in the apostles' days, were informed of their ignorance:
"they knew not the Messiah nor the voices of the prophets which are read every sabbath day". Without the
Spirit of God they abide in ignorance still. Yet our attention is called to the words of unconverted Israeli or
Zionist public men, referring to their quotation of the
Scriptures as though enlightened and specially authoritative! After their Pentecostal enduement with the
Spirit of illumination the apostles never again spoke or
wrote of the kingdom becoming restored to the Israel
nation, either before or following the coming of the
Lord (cf. Acts 1:7).

Daniel calculated from Jeremiah's writing that the
captivity was about to expire, and in answer to his

earnest supplication, and he was not alone in observing the prophetic instruction (Ezek. 36, 37), he was favoured with an answer of peace, a prophecy of immediate release through Cyrus and ultimate salvation in Christ, which all came to pass. Ezekiel ministered during the exile, and Haggai and Zechariah were raised up to encourage their dispirited brethren when their enemies caused the rebuilding to cease, and attempts were made also to annihilate the nation (cf. Psa. 83:4; Esther; Jer. 48:2; 1 Chron. 20). These prophets, for the most part their language symbolical because the goal and realization was in Christ the Redeemer—as the deliverance from Egypt at the beginning pointed to Him, so did this at the end—observed the fulfilment of the literal parts of their prophesyings in their own generation, although the language, as indicated, often exceeded the localized and temporal restoration, "God having provided some better thing" of spiritual and heavenly and of enduring character, of which Ezekiel had written: "I will do better for you than at your beginnings". The prodigious terms employed account for the phenomenal measurements of temple and city, and "show them to be spiritually and mystically understood, Ezekiel's temple delineated larger than all the earthly Jerusalem, and Jerusalem larger than all the land of Canaan" (Patrick Fairbairn quoting Lightfoot, and confirmed by Jamieson, Fausset and Brown, who write: "The Septuagint substitutes cubits for reeds to escape the immense compass given. Fairbairn rightly supports the Authorized Version which agrees with the Hebrew"). Note also the emphasis upon the operation of the Spirit to the exclusion of all human effort, the reverse of the material construction which these very prophets were sent to encourage (Zech. 4:6).

It is claimed by dispensationalists that these postexilic prophecies envisage a return of the Jews to the land in unbelief, distinct from and later than that of their own day, with the re-erection of their temple, and eventual conversion by the second appearing of Jesus Christ. The present Israeli State is said to be in preparation for if not in part fulfilment of this, and passages from Haggai and Zechariah, not to speak of other

Scriptures, are called in evidence. The New Testament, however, provides not the slightest confirmation of it. Haggai's prophecy is not of an earthly and temporary kingdom now being prepared for. The New Testament explanation is that God would "speak yet once more and shake not the earth only but also heaven, signifying the removing of those things that are made, that those things which cannot be shaken may remain"; namely, that believers "receive a kingdom which cannot be moved". So "the latter glory" is not millennial but eternal (*cf.* Hag. 2:6-9; Heb. 12; 27-28; 2 Pet. 3; Rev. 21-22).

Zechariah called attention to the former prophets, to the expiry of the 70 years, as Daniel did, and he makes special reference to the remnant, always a Gospel association (Rom. 9:27; 11:5). Twice he writes of Messiah as "the Branch", as did "the former prophets" (Isa. and Jer.) which in the New Testament is referred to the incarnation and birth of the Lord Jesus Christ (Luke 1:78, "day spring"; Zech. 3:8; 6:12). It is He Who would build the true temple, His church, as He said (Matt. 16). These are said to be "signs", that is, of things to come, for the King-Priest in heavenly glory doth minister peace to those who are "far off" as well as nigh (Zech. 6:15; Eph. 2:13). The humble entry of Christ into Jerusalem, seated upon the ass, so contrary to the Jews' expectation of arrival with pomp and ceremony, seems especially set in opposition to the latter (Zech. 9:9-10; Matt. 21:5). The suffering and crucifixion of Christ, His side pierced, the sword awaking against God's Fellow and His people's Shepherd, and the scattering of the sheep (disciples); the fountain opened for sin and uncleanness; the spirit of grace and supplication, repentance and remission of sins, the living waters of salvation, and entire sanctification — all is found in these prophets wrapped amidst their ministry to local needs and temporal conditions affecting the returned captives. But every such passage the New Testament relates in fulfilment to the first advent and not once to the second. Another return from captivity with millennial earthly prospect is nowhere found in the New Testament interpretation of such Scriptures.

Against the complete historical and spiritual accomplishment, especially the closing chapters of Zechariah are brought forward. But do we know *all* that transpired when God through His servant Cyrus brought back the remnant of all the tribes from "all the countries whither He had driven them" and "from all languages"? A careful reading of the historical substance preserved for us in Scripture alone will show that much of that which is said still to be futuristic is observable in those restored conditions of which the prophet stated the time, saying "in these days". Certainly also there was then bestowed the spirit of grace and of supplication, of national, individual and domestic repentance associated with practical holiness and separation.

We might also enquire, if the Mount of Olives must be regarded with strict literality, what mountain is it which Zerubbabel would have made a plain to facilitate the placing of the headstone with shoutings of Grace, grace unto it? Does not the Headstone represent Christ (Ps. 118:22; Matt. 21:42)? For this accomplishment is "not by might, nor by power, but by My Spirit, saith the Lord of hosts". Therefore the challenge "Who art thou O great mountain?" Perhaps, Babylon the great. Was our Lord's reference to "this mountain" which faith could remove, the mount of Olives (Zech. 4:7, 14:4; Mark 11)? What importance also is attached to the reviving of the Festivals under the Ezra-Nehemiah reformation, and especially Tabernacles? It was on the occasion of this feast that our Lord "stood and cried, saying, If any man thirst let him come to Me and drink". And it was of the spiritual significance, thus symbolized, that He added, "He that believeth on Me, as the scriptures have said, Out of His inward parts shall flow rivers of living waters", using the word which may well have signified the riven rock. So that cloven Olivet might itself symbolize, as did Moses' rock, the Rock of Ages cleft for me, and the living waters, as the apostle later explained, the life of the Spirit poured out at and from Pentecost when Christ was glorified (John 7:38-39). Even the dispensational literalist says, the prophet's "life-giving stream is symbolic of blessing transmitted through Christ to all the nations of the world". Another evangelical association with the feast is the promise of unfading illumination so that even "at eventide it shall (still) be light", agreeable to our Saviour's further invitation on the same occasion of the Tabernacle's festival, "I am the light of the world, he that followeth Me shall not walk in darkness, but shall have the light of life" (Zech. 14:6-7; John 8:12, and *cf.* Rev. 21-22; and Ezekiel's symbolism). There is no exaggeration or fancifulness in such meaning of highly symbolical Scriptures, any more than with the types of Moses which were substantial in themselves but spiritually realized in Christ.

The prophets now considered do not take us beyond this. And if Isaiah's hills and mountains and valleys and places crooked and straight and the wilderness are interpreted of the Forerunner's ministry, humbling and exalting unto repentance and remission, that "all flesh may see the salvation of God"; if the action of making mountains and valleys and paths high and low and rough and smooth, appertain to such spiritual results, and the New Testament says they do (Luke 3:4-6), this is sound guidance for understanding prophecies of similar content.

We have a confirming illustration of this principle in another of the Minor Prophets. The greatest historical event at the beginning of their nationhood is interpreted of spiritual redemption. It anticipates the Gospel, and is guide to the meaning of literal experiences used by the prophets unto this purpose. Here is prophetic spiritualization. Moses' exodus is typical of Christ's expiration, Micah's Gospel interpretation of the Mosaic parallel covers his record as a comparison will show (Ex. 12-14 with Mic. 6:4; 7:15-20). God is He "Who retaineth not His anger because He delighteth in mercy", therefore "He will turn again and have compassion upon us". And how?

In the literal event the Redeemer-Protector paused over (passover) the blood-marked houses, and the "destroyer" *passed by*, sparing from the death-judgment. In the spiritual analogy, according to Micah's Gospel, the pardoning God "*passeth by* transgression".

In the actual event under Moses their taskmasters who had held the people in bondage were all subdued, though they cried, "I will pursue, my hand shall repossess them". In the spiritual conquest Micah's Gospel says, "He will *subdue* our iniquities", a more formidable slavemaster than the Egyptians.

In the historical account the Red Sea at Moses' word overwhelmed Pharaoh, his chariots and horsemen: "the horse and his rider hath he thrown *into the sea*". Giving its intended spiritual meaning, the Gospel according to Micah says, "Thou wilt cast all their sins into *the depth of the sea*", and like their pursuers, they are so covered that "ye shall see them again no more forever" and "there remained not so much as one of them".

Transgression, sin and iniquity, the totality of evil which besets us all are overcome and their victims released, not in consequence of a second advent but effected completely when Christ offered Himself once for all (*cf.* Ps. 32; Dan. 9:24, etc.). This is how God through the prophet says what He meant, even as also through Moses He meant what He said. This is more "marvellous" than "coming out of Egypt" (Mic. 7:15).

Hence, Micah's doxology is in different terms to that of Moses, though both are true; Moses "Who is like unto Thee, O Lord . . . doing wonders?" becomes in Micah's words, "Who is a God like unto Thee that pardoneth iniquity and passeth by transgression?" *In this manner,* and it is to be noted, by the inspired spiritualization of literal events the Abrahamic covenant is completely implemented, not in the repossession of the land of Canaan, but in the redemption that is in Christ Jesus. The prophet's complete assurance that this is what God meant follows in the words: "Thou wilt perform the truth to Jacob and the mercy to Abraham which Thou hast sworn unto our fathers from the days of old".

THE NEW COVENANT is in terms temporal and spiritual. It is acknowledged that the spiritual terms were ratified by the Lord Jesus by the blood of His cross, as He said at the memorial supper, and confirmed through the writings and ministry of His apostles, who were "ministers of the new covenant" (Heb. 8-10; 2 Cor. 3). But, it is said, this covenant is to be fulfilled to the Jewish nation in the millennium, the Church having but prematurely "entered into Israel's spiritual blessings" by Gospel application, whereas to the Jews will be added the literal promises of houses, lands, inheritances, etc. and to this "the returning nation", as it is called, is the prelude and preparation! It is, however, clear, as already pointed out and agreeable to the manner of Scripture, that these were realized in the post-exilic return of the national remnant, while the spiritual awaited the coming of the Redeemer.

This material fulfilment, when the Jews should again possess their inheritances, was guaranteed to Jeremiah by legal deed wherein, at the Lord's bidding, land was purchased just as their captors were to take it in possession and they themselves were to be "carried far away" which, speaking after the manner of men, appeared an imprudent transaction! Yet after the captivity the apparently impossible possession was made good. This, therefore, is not to be postponed to a future millennium, though Judaistic Christians wrongly so used it, but was a strong assurance that, as the temporal promise was honoured, so the spiritual would be in due time. For the 70 years now expired and the temporal fulfilled must be followed by "70 sevens" of years unto Messiah's "It is finished" (Dan. 9). History now attests both.

If, however, it be insisted that the two must have simultaneous realization, the terms and benefits of Gospel discipleship are not irrelevant here. Had the Lord Jesus this in mind when He said: "Verily I say unto you, there is no man that hath left house or brethren nor sisters or father or mother or wife or children or lands, for My sake and the gospel's, but he shall receive an hundredfold now in this time, houses and brethren and sisters and mothers and children and lands, with persecutions, and in the world to come life eternal" (Mark 10:29, 30)? The time-pointer for this is named "the regeneration" (Matt. 19:28). The only other mention signifies that the "regeneration" is this dispensation of the Spirit founded upon the grace of Christ's atonement (Tit. 3:5). And it may be observed

that in the context of the original New Covenant passage, the Redeemer's birth at Bethlehem, exciting enemy
action, is the supernatural focus point upon which the
expectation is founded, and not His second coming in
glory (cf. Jer. 31:15-22; Matt. 1:23; 2:17-18).

It is no outraging of Scripture to apply established
New Testament principles to the interpretation of Old
Testament prophecy. The objective of this is the first
advent of the Messiah Redeemer. The second advent is
not announced save in reference to the judgment of
the wicked and the new creation (e.g. Isa. 65:17-18;
66:22-24; 2 Pet. 3; Rev. 21:1-2). The New Testament
announces that He shall come "the second time". No
Millennium is mentioned. Such is introduced only by
theories which necessitate the abrupt division of chapters, sometimes verses, with Jewish gaps and Church
parentheses, so that when the Jews are in the Church
is out, and when the Church is in the Jews are out. The
truth is that Jews and Gentiles are in together, and
without difference, constituting through faith one body
in Christ, the fulness of Him that filleth all in all. And
so we find the twelve apostles and twelve tribes incorporated in the heavenly bride, the Lamb's wife, new
Jerusalem.

All this is confirmative of an earlier reminder that the
Scriptures emphasize a return to the Lord, the mighty
God, rather than to the land. Generally, we are advised in the New Testament, it was not of a future
state of Israel that the prophets wrote. Salvation, "even
the salvation of your souls", was the subject of their
diligent enquiry; "so great salvation" that all the Scriptures are employed to expound it (I Pet. 1; II Tim. 3).
Salvation is obtained through the merit of Christ's
"sufferings and glory". They so wrote by inspiration
of "the Spirit of Christ Who was in them". The things
thus prophesied constitute the "gospel now preached with
the Holy Spirit sent down from heaven". These things
even angels desire closely to investigate.

This salvation, already described as, in its perfectness,
"ready to be revealed in the last time"; that is, the time
of Christ's second appearing, is assured to addressees
who were Jews scattered throughout the world, and had

become believers in Christ. Their salvation is in contrast with the earthly inheritance which their fathers corrupted and defiled and which therefore faded away or gradually disappeared. Such conception of salvation for Jews is not even hinted. The apostle is enamoured of the heavenly inheritance, a lively hope, obtained for God's elect, and unto which they themselves are "kept by the power of God" (I Pet. 1).

Whether or not the new occupants of the "Home" in Palestine are all true descendants of Jacob is in doubt. It would seem that the identity of exiles who returned under the proclamation of Cyrus, from all the countries whither they were dispersed, was established to attest their descent from "the fathers". Therefore, chronicles were written, and separation from "strangers", wives and families, was enjoined, for they were "a mixed multitude", as they had been also in the original deliverance when they "fell a lusting" (Ex. 12:38; Neh. 13:3; Num. 11:4). Their sanctification of race was strictly necessary then because of Christ Who was to come of Abraham, of David, of Israel. Christ having come, there appears to be no longer any reason for their continued separation from other peoples. Nor, indeed, is it so with them. Never were they so dealt with in divine distinguishing grace for their own sake; no sinners are so regarded of any race; but for Christ's sake alone, and for His sake they may be blessed with others through the Gospel still.

Nevertheless, if it be a question of again being given, under covenant long-standing, the land in possession, with tribal inheritances, statehood, temple, priesthood, sacrifices, the once chosen nation restored to favour and priority in rule over all nations for a thousand years, then the evidence of true descent from "the fathers" to whom promise was made becomes indispensable to support the claim. There are multitudes of Jews content with the lands of their birth or adoption, who have no wish or purpose to return "home". But what of those returned and returning? The Scripture describes the true Jew, and it refers to some "which say they are Jews and are not", which, if taken in its racial literalness may find explication in the following quotation recommending discrimination between "the real Jews and the Zionists". "Zionists throughout the world are overwhelmingly of Eastern European origin. These Yiddish-speaking 'Jews' have no racial connection with Palestine or the ancient Hebrews and are of Khazar origin. Here is a quotation from the Jewish Encyclopaoedia (Vol. 4; pp. 1-12): 'Khazars: a non-Semitic, Asiatic, Mongolian tribal nation who emigrated into Eastern Europe about the first century, who were converted as an entire nation to Judaism in the seventh century, who were conquered in the eleventh century by the expanding Russian nation which absorbed the entire Khazar population, and who account for the presence in Eastern Europe of the great numbers of Yiddish-speaking Jews in Russia, Poland, Lithuania, Galicia, Bessarabia and Rumania'. Jewish historians such as Graetz, Dubnow, Friedlander, Raisin and others support this too. Zionists have long misrepresented that these races of Jewish faith have a right to go to Palestine as their home, misleading these unfortunate people by telling them that in Palestine was their only hope. It is because of political Zionism that anti-semitism spreads, and not because of Hebrew traditions and religion. To that remnant of orthodox Jewry which believes in the authority of the Old Testament and holds fast to the laws of the Pentateuch, we can offer respect and sympathy. To the Zionist who has only the restoration of the land for his personal goal, we can only say that he is endeavouring to frustrate God's unalterable will, an impossible proceeding" (quoted from *The Christian*, 1948).

More recently we have read: "Latterly the flow of European immigrants sank to a trickle; instead, 'oriental' immigrants from Iran, the Yemen, India, Egypt, Algeria, Morocco, and Tunisia streamed in. While the earlier Israelis were largely Ashkenazi or European Sephard— the two main groups defined according to whether their ancestors after the dispersal, settled in Eastern Europe or the Spanish-speaking countries—the new comers were 'oriental', Sephardim of *the most mixed racial origins*, and often on a most primitive cultural level". (*The

Daily Telegraph, London, Nov. 13, 1963).

"Israel" is, indeed, as it is officially described, "an exciting country". In addition to its Biblical and historical and traditional interests, it has all the attractive mixture which other nations advertize and offer to its tourists and visitors. Its transformed economy, industrialization, modernization, improvements due to wise and energetic planning and working, need not, however, and should not be attributed to Scripture incentive and prophetic revival. According to the film popularized on this subject, we suppose it is still "Three Minutes to Twelve", and Christians will be deceived if by such they are led to believe that at the strike of "Twelve" the Messiah will appear. Immigrants to other parts of the world with wastes and deserts and untapped resources have done the like, and countries blasted by wars have put on a renewed appearance and glory in the space of a few years. Material restoration or development is no mark of God's peculiar favour to the Jews or any other people. Of all nations it is written, God "hath determined the times before appointed, and the bounds of their habitation; that they should seek the Lord if haply they might feel after Him, and find Him." The object is spiritual (Acts 17:26-27).

The *Quarterly* of The Free University of Amsterdam (Nov., 1950) contained the comments of their highly reputed and reverent theologian, "the rector magnificus", Professor Dr. G. Ch. Aalders, on Old Testament Prophecy and the State of Israeli. We give the salient parts which are apposite to this subject:

The purpose of the address was to investigate whether the creation of a self-governing state by the people of Israel has to be regarded as an obvious fulfilment of Scriptural prediction. Wide circles of Christians are most fervently attached to this opinion, but the problem is not as simple as many of them imagine. The Speaker has as his particular field of study the Old Testament, but he also pointed out that the New Testament is not concerned with a national restoration of Israel. Whatever the exact meaning of Romans 11:26 may be, it is beyond doubt that it has nothing to say with respect to the national status of the Jewish people on their return to Palestine. Likewise, Revelation 20:9 in mentioning "the camp of the saints" and "the beloved city" does not presuppose the re-establishment of Jewish government in Palestine; as the context makes clear, the passage refers to those who are the disciples of the Lord Jesus Christ. But it cannot be disputed that the Old Testament contains quite a number of places which bear upon the realization of a national future for the people of Israel. In taking a survey of these pronouncements the lecturer called attention to the fact that they are only Assyrians and Chaldeans who are indicated as the instruments of divine wrath by whom the people were carried away from their country; and as the Lord's promise of return naturally has been primarily addressed to this people, it goes without saying that this return was meant as a return from the Assyriar and Babylonian exile. Is it acceptable that such promise at the same time could have had in view a much later return from a renewed exile which had not been explicitly announced? Furthermore, the appeal that has often been made to various expressions like 'I will scatter you among the heathen' and 'the Lord will gather thee from all the nations', or the phrase 'in the latter days' do not imply reference to a later period than that of the Assyro-Babylonian exile. The predictions of return occurring in the writings of post-exilic prophets refer to those who remained back after the edict of Cyrus.

Having thus enquired into the witness of Old Testament prophecy the lecturer proceeded to answer the question whether the State of Israel as it presents itself now can be considered a fulfilment of this prophecy. He carefully traced all available data concerning the State, starting from the Zionist movement to which the origin of the State is greatly indebted, citing the proclamation whereby the foundation of a Jewish State in *Erets Israel* was announced, referring to the project of the constitution, and producing a brief survey of the political parties existing in Israel. All these dates sufficiently indicate that the State of Israel *does not answer* the expectation which many people cherish of a converted Israel restored to its former condition.

Now among those who are inclined to salute the State of Israel as a fulfilment of Old Testament prophecy the idea is prominent that the Jewish people would return to Palestine unconverted, and that after this return Israel will come to conversion, and so the promise of Scripture will be realized. Therefore, they qualify the re-establishment of the Jewish nation as particularly significant, and view it as the sign of the fig tree. But just as well as it can be determined that the State of Israel does not match the picture which has been drawn on account of Old Testament prophecy, it likewise must be stated, that the idea of a restored unconverted Israel which is going to be converted afterwards *is entirely contrary to the testimony of prophecy*. Throughout, prophecy pictures conversion and restoration as closely connected; and when the man of God, Moses, even before Israel had entered Canaan, in the name of the Lord predicts their rebellion and captivity among the nations as well as return from exile, he unequivocally puts conversion as condition for the renewal of God's favour: 'for the Lord will again rejoice over thee for good, as He rejoiced over thy fathers, *if* thou shalt hearken unto the voice of the Lord thy God, to keep His commandments and His statutes which are written in this book of the law, and *if* thou turn unto the Lord thy God with all thy heart and with all thy soul' (Deut. 30:9).

Finally, it is necessary to observe how the Old Testament itself definitely contradicts the notion of a restoration of Israel to its former position of a people of God after having rejected the Messiah. Daniel 9:27 informs us that the judgment passed upon Israel, as the Messiah will have been 'cut off', is a judgment 'even unto the consummation'. In the prophecies of Jeremiah more than once stress is laid upon the fact that in the chastisement of Jerusalem the Lord 'will not make a full end'—in Hebrew the same expression is used—but contrary to this, after the rejection of the Messiah, the divine judgment will reach the full end. A like tendency strikes us in the well-known prophecy of the new covenant: this covenant is contrasted to the covenant of Sinai, resting upon the external bond of belonging to the nation of Israel; the new covenant rests upon the purely internal bond of having the Lord's law in people's inward parts, and this new covenant is realized in the New Testament Church. In that the Lord says, 'a new covenant, He hath made the first old; now that which decayeth and waxeth old is ready to vanish away' (Heb. 8:13). So the particular place which Israel occupied as a nation in relation to God has come to a final end.

In summing up the lecturer drew the conclusion: "the establishment of the State of Israel, though certainly a remarkable event in the historic process of the world's nations, cannot be regarded as a realization of prophetic prediction in the Old Testament; whatever has happened in Palestine and may happen there in the future, it has nothing to do with the divine prophecy which is presented in Holy Scripture."

That Christ will come "the second time apart from sin unto salvation" is a blessed assurance to those who "look for Him", but it was addressed in particular to the Hebrews, that is, to Jews (Heb. 9). Neither here or elsewhere is promise of hope other than of "so great salvation" at first spoken by the Lord Jesus, and confirmed by them that heard Him with powers of the Holy Spirit. It is *now* they "ought to give the more earnest heed" and not "neglect". Otherwise, there is no "escape" from judgment at the Coming (Heb. 2). The solemn word given to unbelieving Hebrews is of "a fearful looking for of judgment and fiery indignation", a "much sorer punishment than those who despised Moses' law and died without mercy", for it is the grace of Christ which is now despised (Heb. 10). The Epistles in general all agree. There is no divergence. The saving opportunity is now, in life upon earth and not after death; while time endures and not in an age to come, while longsuffering waits between the Advents and not upon expiry at the Second Coming. The Lord Jesus insisted upon this in the days of His flesh.

His final word about the Jewish nation was of their dispersal among the nations of the world (Luke 21:24). This came to pass and has since continued. In this dispersion mercy was intended, perhaps, rejoicing against judgment. For settled peacefully and prosperously in Palestine, would they not contentedly abide, still in the rejection of Jesus of Nazareth, as when He was among them, presenting His Messianic claims and calling them to repentance? But scattered among all nations, the Saviour intended they also should hear His Gospel, as many have done, as His great commission has been carried out, by means of which He is taking out from them, from Jews and Gentiles, "a people for His name." Thus are all reached together as would seem to have been His prudent and merciful intention, for "He hath concluded all in unbelief that He might have mercy upon all". When in Oliver Cromwell's day, a proposal was made to Parliament that the Jews be admitted to our Island Home, he remarked, "Since there was a promise of their conversion, means must be used to that end, which was the preaching to them of the Gospel, and that could not be done unless they were permitted to dwell where the Gospel was preached".

The Scriptures, then, do not contemplate that the scattered nation would again become a returning nation, now that the final purpose for which God distinguished them from other nations by His vicarious choice of them has been realized in the bringing into the world of His Son the Messiah, Seed of Abraham, Seed of David, Saviour of mankind (Rom. 9). That end fulfilled, like the types and shadows which accompanied their separated and instrumental appointment, they are now superseded, and the Redeemer having so come, it was prophesied that He died "not for that nation only, but that also He should gather together *in one* the children of God that were scattered abroad", which prophecy agrees with His own word, using another figure, "Other sheep (that is, other than from among Jews) I have which are not of this fold, them also I must bring, and they shall hear my voice, and there shall be *one flock* and one Shepherd". (John 11:52; 10:16).

COMING "FOR" AND "WITH"
THE CHURCH

THE PROGRAMME POPULARLY cherished which dispensationalism has drafted for the Lord to carry out at His coming may be introduced by these two prepositions. The assumption, we think, would not be challenged, that large numbers of Christian believers are indoctrinated with this form of Futurism. Indeed, the order of events presented as that to be followed by the Lord Jesus has been publicly spoken of as His "Agenda". We venture to remark that in no case has humanly unaided Berean-like searching of the Scriptures produced this dividing of the word of truth. It is not a pattern of things to come like those of tabernacle and temple given to Moses and David from above. It is a sketch of things easily reduced to chart form, attracting the eye, into which the details supported by selected texts are nicely fitted. It is a presumptuous venture to "prepare the way of the Lord" by those who, in respect of this subject, are not, like the forerunner, "sent from God" (1 Cor. 14:36; John 1:6).

So assuredly are these views put forth that a negative reaction to them or a question of their Scripturalness may occasion not only some surprise but the marring of Christian fellowship, or even a form of excommunication and, we have noticed, the charge of Modernism! The writer in his youthful unwisdom, accepting the scheme as he had been taught, and before he realized how apposite is the apostle's admonition, "ye know nothing yet as ye ought to know", thought it sufficient to silence all argument merely to say, "This speaker or writer does not distinguish between the Coming For and the Coming With". Was it Moody who remarked that a lie would travel round the world before truth could get her boots on? This dispensational theory was initiated in the early nineteenth century. How it has travelled! It has varied and developed in respect of details, for arising difficulties and apparent contradictions have required explanation, sometimes to be explained away. Theological historians have confirmed the modernity of this form of futurism. But it is rejoined, it pleased God in these latter times to give "prophetic light" which had been lost through many centuries! His Word, of course, is the true light, and does He not ask, "what if the light that is in thee be darkness"?

The man-made distinction between Israel and the Church, the proposition that finds no place in the Old Testament, the recognition that notwithstanding Old Testament prediction does reach unto the end, and even announces the creation of new heavens and earth, the same goal at which the New Testament arrives, and therefore covers the dispensation of the Church, is accommodated by the invention that since the Jews rejected Messiah at His first advent, they have temporarily been set aside, until the parenthetical Church completed at the second advent is removed to heaven, whereupon the Jews will again be accorded priority among the nations in the earth, their formerly rejected Messiah being then received by them at this virtual "second chance". In support of this the continuity of Daniel's "seventy sevens" or 490 years "unto Messiah the Prince" is broken—by an interval which now proves to be four times the length of the predicted period itself—the last period of seven years being conjectured to commence with the rapture of the Church, that it, at the Coming "For"; that this event could be "at any moment", whereas it is affirmed the later Coming "With", placed at the end of the "week", is heralded by premonitory signs! Thus the dispensational gap in Daniel's prophecy of Messiah's first advent necessitates a further gap in the procedure of His second advent. "He shall appear the *second* time" is the word of inspiration, but not a third. The contradiction occasioned by the futuristic theory is, therefore, overcome by the subterfuge of introducing the idea of one second coming in two stages. These "stages" are first *for* the saints, and some years later, *with* them.

During the course of preparing this chapter we have had the opportunity to hear "Advent" speakers up-to-date setting out with every semblance of confidence and certainty the order of events now under review. The mode of presentation differs, but the accepted pattern is the same. On minor points of detail there are variations, but the fabric remains the same within which all is precisely arranged. "For" and "With" are invariably the key-words, and the beginning and ending of the interval determines the stages. Intervening events in heaven for the Church, and on earth for the Jews and the Nations, are given ordered place. The chief Scripture evidence adduced for the former is 1 Thessalonians 4:13-18. The continuing verses, 1 Thessalonians 5:1-11, mentioning the day of the Lord, are assigned to the second stage, as being distinct in time and purpose from the former. So the pattern reads.

At the first stage, and during the interval introduced by the meeting "in the air" the assembling will be followed by adjudication, or the Judgment Seat of Christ, and thereupon, the acclamation or Marriage Supper of the Lamb. Astounding developments eventuate upon the earth during this absence of the Church above; and astonishing, too, for it is said that the Holy Spirit is to be withdrawn from the earth with the Church (1 Thess. 2), while during unparalleled tribulation under Antichrist's reign there will be also unparalleled conversions (Rev. 7). *The Scofield Bible* has a full and sequential note here. "This," he says, "is followed by the return of Christ in glory and the events associated therewith". These events have been conveniently described as the conquest of His foes, the conversion of the Jews and the control of the world. Our present examination is of the former part of this "Agenda". It is just and right to state that there are dispensational teachers who differ upon the proposed "For" stage, while holding to the futurity of Daniel's "week" with end-time developments.

They do not admit any removal of the Church until that end, and hold that the Coming is one without interval interruption.

Apart from the fantastic assumption that in the absence of the Holy Spirit and the Church, and within the surmised interval, though undergoing great tribulation, during the reign of the Man of Sin, "a great multitude which no man can number" shall be converted from among all nations, it may be said that in strict fact the text (2 Thess. 2:7) does not signify 'taken out of the way' at all. 'Become out of the midst' would be more correct. Dr. S. P. Tregelles gives: "Ye know that at present there is that which restraineth in order that he might be revealed in his season and not before. For the mystery of lawlessness is already working (only there is at present one that restraineth) until it become developed out of the midst, and then shall the lawless One be revealed". The dispensational theory of the removal of the Holy Spirit is, therefore, erroneously based. This can be confirmed by an examination of the terms by the Lexicon: (For "*be* taken" see, for example, Matt. 8:24; 13:21; John 3:25; Acts 6:1 etc., and "out of the *way*", Matt. 18:2, 20; John 19:18; Rev. 7:17).

It will not be questioned that the context of any Scripture is always serviceable, often essential to sound exposition. In the main passage before us, the context, and indeed, the verses introducing it, the addressees being the same, a warning to the Church is given touching becoming conduct, and the defaulter, even though he be a "brother" converted from the sinful ways of "Gentiles who know not God", is admonished that "the Lord is the avenger of all such, as we also have forewarned you and testified". Surely, therefore, it cannot be maintained, in view of this immediate context alone, that the Judgment Seat of Christ is with respect to the believer's service only. "Avenger" is a strong word. The defaulter will not only "miss" something as reward for service, but he will "receive for the wrong that he doeth" (1 Thess. 4:5, 6; Col. 3:25).

The passage, however, which is commonly resorted to as upholding the interval judgment may here be examined (2 Cor. 5:10). Scofield's note says, "The judg-

ment of believers' works, not sins, is in question here".
It is usual for dispensationalists to distinguish the occasion from the great white throne (Rev. 20) and the
throne of His glory (Matt. 25). "Judgment Seat" is
given as rostrum, tribunal, throne; the elevated seat of
a judge. Moreover, there is no statement in the context as to the time, though Scofield says, "This judgment
occurs at the return of Christ". The subject mentioned
in the verses which introduce it is that of the believer's
death (2 Cor. 5:6-9; cf. Heb. 9:27-28). In the verse
following the apostle says, "Knowing, therefore, the
terror of the Lord, we persuade men", and he proceeds
to explain the reason for this ministry. He is Christ's
ambassador, and would therefore pray and beseech men
"to be reconciled to God". Everyone is to receive according to the things done in his body, whether good or bad.
There are about ten occurrences of "Judgment Seat" in
the New Testament; most have to do with the civil law,
and the issues in each case, where our Lord and His
apostles are on trial, are guilt or innocence, condemnation or acquittal, death or life; not one has anything to
do with rewards for service (Matt. 27:19; John 19:31;
Acts 18: 12, 16, 17; 25:6, 10, 17). The parallel verse
on the Judgment Seat of Christ quotes in support the
prophet's warning word about universal judgment (Rom.
14:10; Isa. 45:23). Again, there is no suggestion that
the Judgment Seat of Christ is restricted alone to the
"believer's works, not sins". The transliterated *bema*
does not help the dispensationalist's cause. Moreover,
when the Lord comes, His decisions will have already
been made: "Behold, I come quickly, and My reward
is with Me to give every man according as his work shall
be" (Rev. 22:12; Isa. 40:10; 60:11).

The visions of the Apocalypse have not intended fulfilment in the order of record. "They present the unfolding of God's plans for bringing about the grand end
under different aspects, mutually complementing each
other". The writer's introductory words, "after this I
saw" or "And I saw or heard", refer to the order in
which he received the instruction. In the case of the
Marriage Supper there is a time which appears to be
connected with heaven's jubilation over the destruction

of the Beast and his Babylonian regime. Then, the first
recorded Alleluias are resounded, and it is acclaimed
that "the Lord God omnipotent reigneth" and "the
marriage of the Lamb is come", for "He hath judged the
great whore which did corrupt the earth". The marriage celebration, therefore, is in response to the word,
"Rejoice over her (Babylon), thou heaven, and ye holy
apostles and prophets, for God hath avenged you on her".
Therefore, the dispensational placement is incorrect; not
secretly and privately in an interval between the stages
is the Marriage Supper placed, but with sovereignty and
glory and majesty which shall be universally displayed
(Rev. 18:20; 19:1-9; Psa. 45).

RETURNING NOW TO THE key passage, we may notice
that the apostle's introduction of the subject, like the
passage itself, does not employ the popular word, Coming
For His saints. Instead, he writes, "to the end He may
establish your hearts unblameable in holiness before
God, even our Father, at the coming of our Jesus Christ
With all His saints" (1 Thess. 3:13). This, then, is the
Coming which, in a particular aspect of it, the apostle
proceeds to expound in his very next reference (1 Thess.
4:13-17). Contrarily, however, the dispensational timing of this aspect is at the beginning of the alleged interval, at For, the first stage, rather than at With, the
second stage. That is to say, if Paul knew anything of
the stages, he must have confused the first with the
second, for he should have written (if dispensationalism
is correct) "that He may establish your hearts unblameable in holiness at the coming of our Lord Jesus
Christ For all His saints". But Paul says "With".

The passage was written solely because these believers
were in some confusion of mind about those who had
died in faith, especially as to their place when the Lord
should return. They were not so concerned about the
generation of believers still living. They themselves had
been instructed at their conversion "to wait for His Son
from heaven, their Deliverer from the wrath to come"
(1 Thess. 1:9-10). Christ was their hope, but what of
the blessed dead? The apostle, therefore, wrote to ap-
prise and comfort them. It has been suggested that some
had already laid down their lives for Christ's sake, and

that this may have accounted for the expression, "sleep through Jesus". In any case, their confession of Gospel faith had occasioned the experience of persecution, yea, of tribulation, but recompensed, indeed, by "joy in the Holy Ghost". The apostle edified and comforted them by expounding an aspect of the blessed hope concerning which they were in uncertainty. It cannot be maintained from this Scripture, therefore, that the Church is to be translated in order to escape tribulation, nor is it true that this passage has no relation to the tribulation of the saints. It arises from that fact (See 1 Thess. 1:6; 2:14-16; 3:4-8; 4:13; 2 Thess. 1, etc.).

The presentation of the subject here is not designed to announce the Coming or a stage of it, peculiar to the Church as distinct from the purpose of the same event with respect to the world, or that it will be secret and not public, at any moment rather than at the appointed time (Heb. 10:37); nor yet a specially revealed Coming *for* the saints, or previous to and distinguished from "His Coming *with* all His saints" (1 Thess. 3:13). Paul's prophetic burden in this writing was to relieve the heart burden of these beloved believers (cf. 1 Thess. 2:8). The load upon their minds arose from their lack of knowledge about the lot of departed friends in the day of the Lord's return. Thus, in these few verses we read, "concerning them which are asleep", "them that sleep in Jesus", the living "shall not precede them which are asleep", "the dead in Christ shall rise first", and finally, "caught up together with them (the risen saints) to meet the Lord in the air". Each of these five verses refers to the deceased believers, with assurance that precedence shall be theirs, for they "shall rise *first*", rather than that of those still living, whose transformation is not mentioned. This is not a qualification similar to "the first resurrection" (Rev. 20), where it is contrasted with "the second death", but of priority to be given to deceased believers so that those living shall not precede these in meeting the descending Lord.

The apostle's first reasoning word bases the blessed hope upon the Gospel they had heard and believed: "If we believe that Jesus died and rose again", which is the substance of the Gospel according to Paul (1 Cor. 15:1-4), while the word or text which he proceeds to expound is, "them that sleep in Jesus will God bring with Him". He does not write, God will send Jesus *for* them or you, or for you and them together. But God will bring them in conjunction *with* Jesus because they by the Gospel are united to Him. Thereupon the apostle explains, by the authority of the word of the Lord, arrestingly, almost graphically, *how* this miraculous undertaking shall be brought to pass. A question which could quickly prompt itself (were we not so familiar with the words), and as we imagine it did with those early believers might be, "God will bring *with* Him, but *how?*" The simple explanation given is that those then alive and remaining will not be given precedence, for the dead shall rise first. The Lord Himself shall descend away from heaven, not secretly or silently but with tremendous and impressive accompaniment: a shout of command putting all in motion for the assembling; the voice of the archangel, that is, Michael in charge of the angelic myriads (see Rev. 12:7), the angels sent to separate the false from the true in His kingdom, and with a great sound of a trumpet to gather together His elect from the uttermost part of the earth to the uttermost part of heaven (Matt. 13:41-43; 24:31; Mark 13:27). The trump of God is described by Paul in a corresponding Scripture as "the last trump" (1 Cor. 15:52), thereby suggesting that "a well-ordered succession is contemplated". These two Pauline passages concern the same event. "Last" speaks of finality. A succession of numbered trumpets is given in the Apocalypse (Rev. 8-11). The seventh is the last, and announces accompaniments or consequences, including those which the apostle intimates here, but also others; but allowing for no dividing of the Coming into stages. Then "Sovereignty over the world is our Lord's and His Christ's, and He shall reign for ever and ever".

To overcome the timing difficulty thus presented to dispensationalism, some propose that Paul cannot have known of "the seventh trumpet" when he wrote of "the last trump", and they surmise a different set of trumpets of which the Bible has not a word to say. In the liberty and prescience of the Holy Spirit, however, Paul was inspired thus to designate the trump, and John later to write the explanation. Moreover, John, by command of the Lord Jesus, both Paul's Lord and John's, addressed the first of seven letters in this Apocalypse to Ephesus, to whom Paul had earlier written. It was said that at the beginning of the sounding of the seventh trumpet, "the mystery of God" would be completed "as He had declared to His servants the prophets". That doubtless has a Pauline and Ephesian flavour! The mystery concerns the preaching of the unsearchable riches of Christ, and thereby the building of the Church, elect and saved of Jews and Gentiles, the one body, one new mankind, "the fulness of Him that filleth all in all", a completeness indeed. Time for this will be no longer, but thereupon the time of resurrection and judgment and reward and wrath will have arrived. The completion of the one means the institution of the other. The time when the mystery of God will be finished, therefore, will not be reached until the events announced under John's seventh trumpet. And John's seventh is the last, agreeing both in title, time and substance with Paul's "last trump". Of this same time John wrote: "And the nations were angry and Thy wrath is come; and the time of the dead that they should be judged; and that Thou shouldest give reward unto Thy servants the prophets, and to the saints, and them that fear Thy name, small and great; and shouldest destroy them that corrupt the earth" (Rev. 10:5-7; 11:15-18).

At this one and selfsame time, therefore, and not in intervalled stages, the Lord Jesus will finish the building of His Church, against which the gates of hell, through angered persecuting foes, shall not prevail. He will raise the dead unto judgment and reward His saints of all generations—the terms are as descriptively comprehensive as could be in such short space. He will then also, in the same event, at the same time, visit His wrath upon the wicked world. For it is at this time that He comes to take possession, "He Who liveth forever and ever, Who created heaven and the things that therein are, and the earth and the things that therein are, and the sea and the things that are therein". Thus the mighty angel from above was seen with one foot upon the earth and the other on the sea, symbolizing the enforcement of His claim to possession. It would seem that this will be the objective of Christ's descending from heaven, for after judgment, He will create the new universe which other Scriptures predict (2 Pet. 3; Rev. 20-21; Isa. 65:17; 66:22). It is as He is on His way that the Church is blessed in being called into His presence.

The descent of the Lord from heaven, then, will be with a view to joyful release and retributive judgment; release for the righteous and retribution for the wicked will be executed in the event of His one Coming. "When He shall come to be glorified in His saints" is said to be the same time "when the Lord Jesus shall be revealed from heaven in flaming fire taking vengeance", without separating stages and interval of years. He will then release His Church from all the persecutions and tribulations she has endured, especially as the day approaches and antichristianism appears triumphant. At this time He will in righteous judgment visit vengeance upon their foes. The simultaneity is enforced by the repeated "when", and "in that day" reinforces the timing so that the human arrangement of a two-stage Coming is rendered altogether untenable (2 Thess. 1). Indeed, these are the very conditions which explain the reason the Church is to be caught up to meet her descending Lord. Why descend to the air at all if His objective were simply then to assemble His saints without respect to the other events? Why are they to be caught up to meet Him unless to join Him in His mighty undertaking? Why, if His object is to turn about from the air with them there and then to glory, to the Father's house; why not call them to His heavenly presence where He is enthroned and expecting? He Himself ascended up far above all heavens; Enoch and Elijah were taken up but He did not meet them halfway. The descent to the air warrants a reasoned explanation. It is in the day of wrath and righteous judgment, from which believers have been delivered by virtue of His justifying substitution, and their identification with Him, that they shall be raptured to meet Him for Whom they wait. Thus "the saints shall judge the world".

The simultaneous action of God in deliverance and judgment our Lord drew attention to when He spoke of His Coming, and like incidents in Biblical history are not wanting. "The day (*the selfsame day*: Gen. 7:11-13) that Noah entered the ark, the flood came and destroyed them all" ; "*the same day* that Lot went out of Sodom, it rained fire and brimstone from heaven and destroyed them all". "Even thus shall it be when the Son of Man is revealed" (Luke 17). The same waters, raised like a wall for the safe conduct of Israel away from their foes, overwhelmed the pursuing Egyptians (Exod. 14:22-28). The lions whose mouths were sealed unto Daniel's deliverance thereupon devoured his enemies (Dan 6:22-24). And it shall be "in that day" upon which the Lord Jesus shall descend from heaven "in flaming fire taking vengeance on them that obey not the gospel" that He comes "to be glorified in His saints and to be admired in all them that believe" (2 Thess. 1; 1 Thess. 5).

"Thou art coming, we shall see Thee, we shall meet Thee on Thy way". The word signifies to come or go from a place towards a person, and come back with the person met (see Matt. 25:1, 6; Acts 28:15). The Lord is not said to descend in order to meet them, as though thus met He will escort them on their way heavenwards; but they shall be caught up to meet Him and thus escort Him on His way earthwards. "The air" is the trysting place; the air where birds fly and in our times aircraft. This indicates publicity, and so, agreeably it says, "Behold He cometh with clouds, and every eye shall see Him." The terms convey neither secrecy nor silence, but the reverse, which also was "the word of the Lord" (Matt. 24: 26-27). "And so shall we ever be with the Lord" in His continuing descent, for "He shall come *with* all His saints (1 Thess. 3:13), and in His returning still with Him, to the "many mansions" in the "Father's house" (John 14).

This great passage does not terminate with chapter four and should be considered in its wholeness. It is continued, and the parallels and content are to be noted. There are here two sections, though in fulfilment there are not two stages. Of one matter the Thessalonian believers were ignorant; therefore, the apostle gave that priority, ministering the word of the Lord to their comfort. In the other case they "knew accurately", and he had no need further to enlighten them. Of certain issues at Christ's return, chiefly that of resurrection, they had been uncertain. Of the times and seasons, the day of the Lord, that is, the time of His Coming, they were well aware. That day would overtake the world as a thief, but not the Church, for she expected and waited for Him, like as the world in Noah's day, "they knew not until the flood came and took them all away"; but Noah was pre-advised and ready. And so, "that day shall not overtake you as a thief" not because you will have been removed to heaven some years before it arrives; there is no promise of that, nor do these words imply it, only as dispensationalism wrests them. "Sudden destruction cometh" upon the world, or "standeth over them, implying approach". This again confirms the reason for the rapture. Hence the exhortation. Let the Church, therefore, keep awake, alert, clad in the protective armour provided in the Gospel from tribulations and persecutions *around* as the day approaches; namely, "the *breastplate* of faith and love", and security against wrath descending from *above*, "the *helmet* of salvation". Why this provision and admonition, we may well ask, if the Church will not be on earth in the conditions prevailing at the arrival of the day of the Lord? The Gospel of the Lord Jesus Christ is their sufficiency, as the apostle had already expressed in the first section (1 Thess. 4:14), for "He died for us, that whether we wake or sleep, we should live together with Him". And again, as in the first section, he concludes by exhorting them to "comfort and edify one another" (cf. 1 Thess. 4:18; 5:11).

"In His times He shall show Who is the blessed and only Potentate, the Kings of kings and Lord of lords" (1 Tim. 6:15). His exact order in procedure we may not know, and it is presumptuous to arrange an agenda for Him. But the main facts we may discern and assemble. "At the last trump", at the "sounding of the seventh trumpet", such is the hour stated and not at an uncertain "any moment". The Lord from heaven, the last Adam, will appear from above the second time, unveiled in majesty, glory and power, escorted by His holy angels. So descending away from heaven earthwards, His everlasting Gospel purpose reaching completeness, the time will have arrived for His execution of the last things, for He is the Executor of the Godhead. All generations of those who fear God, and all His saints, servants, prophets small and great, shall be raised in incorruption or transformed by immortality, and transfigured like Him then, shall be caught up to meet Him, and to be rewarded by Him. By resurrection "death shall be swallowed up in victory", the enemy last to be destroyed, for all His enemies then shall have been subdued under His feet. The wicked, the apostate nations, the Devil that deceived them, all shall receive their final and eternal judgment and destiny. The called, the chosen, the faithful, from among all nations then "are with Him", even the Church of the Firstborn written in heaven. The world and its evil works shall be cremated, and new heavens and earth created, even "the habitable world to come", for the habitation of the new mankind. Then in His name "every knee shall bow, in heaven, in earth and under the earth; and every tongue shall confess that Jesus Christ is Lord to the glory of God the Father". Corresponding to Paul's victorious announcement is John's apocalyptic vision: "And every creature in heaven, and in the earth and under the earth, and such as are in the sea, and all that are in them, I heard saying, Blessing and honour and glory and power be unto Him that sitteth upon the throne and unto the Lamb forever and ever" (Phil. 2; Rev. 5).

ONE CHURCH, ONE COMING,
ONE CROWN

A foundation principle in seeking a true interpretation, as stated in earlier chapters, is the recognition that quotations from or references to the Old Testament made in the New Testament are not in a manner of application, but of forecast and fulfilment. In the Gospel we may observe "how that the promise which was made unto the Fathers, God hath fulfilled, in that He hath raised up Jesus" (Acts 13:32-33). The divine revelation and activity through Moses and the prophets, the patriarchs and Israel, were designed unto that end. The covenants, promises and prophecies reach their goal in Christ and His Church. The Old Testament cannot be unlocked save with the New Testament key. It is Christ Who opens the Scriptures, and it is He Who opens the understanding (Luke 24). What He did for His disciples before His ascension He continues to do through His Spirit, "another Comforter". Without this ministry of the Holy Spirit, the Jews remain in spiritual blindness even "when Moses is read", the Gentiles being in similar plight when the Gospel is preached (2 Cor. 3, 4). Christ is the Truth, and His Church is "the pillar and ground of the truth" (1 Tim. 3:15). There is no hope for any sinner, race makes no difference, save in a faithful receiving of Christ's Gospel, and all who are so graced now in this accepted time are "sealed with the Holy Spirit of promise" and received by the glorified Head into His

Church, of whom it is written that "Christ hath received them".

The present time is the opportune time, and the last time, whereupon will arrive the end of the world and age, which terms denote respectively the material and temporal nature of the present order. Both will reach the end simultaneously, for these two are one. The "now" and "today" of salvation through the hearing of faith will be terminated at the Second Coming of Christ, now Saviour, then Judge (2 Cor. 6; Heb. 4). While this remains a "promise", though it be met with scepticism, the longsuffering of God is unto salvation. When that expires, and it will do so at the Return of the Lord Jesus Christ, the lengthened opportunity to be saved will expire with it. The apostle has affirmed this with no uncertainty, and claims his fellow apostles and the prophets in witness thereto. And he would have the Church "be mindful" and "beware" and not "wrest the Scriptures" (2 Pet. 3; 2 Thess. 1). Thereupon, the day of the Lord will have come, and with it the day of judgment, and not an intervening added millennial or national salvation. All will be headed up in Christ Jesus and time shall be no more (Eph. 1:10). The fallen ruined world will be cremated and a new and eternal world created, the habitation of Christ and His Church; this while on earth and on pilgrimage she expectantly waits for. Such is the testimony of the Scripture. Then "He will present her to Himself a glorious Church, faultless, with exceeding joy" (Eph. 5; Jude 24). The one and selfsame "promise of His Coming" incorporates all. These arrive in the one momentous event of the end (2 Pet. 3:4, 9, 13). Then, beyond all capability of human thought or speech, to God in Christ will be glory through no other instrumentality than the church "throughout all ages, world without end" (Eph. 3:21).

Emphasizing the instruction "rightly to divide the word of truth", dispensationalists naturally made dispensational divisions, but in so doing they themselves are divided. Superseding the "church age", they say, will be the "kingdom age", when the Jews will be nationally re-instituted as the earthly people of God, and nations will be saved. It is claimed that the continuance of the

Church on earth is a preventive to the "kingdom age" development or establishment, hence the necessity for the Church to be removed. Preceding the "church age", it is said, the nation of Israel was in acceptance, but this ended with their rejection of the Messiah, being "cut off" by them; they were cut off by Him, yet it is said, but temporarily, until the completing of His building the Church. If it be pointed out that the finality and fulness of God's revealed purposes are attained in the Church, it is speculated that after the "kingdom age" (millennium) the Jewish nation will be immortalized and incorporated in the Church previously glorified. And also, we suppose, the "saved nations." There is no promise of this. The Church consists not of saved *nations;* she is herself "an holy nation", and is composed of sinners "called out" from all nations: hence "Church" (Exod. 19:5-6; Matt. 21:43; 1 Pet. 2:9). Moreover, our Lord in His own parabolic illustration declared of the Jewish nation that her last state would be worse than the first (Matt. 12:38-45) and that His "brethren" were those only in spiritual relationship with Him through faith expressed in discipleship. This He followed with His parables of the Kingdom, the course of the Gospel among the nations until the end of the world. Then, with the judgment of the wicked, not an earthly kingdom-age instituted, but "the righteous shall shine forth as the sun (as He did when transfigured, see Matt. 17:2; Phil. 3:21) in the kingdom of their Father" (Matt. 13:43).

But dispensationalism is characteristically divisive. Indeed, resurrections are duplicated, "firstfruits" are given a rapture to themselves, though part of the harvest. Again, viewing the Church to be raptured some years before the end, when it is said Christ comes for her, the uncountable "great tribulation" converts are said to be post-church, but seen in heaven before the millennium! And how do they get there? By yet another resurrection and rapture? In dispensationalism every proposition demands another proposition to accommodate a former. It is a matter of common sense, therefore, as well as of spiritual discernment, to enquire whether a mistaken proposition did not invent the whole scheme?

But the dividing is not finished with the general pre-millennial views. There have arisen the "mystery" and "body" theories. We are told of separate "churches", of the Acts, and of the Gospels, and of course, in Israel of old, distinct from the Church of which Paul wrote in his "prison epistles", that is, his letters after Acts 28. "Three spheres of blessing" are proposed, all founded upon redemption, but built in tiers thereon: at the foot, the Jews and saved nations on earth; in the centre, the heavens, the bride, the heavenly Jerusalem; and at top, the heavenlies, the Church which is His body. The group at the top will be "the nearest to Christ" and occupy "the most glorious position". All this seems very fanciful, but it is to be attributed chiefly to the late Dr. E. W. Bullinger, a scholar of no mean theological reputation. *The Companion Bible* and other works represent his industry. He wrote (re Phil. 3:10, 11): "Such as had attained to what Paul was pressing forward to might receive their glorified bodies soon or immediately after death, so that they are already with the Lord instead of sleeping until His coming". The text, he says, "promises for the saints here and now an out-resurrection from among the dead and a rapture on high. And these are in place of and in advance of 1 Thessalonians 4:16, which has been postponed on account of the non-repentance of Israel.

To such lengths does dispensationalism conduct us. Dr. Oswald Allis has testified to Dr. Bullinger's consistency in carrying dispensationalism to its logical extreme, although the Scofield party consider him "ultra". We are presented, then, with divisions between Israel or the Jewish Church, the "bride" Church and the "body" Church. Yet it is in the very writing of Paul, Ephesians, regarded as the chief avenue of this "revelation", that the apostle affirms that all divisions are now in Christ Jesus broken down among believers of all ages and races, in the unity of the Spirit and of the faith and knowledge of the Son of God, in the fellowship or partnership of the "one new man" or mankind. It is here too that believers, aliens and foreigners to favoured Israel beforetime—for hers was then the advantage of possessing the divine oracles—and without hope, become in Christ Jesus fellow-partners in Israel's "commonwealth". It is here the Church is presented under the figure of a bride, illustrated in the union of husband and wife, the announcement first made in Eden before the Fall being described by Paul as "a great mystery concerning Christ and the church". So the redeemed from among the Jews, and the nations, the chosen of God, whatever figure describes them, the bride, the body: all are one. How many soever "spheres of blessing" there may be, all alike being graced in Christ Jesus, shall equally share them. Moreover, silencing all controversy and healing all divisons, Paul summarizes thus: There is one Spirit, one Lord, one God and Father of all, Who is above and through and in all; and there is one body, one faith, one baptism, one hope of your calling. If, therefore, liberty is taken to put asunder what God has joined together, if there be more than the one body and faith and baptism and hope, by dividing the redeemed into these dispensational groups and spheres, logically this could be extended to a multiplication of the persons in the Godhead: "gods many and lords many"! Against all this wrongly dividing the word of truth, its unity of teaching unites in their entirety all believers, "the fulness of Him Who filleth all in all".

In previous chapters we have examined some aspects of the popular dispensational theories; we now attempt an examination of the extreme view, "mystery-dispensationalism", as it has been called. In the first place, it is clear that Paul was not alone in receiving the revelation. As the one Gospel was revealed to Paul but not to him alone (Gal. 1:12), and the memorial ordinance, previously committed to others (1 Cor. 11:23), and as Paul was joined to the existing apostles, "last of all" (1 Cor. 15:8), in similar manner he wrote that the "mystery" or secret was communicated by revelation, "which was not made known in other ages as it is now revealed unto His holy apostles and prophets by the Spirit" (Eph. 3:3-5). The "mystery", therefore, was not altogether previously unknown, nor was it revealed through Paul, but to Paul and to others "by the Spirit". He had just written of the resurrection and ascension into the heavenlies of the Lord Jesus, upon which He was given headship over the Church, so that "the church, which is His body" was already in being when He ascended on high. Again, it was not the fact of the Church which had been hitherto partially a mystery, but her constitution. The revelation made was that with believing Jews, the first to be evangelized, "the Gentiles should be fellow-heirs, and fellow-members of the same body, and fellow-partakers of His promise in Christ by the gospel" (Eph. 3:6).

The emphasis is upon the fact of the fellowship, the partnership. Centrally we have the phrase, "fellow-members of the same body", or one body. The purpose of God was now fully revealed, that "He might reconcile both (Jews and Gentiles) in one body by the cross", that is, those "who were afar off with those who were nigh", the circumcision and the uncircumcision. When the apostles received commission to evangelize the nations, the order of procedure was laid down; "in Jerusalem, all Judea, Samaria, and unto the uttermost part of the earth" (Acts 1:8). The Lord's instructions were precisely followed, and the Acts of the Apostles is the record. Jews, therefore, were the first converts, then Samaritans and the Gentiles. When "the uttermost part" will have been reached, as God intends it, presumably the Lord will come!

To be "fellow-partakers of His promise" was another privilege of grace. "In time past", the Gentiles "were without Christ, being aliens from the commonwealth of Israel, and strangers from the covenants of promise", words which make it clear that being in Christ, and partakers of the promise, and having hope, means the position is reversed, and "ye are no longer strangers and foreigners, but fellow-citizens with the saints and of the household of God", which cannot mean other than that all such share in the "commonwealth".

But to whom were the promises initially made? God in His sovereign will selected Abraham, called and saved him by His grace to be in his exemplary faith "the father of all them that believe" without distinction of privilege or race; which is the New Testament explanation of the promise, "I have made thee a father of many nations" (Rom. 4). In this connection He made him "heir of the world". All believers, therefore, "are blessed with faithful Abraham", since it was said, "In thy Seed, which is Christ, all families of the earth shall be blessed" (Gal. 3). And in this the Gospel was thus announced to Abraham. There is no more justification for dividing the favoured beneficiaries of God's redemption into separate groups with ultimate graded spheres of blessing than for divorcing from Abraham's covenanted blessings the generations of believers; pre-and-post-Abraham who partake of his faith. As Christ was his Seed par excellence, so all in Christ are his spiritual seed, for "if ye be Christ's, then are ye Abraham's seed, and heirs according to the promise" (Gal. 3). Heirship is within the covenants of promise. These, however, were not Israel's possession; they were hers only in so far as Israelites believed as Abraham believed, sharing his faith. To Israel was given the law four centuries later, whereas the covenants of promise were made to Abraham that in Christ they might be "sure to all the seed" (Gal. 3:17; Rom. 4). The law, being "added", was the parenthesis, if such there be, and not grace.

The promise would also embrace the being "fellow heirs and of the same body". Heirship is included according to the revelation of the "mystery," and this agrees with the earlier statement, from a non-prison epistle, "if ye be Christ's, then are ye Abraham's seed, and heirs according to the promise" (Gal. 3:29). But how do the Gentiles become fellow heirs? By reason of their having become "in Christ" Abraham's seed, and this, therefore, determines that the term "seed" is to be viewed spiritually and not racially. Jews, therefore, are only included as beneficiaries of the promise if they, as the Gentiles, become the seed of Abraham in Christ. "In Christ Jesus, neither circumcision availeth anything, nor uncircumcision, but a new creation" (Gal. 6:15). Thus Abraham, and all God's believing people of the past dispensation were already in the Church, although the full revelation concerning the incorporation of Gentiles was not completely known. The statement about heirship attaching to Abraham's seed in a non-prison epistle is parallel with a passage in another prison epistle (Gal. 3:28; Col. 3:11). And these words are vital to the revelation of the mystery. Consequently by this and other comparisons, the divisive method of special and privileged grouping and sphering breaks down.

Can there be any promised blessing greater and higher, larger and richer, than that conveyed in the title, "heirs of God", and can there be any relationship nearer and dearer than that of being "joint-heirs with Christ"? Yet mystery-dispensationalism places non-prison-epistle believers, of whom such is spoken, in a lower category (Rom. 8:17). They are justified, and this is the assurance of their being "glorified together". And when the apostle would show how guilty sinners are justified, he again cites Abraham who "believed God, and it was accounted unto him for righteousness". That Abraham was thus justified "was not written for his sake alone, but for us also to whom it shall be imputed if we believe" (Rom. 4:23). Justifying-faith is faith-obedience, and "by faith, Abraham, when he was called, obeyed", and the apostle writes that this very Gospel of the mystery, as it has been called, once secret, is now "made known to all nations for the obedience of faith" (Rom. 16:25-26). Now more confusion! How did this prison-epistle revelation get into the Roman epistle? We are treated to the "suggestion" that Paul's "postscript" was added later, during his writing in prison. It were more satisfactorily explained by the counter suggestion that the Holy Spirit, foreseeing this wrongly dividing, inspired Paul to introduce the subject and later to unfold and develop it in his prison writings, for the Church of Christ is one. Following the reference to Abraham's justification and all believers with him, we read, "being justified, we rejoice in hope of the glory of God", and Abraham rejoiced in this hope of glory. When he was called, "the God of glory" appeared unto him (Acts 7:2). He had not the fulness of the later revelation, but he had the promise of fulness of blessing.

THE FEW SCRIPTURES already reviewed direct us back to Abraham, and associate him with all who are Christ's through the Gospel, and in the glory. The question arises as to the position of those who lived before Abraham and the Israel nation. From Abel downwards (perhaps, Adam) "these all died in faith, not having received the promises, but having seen them afar off, and were persuaded of them, and embraced them, and confessed that they were strangers and pilgrims on the earth." Wherefore? Because they were called unto and looked for that which was heavenly both in character and location. And why have they not received the promises? Because God, foreseeing, provided "some better thing for us that they apart from us should not be made perfect", words which declare the unity of the faithful from first to last (Heb. 11:39-40). This unity is again spoken of in the words, "Ye are come to the general assembly of the church of the Firstborn, written in heaven" (Heb. 12). "The term, 'general assembly', implies not merely a great, but the full number" (Dr. Saphir).

It is clear from the Scriptures that the *ground* of salvation in all dispensations is the meritorious value of Christ's obedience and blood, that the *means* is faith which apprehends and depends upon Christ alone; and it is equally clear that all are promised, and made heirs of the same hope. Abraham and the patriarchs "looked for the city which hath foundations, whose builder and architect is God." Even the "land of promise" was to him "a strange country" in which he dwelt as a pilgrim, "with Isaac and Jacob, heirs with him of the same promise." For believers before the coming of Christ "confessed that they were strangers and pilgrims on the earth", that they sought a native, that is, a heavenly country, for which they were born anew from above. And so "God hath prepared for them a city." Thus in Paul's "allegory", all born of the Spirit and "children of the promise" belong to "Jerusalem which is above, is free, and is the mother of us all" (Heb. 12; Gal. 4).

The city is described in vision in the Apocalypse. She is "the bride, the Lamb's wife", which accords with kindred revelations (e.g., Psa. 45; Rev. 19; Eph. 5; 2 Cor. 11). The one church is "built upon the foundation of the apostles and prophets, Jesus Christ Himself being the chief corner-stone", and in the foundations of the city their inscription was seen. On the gates of the city are seen inscribed "the names of the twelve tribes of Israel". All the redeemed of all time are connected with this heavenly city, and He writes the name upon them (Rev. 3:12; 21:12, 14; Eph. 2:12). To have no participation in that city is to be without hope (Rev. 22:14, 15, 19). The hopeless estate when "without Christ" is remedied by His cross, with reconciliation and peace and the Spirit, and citizenship with the saints, implying membership of a state or city, a freeman; which "citizenship is in heaven, from whence also we look for the Saviour" (Eph. 2:12-19; Phil. 3:20; Heb. 12). The varied Scriptures agree; each adds its own contribution; they were inspired by the one and self-same Spirit. Why dismember and dissociate those and that which God hath joined together? There is no more grander or more glorious goal for the pilgrim Church. Yet the mystery-dividers give the bride and the heavenly city an inferior place, with superior sphere in glory and nearer relationship to the one Redeemer to those whom they distinguish as "the body". Are not these and other terms just figures of speech; is not Christ Himself the bearer of many titles and offices designed to set forth His fulness? And likewise His Gospel? So also the Church which "He will present to Himself"?

"The God of all grace hath called us to His eternal glory by Christ Jesus" (1 Pet. 5:10). There are too many references to this goal of glory to allow of quotation here; a concordance will indicate the wide-embracing array, in promise, in objective, in vision. It is glory, glory, glory, and ultimately, the city itself is seen "having the glory of God" which did "lighten it, and the Lamb is the light thereof". A heavenly calling; the hope is of glory; the Church will be manifested with Christ in glory; the Gospel is altogether unto the praise of His glory; it is Christ's ultimate for His own whom the Father had given Him; they shall be "glorified together" in the unity and oneness of the Father, the Son and the Spirit. He will be "glorified in His saints and admired in all them that believe in that day." The "day" is that of His coming, the last of the present evil age, the first of the age to come. Then, with the creating of new heavens and new earth, the city is seen to descend, and He will have made "all things new".

To recapitulate: The Secong Coming of Christ will be one majestic, momentous event; its beneficiaries, the uncountable myriads of His redeemed from Time's beginning, "that they all may be one" (John 17). The new and heavenly Jerusalem, of which the Lamb is all the glory, is their conversazione. Title is theirs alone who in Christ are "made meet for the inheritance of the saints in light." There are no additional groups of the saved or spheres of glory. From Abel to Abraham and onwards, all who "died in faith" shall be there in resurrection glory, for on pilgrimage the heavenly city and country was their hope (Heb. 11, 12).

"The twelve tribes of the children of Israel" receive special mention. Contrary to such as ascribe to them a restored Jerusalem on earth, their names are inscribed in Jerusalem in heaven, and on the "gates" of entry, their "right" of entry being the blood and righteousness of the Lamb. Dispersed among the nations, from the nations they are gathered by the Gospel. Hence in the epistles of the Church they are promised heirship to the kingdom and inheritance reserved in heaven. Are they not the "firstfruits"? It was necessary to divinely-ordered procedure that the Gospel be first preached unto them (Acts 3:26; 13:46). May not, therefore, the Pentecostal harvest and the evangelization of "all Judea" have outgathered the firstfruits from Israel's scattered twelve tribes? "This is the hope of the promise made unto our fathers" spake the Hebrew apostle Paul, now fulfilled in the Gospel which he preached, "unto which, our twelve tribes, instantly serving God day and night, hope to come" (Acts 2; Jas. 1:1, 18; 2:5; 1 Pet. 1:1-4; Acts 13:32-33; 26:6-7; Heb. 12:22; Rev. 14:1-5). This, then, is what God ultimately meant by what He said concerning tribal reinstatement, looking beyond the literal rehabilitation of People, City and Temple, still typical, after the captivity to the heavenly and eternal reality.

"The twelve apostles of the Lamb" are inscribed in the foundations. How appropriate! The vision of the glorified Church agrees with the doctrine of the Church, written in the very epistles which super-dispensationalism associates with a distinct and "higher" group, the "body" say they, but not the "bride". The fact is these two are one. In continuation of their "citizenship" Paul wrote, "ye are built upon the foundation of the apostles and prophets, Jesus Christ Himself being the chief cornerstone." For it surely is on the great doctrinal confession of the Person of Christ expounded in the writings of apostles and prophets that the invulnerable foundation is laid (Matt. 16:16; 1 Cor. 3:11; Eph. 2:20; 1 Pet. 2:6).

Having described the grandeur of the city in some detail, with its twelve gates and foundations, representatively incorporating the Gospel fulness of the Jews and of the Gentiles, together constituting the fulness of the Church (Rom. 9:23-24; 10:12; 11:12-25), the vision generally summarizes the whole by its mention of "the nations of them which are saved" and their "healing" which, not the equivalent of saved nations as such, but interpreted by the terms of the great commission, would mean those saved from among all nations, including some in high places as "kings", which "bring their glory and honour into it" (to the interior). The commission that disciples should be made of all nations did not mean nations as such, but individual sinners from among them; so the Gospel is to be "preached among all nations". Some audiences would include kings and rulers and others in authority, before whom Paul especially was privileged to bear witness, and John on Patmos also received instruction. Therefore, are those in high places to be subject of the intercession of the Church, not alone for her peace in this world, but also because God will have all classes of men to be saved and come unto the knowledge of the truth (Luke 21:47; Acts 9:15; Rev. 10:11).

Here, then, is presented to our view as a figure of the true, the one Church inclusive of all the redeemed. He will "have gathered together in *one* the children of God which are scattered abroad" for to this end He died (John 11:52); His "other sheep" will have been brought home, joined to those "before" Him, and of His earthly ministry, "and there shall be *one* flock and one Shepherd" (John 10:8-16); His prayer will then be answered, for all those who are His Father's gift to Him (as bride to Bridegroom) "that they all may be made perfect in *one*" seeing and sharing His glory (John 17: 21-24). These all constitute the "*one* new man" and the "*one* body" (Eph. 2:15-16). the names of each and all being inscribed in "the Lamb's book of life". To crown all the spiritual blessings with which they are blessed in Christ Jesus, "they shall see *His face*, and *His name* shall be in their foreheads", and "they shall reign for ever and ever" (Rev. 21:4-5).

DANIEL'S PARENTHESIS

SINCE our preparation of the chapter "Gaps and Guesses", including consideration of Gabriel's prophecy of the seventy weeks (Daniel 9), we have been introduced to current articles under the above title (*The Harvester*, from which quotations are made, unless otherwise stated). The views expressed, with some minor variations, follow mainly Dr. Tregelles and some Brethren, Sir Robert Anderson, Ironside, Gabelein, Futurism, and as presented in notes in the Scofield Reference and Companion Bibles. The prophecy is made to befit the general dispensational theory. The main difference between this and a historical view seems to lie in the interpolation of a time-parenthesis and the assignment of the 70th seven to Antichrist rather than to Christ, Whose appearing the 69 sevens and, indeed, the entire 70 had in view. The parenthesis theory allows for the invention of an intervening "Church period", since Messiah was "cut off", at which time Israel's "clock ceased ticking", to be set agoing at the beginning of the 70th seven, when, upon the expiry of the parenthesis the Lord will come *for* His Church — some say, to include the withdrawal of the Holy Spirit Who, till then, holds back the appearing of the Man of sin (2 Thess. 2) — and *with* the saints at the termination of the last seven years to establish the millennial reign. It is a superficially attractive hypothesis, but it is not found in Gabriel's inspired answer to Daniel's prayer, nor does it find support in the Scriptures.

Daniel concluded his intense intercession with the appeal: "O Lord, hear; O Lord, forgive; O Lord, hearken and do; defer not, for thine own sake, O my God: for thy city and thy people are called by thy name" (Dan. 9:19). His chief burden was for Israel's sin with which he identified himself. Before he had finished praying, Gabriel was "swiftly" dispatched in response, and Daniel was made "skilful in understanding" (vv. 20-23). He had sought with worshipful emotion "about the time of the evening oblation" (worthy of note) an answer of grace assuring divine forgiveness. Accordingly and graciously Gabriel announced a limited period of time in which remission would be finally, abundantly and eternally provided (v. 24). Daniel had requested that there be no deferment, no procrastination. The dispensational proposition, postponing Israel's blessings by a lengthened parenthesis (still continuing) is tantamount to divine procrastination in view of the unity of the period decreed. Surer and safer was Daniel in the lion's den than he would be in the dispensationalists' camp.

The remarkable similiarity of terms and numerals, surely designed, between Jeremiah and Gabriel (70 years - 70 sevens) may represent a "round period". There is no necessity to fix precisely when and with what event may come the termination of the 70th seven, unless the Scripture so advises. Following the mention of the 69th and 70th there are particulars about "desolation", and "end" and "consummation". Beyond this Daniel was given no information. Certain it is that Gabriel's chronology contains no hint that a "little horn" (Antichrist) would "make" with the Jews a seven-year covenant which he would "break" half-way through. In fact, there is no suggestion in the text of *making* or *breaking* a covenant at all. The words are, "He shall cause to prevail a covenant for the many one week". It is also certain that Gabriel announced a period of "70 sevens" as consecutive as Jeremiah's "70 years". Any interruption by an unmeasured or immeasurable parenthesis would make it impossible for Daniel or any one else to "know and understand" as the prophet had "understood the number of the years" of the earlier prophecy. Daniel could reckon with certainty that God meant what He said, whereas gaps and guesses mean, perhaps, they have guesses who have gaps.

"We lay it down as an absolute rule", wrote Philip Mauro, "admitting of no exceptions, that when a definite measure of time is specified by the number of units composing it, within which a certain event is to happen or a certain thing is to be found, the units which make up that measure are to be understood as running continuously and successively". He gives the following examples: Gen. 15:13; Exod. 12:40; Gal. 3:17: — 430 years. Gen. 45:6: — 7 years. Numb. 14:34: — 40 years. Our Lord's burial: — "3 days and 3 nights". And we might add, Jeremiah's 70 years.

Daniel was given to understand that within the period of time stated blessed events for his people and city would be accomplished, and that for this the 490 years had been appointed of God, and further, that they concerned the coming and cutting off of Messiah the Prince. So it proved in the course of the time decreed. Daniel understood when others did not (cf. 8:27; 10:1). A distinction is made between the wise and understanding ones or the remnant, and the nation in general. We repeat as important that the blessings of v. 24 are to be achieved within the 490 years. It is not said that the period will elapse *before* their realization, or that 70 sevens are decreed *after* which transgression shall be finished. Rather 70 sevens are decreed *to accomplish* them. The casual "therefore" of v. 25 requires the Messianic undertaking. If the final 7 years of the total 490 are not consecutive, but disjoined by an unmeasured gap; namely, the prolonged time-course between the Advents; if "after" (v. 26) does not place the crucifixion within the last 7 years, then neither the death of Christ, which atoningly secured the promised blessings, nor the Second Advent, which in the postponement view will supply or apply them, is within the period ordained and specified for this very purpose.

Moreover, the parenthetical hypothesis divorces the blessings from the only Coming of Christ here announced, namely, unto the cross; and makes them consequent upon His Second Advent in glory, which is also beyond the limit of Gabriel's period. We quote: "I do not regard any of them (v. 24) as referring strictly to the work of Christ on the cross; they all belong to the time of Israel's blessing (i.e. the millennium), when they will be applied" (Tregelles). Again, "These events did not happen at the cross: the nation is still sinning"; they "await our Lord's return, the words plainly demand a period such as that foretold in Rev. 20:4-6". Further, "Gabriel surely spoke of God's action in restoring the shekinah glory to the future temple". Yet it is admitted by premillennialists that sin and the curse are not entirely removed in their millennium: "the sinner being an hundred years old shall be accursed", and even death, for "the child shall die an hundred years old" (Isa. 65). The futurist theory therefore means that the fulfilment of v. 24 is postponed beyond the cross of Christ; beyond the conjectured parenthesis, still current; beyond the entire predicted period, unto Messiah's second manifestation and into the millennium!

"It will not do", it is averred, "to insert within this 70th seven a period of grace"; perhaps not, but the 490 years cannot but represent or lead to a reign of grace, the promised blessings being witnesses: — transgression, sin, iniquity completely expiated (cf. Psa. 32; Rom. 4); righteousness everlastingly brought in (Rom. 5), "for if righteousness were by the law, then Christ died in vain"; vision and prophet ratified in Christ and the Gospel (Luke 24:44-47; 1 Pet. 1:10-12); access into the holiest by the blood of Jesus, and worship in the Spirit (Heb. 10; John 4; Phil. 3). Christ being "cut off" or crucified, the new covenant prevailed and will do for He is its Mediator, and the blessings of v. 24 are guaranteed by it. These are comprehended in "the fulness of the blessing of the gospel of Christ" and are "the promises made unto the fathers", agreeable to Daniel (Rom. 15). Consequently and essentially the old covenant requiring typical "sacrifice and oblation" was "caused to cease".

The references to the covenants and all that is comprehended in them in the Hebrews Epistle of the New Testament are significant. The old covenant, formed or produced under Moses, was declared obsolete as worn out: hence it could not prevail, and the prediction was fulfilled, "He shall cause to cease" (Heb. 8:9, 13; Dan. 9:27); whereas the verbs "to make", used in the same context of the new covenant are given, "to assign, place apart; to execute, complete entirely, fulfil"; hence the accurate forecast, "cause to prevail" (Heb. 8:8-10; 10:16 with Dan. 9:27). Verbal inspiration again, so that in the Hebrews Epistle God said what He meant by what He said to Daniel through Gabriel. The principle has been advanced in earlier chapters that there is no warrant rigidly to reason, because terms common to Old Testament habit in the age of types are employed in the prophecies of the same period, that their fulfilment in Christ Jesus must conform to the same grammatical pattern. His coming and cross have made all the difference. Sovereign liberty belongs to the Spirit of God in interpretation as well as inspiration of the word of prophecy.

To overcome difficulties further time-parentheses are introduced. We are reminded of the Cabinet Minister (Birrell) who in reply to an M.P. who had presented part of his question in Greek, replied: "Quoting Greek is a convenient thing to do when one is in difficulty"! The same might be said of "gaps". An important matter to notice however is this. The dispensational theory identifies the covenant of Dan. 9:27 with that mentioned in Isa. 28, and further reference is made to Isa. 10. Historical fulfilment as to the Assyrian is overlooked. But what is more conclusive against this reasoning is that these chapters are quoted in the New Testament of the Gospel, the Church, the Holy Spirit, the purpose of grace, and given an entirely evangelical fulfilment "now in this present time". Compare with Isa. 28, Rom. 10:11; 1 Cor. 3:11; 1 Cor. 14:21; 1 Pet. 2:6 (and Isa. 8, Psa. 118 also) and Isa. 10, Rom. 9:27-28, where Paul declares that the salvation of Isaiah's remnant, which dispensationalists give a future fulfilment, is indeed the work of their salvation which He will finish now in righteousness, in the Church composed of those (quoting Hosea to support Isaiah) "whom He hath called, not of the Jews only but also of the Gentiles". There is no appeal beyond the New Testament.

From the "commandment" or "word" to turn again
the capitivity and rebuild the city "unto Messiah the
Prince", 483 years. That the decree of Cyrus was the
commencing date of reckoning seems evident, for he
"made a proclamation", or (as margin) "caused a voice
to pass"; that is, a word (Isa. 44:28; 45:1-4); Ezra 1:1-
4). "Unto Messiah the Prince", that is, His "manifestation in Israel", reached the measure of 69 sevens (John
1; Isa. 40; Mal. 3). Three-and-a-half years "after",
that is, "in the midst of the 70th seven", He was "cut
off". Not His birth or youth but His maturity was indicated in the title, "Messiah the Prince". Historically
it is confirmed that three-and-a-half years after His public ministry began He was crucified. It is strange, indeed, if the two sentences, "unto Messiah the Prince"
and "after . . . shall Messiah be cut off", refer to the
same point of time, namely, His crucifixion, that it
should be so stated. Obviously, "after" denotes a different and a later point of time than "unto". Gabriel gives
no details of the brief time to elapse between "unto" and
"after", but the Gospel records tell the story of His repeated rejection by Israel until finally He was "cut off".
"By wicked hands He was crucified and slain", but this
deed was also "according to the determinate counsel and
foreknowledge of God" (Acts 2:23). As of Joseph in
Egypt it might be said, "Ye meant it unto evil, but God
meant it unto good". The human, malicious aspect: "cut
off"; the divine, merciful aspect: a covenant of grace
confirmed and the covenant of works abolished. How
and when effected? "After" the 483 years and within
the last 7 years. At what point? "In the midst of the
seven", that is, correspondingly, His public ministry of
three-and-a-half years ended with the cross when He
cried, It is finished.

Information is now given concerning the destruction
of the city and sanctuary by the people of the coming
prince. The prediction is stated before the events of the
70th week. It is generally acknowledged that A.D. 70
is referred to. This does not come within the decreed
Messianic period. It is, however, placed where it is,
somewhat relevant to Messiah's being "cut off". Did
not Christ on earth foretell this, confirming Daniel? But
now, at the date of fulfilment, (A.D. 70), risen, en-

throned, vested with all authority in heaven and earth, did not He watch over His word to preform it? Like Cyrus, Nebuchadnezzar and others, though pagan, even describing them as His servants, whom Christ could commandeer to do His will, so also Titus (Dan. 4:35; cf. words uttered in the context of His Own sovereignty (Luke 15:41-46, etc.).

A comparison will show the similarity of subject and of terms, so that the Subject of 26A and 27A are the same, and the events of 26B and 27B are the same. But it is asked, "If the cutting off of Messiah and causing sacrifice to cease are one and the same event of the cross, why is the destruction of Jerusalem sandwiched out of its chronological order? Should not Gabriel have said, After Messiah shall be cut off and have caused sacrifice to cease, without the intervening prediction about A.D. 70?" The explanation is clear. Whereas chronological parentheses are not common in Scripture, grammatical parentheses are. Examples are not difficult to find: Psa. 49:8; Mark 2:10; John 4:2; John 7:39; Rom. 5:13-17; Phil. 3:18-19). In these (and others) the sentence following the parenthesis should be joined to that preceding, to continue the main narrative, and the like rule applies to Gabriel's prediction. Without and beyond the boundaries of the time period of the sevens, judgment is announced upon the apostate nation, appropriately placed where it is because the cutting off of Messiah occasioned it. Here are cause and effect. So, bracketed, the Messianic particulars are continued thus: "Messiah shall be cut off" (parenthesis announcing the judgment merited) "and He shall cause to prevail".

There is at hand a simple example of this manner of revelation (v. 25). 483 years unto Messiah are divided into 49 and 434 years. The reason for this is found in Jerusalem's rebuilding. Yet Gabriel did not say, "49 years during which the city shall be rebuilt in troublous times, and from thence 434 years unto Messiah". No, he puts 49 and 434 together, making 483 unto Messiah, and then adds a *parenthetic* explanation of the first 49 years. The reason, of course, is that the coming of Christ is the overriding momentous event through Whose mediation of the new covenant all the promised blessings (of v. 24) are secured.

Parallels may be outlined thus:

Psa. 49. vv. 7, 9: "None . . . can give to God a ransom for him:
that he should live forever . . ."
v. 8 (parenthesis): "For the redemption is precious".
John 7: vv. 38, 40: "shall flow rivers of living water. Many of
the people, therefore, when they heard . . ."
v. 38 (parenthesis): "But this spake He of the Spirit . . ."
Daniel 9: vv. 26A and 27A: "After . . . Messiah shall be cut off:
And He shall cause to prevail . . ."
vv. 26B and 27B: "and the people of the prince . . . unto
the end desolations are determined. And for the over-
spreading of abominations, he shall make it desolate until
the consummation . . ."
vv. 25A and 26: ". . . commandment to restore and build
Jerusalem unto Messiah the Prince, 7 and 62 sevens . . .
and after the 62 Messiah cut off".
v. 25B (parenthesis referring to the 7 sevens): "the street
. . . in troublous times".

The time-parenthesis view requires that the pronoun,
"he" (v. 27) be referred back to a Roman prince, and,
therefore, connects the person of the last seven with
events not within the sevens at all but in the proposed
parenthesis. Thus it presents the incongruity of associating the armies of A.D. 70 with a coming prince, say,
two thousand years in the future, not yet arrived A.D.
1964! The events of the seventy sevens must be confined within their own bounds. The person of the 70th
seven, whoever he may be, must be the person of the
69th seven, whoever he may be; but not a person forty
years removed from these boundaries and in the
parenthesis.

It is insisted in support of the time-parenthesis theory
that Gabriel's announcement strictly concerned Daniel's
people and city, and cannot refer to the Gospel in general. Was not Daniel's burden for his captive people
and ruined city relieved by the assurance that the proximate event, for which the time was divided, would be
the turning of their captivity? But Gabriel's message,
the divine burden, was the true hope in Christ, in preparation for which the rehabilitation of the nation was a
providential necessity, for "of Israel, as concerning the
flesh, Christ came" and "our Lord sprang out of Judah".
Moreover, Jerusalem is the city "where also our Lord

was crucified". As He approached the time of His being "cut off", Caiaphas prophesied "that one man should die for the people, that the whole nation perish not". He thus spoke of the death of Christ, Who would thereby "gather together in one the children of God that were scattered abroad" (John 11:49-52; 18:14). Thus also was anticipated Paul's revelation that by His death Christ broke down the middle wall of partition and made both one. Daniel's people, in the decision of the New Testament, were not the unbelieving but the remnant, to which in Daniel's day he belonged, and to these only the blessings of v. 24 applied. The covenant was made for the "many". Isaiah confirms this (ch. 53), so did the Lord Jesus (Matt. 26:28); and so does Paul, quoting Isaiah and Hosea, declaring the divine principle of differentiation and selection (Rom. 9-11).

The payment of the ransom completed on the cross, accomplishing and confirming the promises of Daniel 9:24, the Gospel was preached to Israel "first", that is, to Daniel's people; and the apostles were commissioned to "begin at Jerusalem", that is, Daniel's city (Luke 24:47; Acts 1:8). Their preaching was effectual "in demonstration of the Spirit and of power" unto the outcalling of "many". Eventually, the chosen remnant, the firstfruits from the twelve tribes were reached and saved, the nucleus of the Church (Jas. 1:1, 18; Rev. 14:4). They were the first citizens of the commonwealth of grace, to whom believers are added without distinction, for they all are Daniel's people: Daniel belongs to them and they to Daniel (Heb. 11:33-40). There is no promise in Gabriel's prediction of an earthly establishment again for Israel as a nation: not the slightest surmise or sign of it. Dispensational guesswork superimposes it upon the gap, but Gabriel is silent about the whole thing.

By divine decree 490 years were to run between Jerusalem's rebuilding and the coming and crucifixion of the Messiah. Within that period, and three-and-a-half years after His manifestation but before the expiry of the whole, the blessings announced would be by Him secured. History verifies the reliability of the prediction and accuracy of the chronology. The Hebrew apostles were commissioned to preach this Gospel first to the Jews and at Jerusalem. This they did, agreeably with Gabriel's Gospel and, as it would have been, to Daniel's delight. Therefore, we read the representative passages: "Unto you *first*, God, having raised up His Son Jesus, sent Him to bless you in turning away everyone of you from his iniquities. The God of our fathers raised up Jesus, Whom ye slew and hanged on a tree. Him hath God exalted with His right hand to be a *Prince* and a *Saviour* for to give repentance *to Israel* and forgiveness of sins" (Acts 3:26; 5:30, 31; Dan. 9:24).

DISPENSATIONALIST
MISCONSTRUCTIONS

THE HEADING IS ITSELF an admonition, and we are not ourselves unmindful of the danger, desiring always to be amenable to the Scripture of Truth. It is our experience that Christians accept proposed proof-texts very superficially, and mostly without themselves searching the Scriptures whether these things be so. Texts are claimed as declaring this and that when neither that nor this is within the text. We proceed to comment with some recapitulation upon examples of misconstruction, introduced to us or which we have happened upon in current prophetic papers and magazines since the previous articles were written.

We quote: "God promised that through Abraham and his seed all nations would be blessed. Through the Lord Jesus Christ many individuals from many nations have been blessed; but the whole Jewish nation must yet be a blessing to all the nations of the world. This is God's promise for Israel in the millennium" (Gen. 22:16-18, etc.).

It is implied that saving blessing during a Jewish millennium will be greater, as nations are greater than individuals, than through present worldwide Gospel ministry; that Jewish nationalism will somehow effect results in excess of Christian evangelization. We must bear in mind that, howsoever the millennium is understood, upon its expiry the nations from the four quarters

223

of the earth in number as the sand of the sea will be found in rebellion against Christ and His people (Rev. 20). The failure of Christendom, therefore, which futurism expects, would seem to be followed by the failure of a Jewish millennium!

In the promised seed God neither said nor meant the construction above quoted. "He saith not, 'And to seeds', as of many, but as of one, 'and to thy Seed', which is Christ" (Gal. 3:16). If the seed intended had been a plurality, whether by Hagar, Sarah, Keturah, or Isaac, Jacob, Esau, He would have said "seeds". But this "He saith not" because He meant none of them, not even the twelve tribes of Israel. He said "Seed" because He meant Christ. The Spirit's guarded inspiration omitted one letter which made all the difference, the purpose being "that the blessing of Abraham might come on the *nations*—not through the Jews, but— through Jesus Christ". Moreover, the means of blessing to the nations is plainly stated, namely, the same Gospel of justification by faith, which by Scripture foresight was preached before unto Abraham (Gal. 3:8; Rom. 4:16).

The failure and rejection of the disobedient Israel nation as God's witness to the nations is on record in a context which by contrast calls the attention of all nations unto earth's end to the ideal "Israel", the "true and faithful Witness", God's Servant and Messiah, *the* Seed of Abraham, by Whose redemption all without distinction are blessed. The time is the present "acceptable time", the "day of salvation", and not a fictitious future after His second advent. This God said through His prophet, and this, the apostles explain, is what He meant (Isa. 48:49; Acts 13:47; 2 Cor. 6:2).

Pre-eminently, Abraham's Seed is Christ. Consequently, all blessed in Christ are Abraham's spiritual seed. These are a new creation whom Paul calls "the Israel of God" (Gal. 6:15, 16). Jews, racially, naturally, outwardly, are not now in God's esteem, the seed or children of Abraham, any more than Ishmael and Esau; Zimran, Jokshan, Medan, Midian, and Shuah (Gen. 25:1-2; Matt. 3:9; John 8:37, 44; Acts 13:41;

Rom. 2:28, 29; 9:6-8; Rev. 2:9; 3:9). The Israel nation's service to God and the world ceased with the coming of Christ, in which sense, as He said, "salvation is of the Jews", for He Himself was the end or object of the law in its wide embrace and significance (Rom. 9:5; John 4:22; Rom. 10:4).

Moses and David both declare that the covenant made with Abraham and the fathers He "commanded to a thousand generations". The covenant, however, is not unconditional, as is often said (see Scofield), for Moses added: "if ye hearken and keep and do the judgments", "the Lord shall keep unto thee the covenant and mercy which He sware unto thy fathers". The gift of Canaan is included "for an everlasting possession", the covenant also being "everlasting". As, therefore, the true "Seed" was not the Jews but Christ, so "Canaan" was not the true inheritance, but the "heavenly country", and this the patriarchs understood. Moreover, if literalness is a guiding principle, may not "a thousand years", named only in a book of symbols and figures, also indicate a prolonged and indefinite period (Deut. 7:9-12; Psa 105:6-11; Gen. 17:7, 8; Heb. 11: 8-16)?

As to the extent of the land the claim is made, and we quote, "God promised to Abraham a material kingdom, the size and glory of which have never yet been realized. Such promises require resurrection for their fulfilment. Abraham, Isaac and Jacob must be raised from the dead to receive this inheritance". The Scofield Bible has a note discriminating between "river" and "border" in support of this theory, whereas a boundary was commonly determined by the course of a river. Of 2 Chronicles 9:26 he says, "to the border of Egypt, but not to the river of Egypt, yet to be fulfilled". He had only to turn back a page to read that the "border" was, indeed, the "river" (2 Chron. 7:8).

The evidence of Moses, Joshua, Samuel, David, Solomon and Nehemiah is conclusive. The original promise was literally fulfilled to the letter. It is, therefore, a matter of history that the land was possessed "from the river of Egypt unto the great river, the river Euphrates" (Gen. 15:18; Exod. 23:31; Deut. 8:8-21; 11:24; Josh. 15:4-23; 21:43-45; 23:15, 16; 2 Sam. 8:3; 1 Kings

4:21-24; 2 Chron. 7:8; 9:26; Neh. 9:7, 8).

The patriarchal hope, the New Testament avers, was not a material kingdom at all, but a heavenly country, the promise of which was "embraced" (Heb. 11). It is also true that the state of immortality, the spiritual resurrection body, is not compatible with material conditions (1 Cor. 15). Perhaps, if we could enquire of Abraham he would answer something like this: "I would not change my blest estate for all the Jews call good and great; and with the heavenly country's joys, I covet not fair Canaan's toys".

What, then, is the inheritance of the natural seed of Abraham? The remnant of the twelve tribes are by divine ordination and grace within the Church. Thus they enter into the true "rest", which the nation failed to do under Moses and Joshua and David because of unbelief (Jas. 1:1; 2:5; Heb. 4). Chosen of God, redeemed from Egypt, conducted through the wilderness, settled in Canaan, guided along a distinguished and typical course, as was no other nation, their appointments and providences were all "for His Name's sake", that is, for the unveiling of Jehovah in His character, purpose, activity, recorded in the oracles of God committed to their trust. The unique and miraculous history of national Israel was completed, and the goal reached. That goal is Christ (Exod. 33:18-23; 34:5-8; Deut. 4:7, 8, 31-40; Rom. 3:2; 9:5).

The Church in heavenly glory, Jerusalem above, is the habitation of all the faithful from the beginning. They all shall be "made perfect" together. On her gates and foundations are inscribed the names of the twelve tribes of Israel and the twelve apostles of the Lamb (Heb. 11:12; Rev. 21:12-14). Through the twelve tribes the way of the Lord was prepared; through the twelve apostles the foundation of the Church was laid. There is no tribal succession; there is no apostolic succession. The twelve tribes have no future earthly country; the twelve apostles have no future earthly calling. The appointed service of Israel closed with the appearing of Christ, and the ordained ministry of the apostles finished with the founding of His Church. The Old Testament was Israel's preparation for Christ and

His Gospel; the New Testament is the apostolic exposition of Christ and His Church. The twelve tribes withdraw, the Saviour has come, good tidings to all people. The twelve apostles withdraw, the Spirit has come, poured out on all flesh. So, the abiding commemoration of both Old and New Testament revelation, both twelve tribes and twelve apostles, is represented in their inscription upon the gates and foundations of the Eternal City. "Behold, I make all things new".

— — — — — — — — — — —

A Hebrew-Christian editor writes as follows: "In Deuteronomy 4:25-31 and chapter 28, God definitely said that Israel, after remaining a long time in the land and being blessed there, would turn to idols and be cursed. This is what just did happen, and the curse of being scattered from their land is still upon them. However, in Deuteronomy 4:29 and 30:1-10 Moses wrote that *a time would come* when Israel among the nations would return and repent, and then they would be brought back to their land for blessing. These are the promises reiterated by all the prophets and confirmed in Romans 11:25-27."

It is to be observed that these words ignore the conditional character of the Scriptures cited. Wrote Moses: "*If* from thence thou shalt seek the Lord thy God with all thy heart and with all thy soul: *if* thou turn to the Lord thy God and be obedient to His voice: *then* the Lord will turn thy captivity and gather thee from among the nations: *if* thou shalt hearken unto the voice of the Lord thy God, and *if* thou turn unto the Lord thy God". Genuine conversion is here expressed, not as a post-return blessing but as an essential prelude to it, while scattered among the nations. Moses' conditions for restoration were honoured in the return from the Babylonian exile (e.g. Ezek. 36:32-38), . . . "I will yet be enquired of by the house of Israel to do it for them". Thus did their captive leaders penitently confess and seek His mercy. Upon return they were sorely tested by the enemy, but their backslidings were healed through the ministry of Zechariah and Haggai, especially raised up to encourage them, "the prophets of God helping them" (Ezra 5:1-2). The very tenor of these writings suggests, as of course direct prophecies declare the anticipation of the Redeemer's coming and work, the Gospel, and the dispensation of the Holy Spirit. The Israeli conjectured fulfilment at the present time, judged by these Mosaic and prophetic pre-return conditions, is weighed and found wanting.

Paul, who is claimed in support, also wrote conditionally: "*If* they abide not still in unbelief". Moreover, the very language of Moses as to Israel's "return" (cf. Hos. 7:16) is used by Paul to show that God meant what He said in Moses but said what He meant in the Gospel, and, therefore, quoting Moses' authority to buttress his argument, Paul wrote to the Jews in particular: "*If* thou shalt confess with thy mouth the Lord Jesus, and believe in thine heart that God hath raised Him from the dead, thou shalt be saved". This, according to Paul, written in the midst of his classic treatment of the Jewish problem, is what Moses' words signified, to hearken to the voice of the Lord (for "faith cometh by hearing the Word of God"), to be obedient, to seek the Lord with all the heart and soul. This was Paul's insistence, that by preaching and believing the Gospel, and nothing else, could "the hope of Israel" be fulfilled to his kinsmen according to the flesh (Rom. 9-11).

— — — — — — — — — — —

Psalm 89, being Messianic, is dispensationally treated as millennial. It is reasoned that as upon His ascension Christ sat down in His Father's throne, so at His future descent He will sit upon David's throne, otherwise, "His Own throne"! The Psalm is "the confirmation and exposition of the Davidic covenant, and looks beyond David". This is true, but it may the rather be described as evangelical, fulfilled in Christ ascended, His work finished on the cross, proclaimed now in the new covenant of the "joyful sound" (v. 15). It is written, not of Solomon, though there is proximate reference to him, but of Christ" of the seed of David according to the flesh, declared to be the Son of God with power according to the Spirit of holiness by the resurrection from the dead", and "Remember Jesus Christ, of the seed of David, raised from the dead according to my gospel". "The Scriptural ideal is not like that of the poets. They take the things of earth and lift them up to heaven. The Bible does the very opposite; it takes the invisible only as reality and the visible simply as the shadow of real things. It considers all things from God's point of view" (Adolphe Monod, 1855).

According to the New Testament David's covenanted blessings are Gospel mercies, bestowed through faith in a risen, reigning Saviour (Isa. 55:3-4; Acts 13:33-34; Psa. 89:1-2). Accordingly we read, "Blessed is the people that know the joyful sound" (the Gospel), that understand and appreciate the spiritual benefits symbolized in the festivals to which the people were summoned by the trumpets (Psa. 89:15 with Lev. 23:25).

"I will make Him My firstborn, higher than the kings of the earth" (v. 27). The title is given to Christ, firstborn of all creation, as Creator; "as firstborn He has pre-eminency among the children, so Christ is He to whom pre-eminency belongs. The pre-eminent One, the firstborn, the King of kings, are His titles of excellence". He is "firstborn among many brethren", therefore, "He is not ashamed to call them brethren"; they constitute "the church of the firstborn" and are the "many sons" He is bringing to glory (Rom. 8:29; Col. 1:14-18; Heb. 1:6; 2: 10, 11; 12:23).

As the Firstborn He is "higher than the kings of the earth", for His throne, "the throne of the Lord", is "established in the very heavens". So that upon His enthronement, "from the seven Spirits which are before His throne, and from Jesus Christ Who is the faithful Witness, the first-begotten from the dead and Prince of the kings of the earth", His apocalypse is given, for there on the antitypical throne of David He reigns in excellent glory. The words are parallel. No thronal type on earth is for Him. He is Reality, "How well Thy blessed truths agree" (Psa. 89:2, 4, 5, 14, 18, 19, 27, 29, 36, 37; Rev. 1:4, 5).

We are justified therefore, in esteeming the throne of David in Jerusalem, with the temple and all other institutions of a typical and preparatory age, as "patterns" of heavenly realities. The originals were in heaven and still are, and Christ's is not to be the humiliating association with a reinstitution of the "beggarly elements". David himself understood this and wrote thereof by inspiration in his last words. The covenant is "everlasting", not for a measured thousand years, and fulfills all David's desire and salvation, though he did not expect to see it on earth or to be realized in his own house (2 Sam. 23). Confirmation was undoubtedly given by the same Spirit through Peter at Pentecost, who quoted David as understanding that "of the fruit of his loins according to the flesh" would Messiah be raised from the dead "to sit on his throne". Christ, therefore, reasons the Apostle by the Spirit, and not David, "ascended into the heavens" being "by the right hand of God exalted". By this, His ascension to the throne, "let all the house of Israel know assuredly that God hath made that same Jesus, whom ye have crucified, both Lord and Messiah" (Acts 2).

In antithesis to the establishment of the throne of David in the heavens by terms of the covenant of grace, a lamentation is written for the ruination of David's throne on earth. "But Thou hast cast off and abhorred; Thou hast been wroth with Thine anointed; Thou hast profaned his crown by casting it to the ground; Thou hast made his glory to cease and cast his throne down to the ground". Surely, "He taketh away the first that He may establish the second". God's pleasure is realized not in David but in Christ, and of this David also wrote (Heb. 10:7-9; from Psa. 40). Finally, it is complained: "Lord, where are Thy former lovingkindnesses which Thou swarest unto David in Thy truth?" Where indeed? The answer is in the foregoing, the everlasting establishment of the throne of the Lord Jesus Christ" in the very heavens" of which David's in Jerusalem was set up as a figure. As lasting as that glory are the lovingkindnesses of the Gospel. Hence, the final word of the Psalmist, "Blessed be the Lord for evermore" (vv. 38-52).

——— ——— ——— ——— ——— ——— ——— ——— ———

Of the Scripture forecast of the sufferings of the Lord Jesus Christ, we quote the claim which has no Scriptural support:: "The Jewish nation will yet say it as their confession: the application is for us now" (Isa. 53).

The prophecy, since so remarkably fulfilled, is introduced by the effect upon "many nations" (Isa. 52:13-15). It commences, "Who hath believed our report?", which Paul interprets of the Gospel now preached for the sake of faith which cometh through hearing the Word of God (Rom. 10:6). In demonstration of its effectuality, Philip the evangelist from this chapter preached Christ, not to a Jew, but to an enquiring Ethiopian, who through its virtue believed and was baptized and "went on his way rejoicing" (Acts 8). Apparently the evangelist but "applied" the Gospel, not strictly for a Gentile!

So far as the Jews were concerned, being stiffnecked, obstinate, unbelieving, our Lord used these words, not as a confession of their faith, but as confirming their unbelief, the very reverse of the Jewish futurist claim, for "though He had done so many mighty works before them—though He demonstrated the proofs of His Messiahship (Luke 7:19-22)—yet believed they not on Him, that the saying of Isaiah the prophet might be *fulfilled* which he spake, Lord, who hath believed our report?" (John 12:37-41, quoting Isaiah again from chapter 53).

The words have a Gospel context, report or record and faith are essentials and are opposed to sight and sign and demonstration. Faith so-called, born of the latter, our Lord rejected (John 2:8). And did He not say to sight-seeing doubting Thomas, "Blessed are they who have not seen and yet have believed"? Abraham's faith is the pattern, and should be especially to those who prided themselves upon their descent from him. Abraham "staggered not at the promise of God through unbelief". It is sometimes also claimed that Paul's conversion was a foreview of his nation's. But when Paul spoke of himself as "one born out of due time", his reference was to his apostleship:: "the least of the apostles" (1 Cor. 15:8-9). When he does relate his conversion, he was a "pattern", not for Jewish national conversion at the Second Advent, but "to them that should hereafter believe". Hence, being "of sinners the chief" and having "obtained mercy", he commended the faithful saying that Christ Jesus came into the world to save sinners as being "worthy of all acceptation" (1 Tim. 1).

If the words do form a confession, they truly befit every penitent heart hearing the Gospel report or reading the written record, every sinner genuinely converted believing the report, who worships as he reviews "how deep were the waters crossed, and how dark was the night that the Lord passed through ere He found His sheep that was lost". But we search in vain for any Biblical futuristic ascription of this chapter to the Jewish nation. It belongs to Christ's Church.

— — — — — — — — — —

It may be relevant at this point to comment upon the complaint so frequently made, and repeated in the sources already referred to, What saith the Scriptures as to the blessings of grace and the curse of the law? "The law and the gospel are two keys", remarked a Puritan preacher: "the law is the key which locks sinners up to condemnation: the gospel is the key which opens the door to their freedom". That curses should be pronounced upon the Jews and blessings upon the Church, of course, may appear inequitable, and the Bible is, if anything, a balanced book. Turning at random the pages of the Old Testament, the following headlines met our gaze: Judgment upon Jews; Calamity of Jews; Curses for disobedience; Blessings for obedience; Jews and Gentiles threatened; Christ promised; the Remnant saved; the Privilege of the Church; the Church's complaint; the Church's confidence in God; God's majesty in the Church. If, of course, the assertion were true that "the Church nowhere appears in the Old Testament", the headlines are wrong. The curse is, indeed, solemnly pronounced upon Jews who are found in unbelief and disobedience: it is removed only in the grace of the Gospel. But not to the Jews only for now "there is no difference between the Jew and the Gentile" and "cursed is *everyone* that continueth not in all things that are written in the book of the law to do them".

On the other hand, it is true that God's blessings are upon the Church, and for the Church only. All her members are saved by grace. The Jews, "the remnant according to the election of grace", the remnant which in the Old Testament is repeatedly distinguished from the apostate nation, are blessed as Gentiles are blessed, only by union with Christ, and therefore, in His Church. Together, believers all in Christ Jesus are denationalized, but "blessed with all spiritual blessings in heavenly places in Him". On the unbelieving, without distinction of race, the curse remains. Sinners of all races are blessed through faith in Him. Bible headings may not be wrong.

— — — — — — — — — — —

The words, "Behold, I am the Lord, the God of all flesh, is there anything too hard for Me?" are as a rejoinder to the prophet, whose earlier asseveration, "there is nothing too hard for Thee", was supported by his taking account of God's omnipotence, wisdom, and faithfulness; recalling His creative power; His providential conducting of His chosen Israel, miraculously redeeming them from Egypt and bringing them through the wilderness to establish them in the land promised to their fathers (Jer. 32). Now, however, they were at the point of being expelled; the judgment had already commenced for after longsuffering and repeated remonstrance, misused and mocked, "there was no remedy" (2 Chron. 36). The evil events prophesied weighed upon the prophet's heart in heavy grief; yet redemption would come at the appointed time in the people's return, re-establishment, possession and prosperity. Scattered Israel would be gathered home again. This assurance given by the Lord, Who, being also "the God of all flesh", had all nations in His control, was set over against a measured captivity of seventy years, upon the expiry of which, no less and no more, He would, to use the words of another prophet, "set His hand again the second time to recover the remnant of His people" (Isa. 11:11-16).

This, as was the case with the first deliverance, and as is the burden of all prophecy, was necessary to Messiah's coming. He would come to effect the real and eternal redemption. Described as the "stem of Jesse", the "Branch" to grow out of his roots, the fulfilment is given in His first advent, recognized and by inspiration testified, "whereby the dayspring (branch) from on high hath visited us" (Isa. 11; Jer. 33; Mic. 7; Heb. 4; Luke 1). This is the longer view of prophecy, of which Jeremiah's context, and also Isaiah's, take account. But the proximate chastisement would not be prolonged beyond the seventy years. All nations served Babylon as God determined, and among them all Israel was scattered (Jer. 25:12; 27:5-8). But "He that scattered Israel will gather him", and "out of all the countries whither I have driven them in Mine anger, saith the Lord" (Jer. 31:10; 32:37). It is to be noted that another and final "scattering" was predicted upon them by the rejected Messiah, without promise of a further regathering (Luke 21:24).

We are challenged by a Hebrew-Christian writer, who postpones fulfilment to the 20th century, "not to spiritualize this". There is no Scriptural case for so doing. Nor is there any case for his postponement from the stated time of which Jeremiah wrote unto a conjectured period two-and-a-half millenniums beyond the prophet's time. God scattered Israel for seventy years: He also gathered Israel after the seventy years. To impress the reliability of this promise upon Jeremiah's tender heart, the Lord pre-advised him of an event he never would have expected. His relative would arrive, requesting him to purchase in accord with his right of redemption property which, if not already in the enemy's hands, would assuredly be so. It was located in Anathoth. Human wisdom doubtless would consider this a most imprudent and foolish proposition. However, having been instructed by the foreknowing word of God, the business was legally signed, sealed and settled.

At the expiry of the seventy years God fulfilled His promise, and "men bought fields, subscribed evidences and sealed them, and took witnesses in the land of Benjamin, and in places about Jerusalem, and in the cities of Judah" (Jer. 32:43-44). This restoration, for there is nothing too hard for the Lord, "out of the hand of the Chaldeans", Scripture and history verify. In face of this historical fulfilment we are asked to believe that here is "the future of the Jews according to Scripture", the fanciful suggestion being made that Jeremiah's "earthen vessel" in which the documents were preserved according to custom, during the "many days" of the seventy years, "may yet be discovered by archaeologists", for "fields must be acquired before the second advent of Christ" because in the Millennium "Christ will be reigning and He does not sell anything"!! And it is added, "that when in 1922 a national home for the Jews was announced, then commenced the time for buying fields. High prices were paid to Arab landlords for their soil". So, the complement to the predicted seventy years' "scattering" was not the duly implemented "gathering" at its expiry about B.C. which Scripture testifies but by the expulsion of the Arabs in A.D. 1922!!

The prophet's nephew had said, "Buy my field, I pray thee, that is in Anathoth . . . for the right of inheritance is thine, and the redemption is thine: buy it for thyself". And if Jeremiah himself did not repossess it, his "heirs and assigns" surely did (cf. Ruth and Boaz). The assurance thus was given that tribal and family inheritances would again be instituted upon the exiled nation's release from captivity. And indeed they were. Included in these were Anathoth and those who legally could claim redeemed property (See Ezra 2:23; Neh. 7:17; Jer. 1:1; 29:10-14; 30:8-10; 32:8).

It has already been said that the burden of all prophecy is the Lord Jesus Christ and that, in Him God says what He means. In the immediate context of this Scripture we are directed, not to any Jewish national resettlement beyond that of the post-captivity return, but to the great event unto which that return was appointed, namely, the First Advent of the Redeemer, His incarnation and virgin birth, with the grievous and hostile circumstances occasioned thereby through Herod's malice; to the Saviour's obedience and blood, procuring the blessings of the new covenant to the house of Judah and Israel, by means of the Gospel, so that by the covenant ministry of the apostles, Israel in her "twelve tribes", united in Christ, were the "first" so to be blessed, "a kind of firstfruits of His creatures" (cf. the ref. Jer. 31:15 with Matt. 2:18; Jer. 31:22 with Isa. 7:14 and Matt. 1:23; Jer. 31:31-34 with Heb. 8 and 10; 2 Cor. 3; Acts 2:5; 26:6, 7; Rom. 9:24; Eph. 2; Jas. 1:1; 1 Pet. 1:1, etc.).

— — — — — — — — — —

"The abomination of desolation spoken of by Daniel the Prophet", to which the Lord Jesus Christ added his own predictive confirmation, was then a future event which long since has passed into history. To dispensationalists this is not so. They associate it with the act of the man of sin (2 Thess. 2) and the last seven years of the Messianic time-table, a total of 490 years, revealed to the prophet (see previous chapters), by breaking the connection with a prolonged parenthesis, beginning and ending with the coming of the Lord in two stages, "for" and "with" His saints.

How did the prophetic confirmation arise? His attention having been directed to the attractiveness of Jerusalem's temple, our Lord predicted its overthrow, whereupon the apostles, apparently associating this with His own Messianic advent, enquired as to the time of the catastrophe and the sign of His c o m i n g. They rightly understood that His coming would be at the end of the world, and these they related in the question. They may have wrongly thought of this as coincident with the destruction of the temple, and indeed, our Lord's answer showed like characteristics. The first part of His informative answer concerned the course of the world, especially as affecting His Church, unto the end. He thereupon depicted the nearer event of judgment upon the Jewish nation which rejected Him. According to His forewarning word, and by His Own sovereign administration "when He ascended on high", the desolation of the city and temple took place with the evil accompaniments He forecast.

It is historically recorded that the unparalleled tribulation spoken of in our Lord's prediction was visited upon the Jews when the Roman destruction took effect about 70 A.D. It is said that the "abomination" indicates an act of profanation or idolatry. Luke associates this with the Roman encompassing "armies", of which Daniel also had written, "with the abominable armies" (Dan. 9:26-27 mg.). The Church of Pentecost, located in Jerusalem, chiefly Hebrew-Christian, aware of and acting upon her Lord's instructions given in this discourse, escaped the terrible destruction. The Jews, however, ignoring His directions, crowded into Jerusalem, and over a million perished. The Jewish historian, Josephus, has recorded these events, by no means written to confirm the words of Christ, yet it is remarkable how they do so in much detail. And yet again, is it remarkable in view of the fact that the Lord "watcheth over His word to perform it"? Josephus writes of a false prophet declaring miraculous (but false) signs of deliverance; of a great number of false prophets, seducers, bidding the Jews wait for the deliverance of God; that the miserable people were persuaded by such deceivers; that they did not give credit to the signs; that a star resembling a sword stood over the city and a comet continued a whole year; that at the feast of unleavened bread, a great light shone round the altar for half-an-hour; that before sun-setting chariots and troops of soldiers in their armour were seen running about among the clouds; that the Jews came upon an ambiguous oracle in their sacred writings; that about that time one from their country would become governor of the habitable earth, which they took to belong to themselves in particular, and they interpreted some of the signals according to their own pleasure. Further, the Romans brought their ensigns to the temple and set them over against its eastern gate, and there did they offer sacrifices to them, and there did they make Titus *imperator* (Prince, Dan. 9:26?).

The tribulation arising in connection with the desolating abomination, therefore, is past, and the predictions of Daniel and his Lord are verified. Postponement to the yet future is unwarranted. The association of evidently future events respecting Christ's coming with the past-event of Jerusalem's destruction, which arose from the apostles' enquiry, and which seems to appear in our Lord's answer, may be explained by the revelation to Peter that to the mind of the Eternal God there is no distinction between a thousand years and a day. The Coming may be spoken of as though it were a related event, which, indeed, in the question, it was. "That day seems to us short-lived beings long in arriving, but with the Lord the interval is irrespective of any idea of long or short" (Jamieson).

There are several mentions of affliction or tribulation in this reply of our Lord. "The tribulation of those days" may be the sum total of the Church's endurance during her universal preaching of the Gospel from the time of the commission unto the end. The whole passage portends perilous times among all nations, probably increasing in intensity at the end. This would be accordant with "the great tribulation", great in extent. Tribulation is common to all generations of believers, the experience of the Church in all parts of the world as she has faithfully borne witness for Christ. Those who determine to live godly in Christ Jesus shall suffer persecution (2 Tim. 3:12). To suffer for His sake is as much God's appointment for His people as is faith. Believers rejoice in tribulation for Christ's sake, and there is no promise of release from it until the Coming of the Lord, giving "rest" to His oppressed people, "taking vengeance" upon their foes in the same day (Acts 14:22; 2 Tim. 3:12; 1 Pet. 2:21; Phil. 1:29; Rom. 5:3; 2 Thess. 1). Tribulation may not be upon the world, but arise from the world; certainly "in the world". It comprises any form of testing permitted to the saints for His Name's sake. It may be common; it may be exceptional, "much'" or "great", which may denote its extent through all operations as well as, perhaps, its intensity at times or at the end. It is called "the tribulation of the saints," and the apostle John, who wrote of Christ's Apocalypse and addressed it to "the churches", was himself their "companion in tribulation" (John 14; Matt. 5:10-12; Rev. 12:12; 1 Thess. 5; Rev. 1:9). It is not to be confused with divine wrath from which believers are saved. It may be occasioned, however, by Satanic wrath. Out of tribulation believers will be rescued. The redemption of spirit, soul and body will be entire (1 Thess. 5:23; Rev. 7:14).

Circumstances will prepare the Church for Christ's coming. She may not know the "day or hour", but she will recognize the signal of His approach (Heb. 10:25). It will not be in "secret"; He has anticipated this deceit with a denial, nor can it be at any moment.

It is impossible that Paul was guilty of "the contradiction of Christ" when he declared, "this we say unto you by the word of the Lord" (Matt. 24:26; 1 Thess. 4). His mention of the "carcase" and "eagles" may time the event with "the supper of the great God"; in any case, when the hour is come "He will not tarry" (Matt. 24:28; Rev. 19:17; Heb. 10:37). The budding fig tree, harbinger of summer, is His illustration in the Gospel's context. This tree, however, is not intended, as so many assume, and was never said to portend a revival of Jewish nationalism. By the budding fig "ye know that summer is nigh", so "when ye shall see all these things, know that He is near". In His full statement, to "the fig tree and all the trees" direction is called. There is no special reference to a Jewish revival, therefore, for "all the trees" alike serve His purpose (Matt. 24:32-33; Luke 21:29)!

His coming will be "as the lightning", that is His corrective of all false theories, illuminating from east to west, and maybe destructive also. For it is not to be overlooked that whereas Christ prospects no earthly or millennial reign in His Olivet discourse (or elsewhere), He does however foretell—and significant it is— in association with His coming, *the passing away of the heavens and the earth*, that is, the dissolution of all that is temporal to give place to the eternal. "Heaven and earth shall pass away, but My words shall not pass away" (Matt. 24:35). Noah and the judgment of the deluge, Lot and consuming judgment by fire, deliverance and destruction in "the same day": these are His forewarnings. Peter, who heard his Lord thus speak, wrote of and repeated the same facts respecting "the promise of His coming", with the passing of the heavens and the earth, "reserved unto fire against" this same "day", and by "the same word", which shall never pass away (Luke 17:23-30; 2 Pet. 3). The apostle John, who also heard his Lord's Olivet discourse on earth, received His confirming testimony from heaven, agreeable as to time, manner and consequence. This he was to communicate to "the churches". The facts are thus established in the mouths of many witnesses. At His coming His redeemed the world over shall be rescued from and recompensed for all their tribulation for His sake. The flaming fire of vengeance shall equitably reward His enemies, all then subdued unto Him, and the last, death itself. Then shall heaven and earth pass away. Until then His word shall sustain the universe that His purpose may be completed. All is graphically brought to the issue in "the revelation of Jesus Christ", confirming His Own testimony on earth and that of His apostles. Relieved of dispensational confusion, therefore, one Second Coming is indicated, "when He shall have delivered up the kingdom to God, even the Father" (Matt. 24:35; 2 Pet. 3:7-12; Luke 17:29-30; 2 Thess. 1:8; 1 Cor. 3:13; Rev. 20:9; Heb. 12:29; 1 Cor. 15:24).

With these words "so all Israel shall be saved", the apostle approaches the conclusion of his treatise respecting the salvation of his kinsmen according to the flesh (Rom. 9-11). He had already written in these chapters of "Israel" and her "blindness." He placed in opposition the elect or remnant appointed to salvation and "the rest" in their hardened spiritual condition, quoting David and Isaiah in support, and Elijah in analogy. Summing up, he reaffirms the abiding blindness or hardening of this "part" of the nation. And then, "as touching the election" (11:28), he intimates *the manner* in which all "Israel shall be saved." For this "all Israel" must of necessity be qualified by the apostle's initial ruling, involving divine election, that "they are not all Israel which are of Israel" or "children of the promise" (9:6-13).

The apostle has also defined his understanding and use of the word "salvation". It is not of the nation as such that he speaks, the salvation of restored national status in Palestine, but spiritual and eternal salvation individually conferred by the grace of faith confessed in the Lord Jesus Christ (10:9,10). This salvation he had himself received, and he sought it for his brethren with earnest desire. Of this one and only salvation for "all Israel" he expresses confidence, and he extols the wisdom of God, the Source and Means and End of all things (11:33-36).

But *how* shall their salvation be effectuated? It is here that we meet with a misconstruing of the sense of the words. "SO all Israel shall be saved", is not the "so" of argument as, therefore; or the "so" of consequence as, thereupon. It signifies not time but *manner*. A familiar illustration of its use is, "For God *so* loved the world" (John 3:16). That is, He so loved after the manner typified in the uplifted serpent by Moses and fulfilled in the uplifted Son of God on the cross. It is as unwarrantable to interpret Romans 11:26 as though it read "And then all Israel shall be saved", as it would be John 3:16, "For God *then* loved the world". Yet Judaistic dispensationalism foists upon the Israel passage this meaning. For example, part of the "aim" of a missionary agency to Jews reads: "to prepare the nation for the time *when* 'the Redeemer shall come out of Sion and all Israel shall be saved' ". Thus the "when" of time is substituted for the qualifying "so" of the text which does not appear. Moreover, the Isaiah prophecy is given futurity, whereas Paul simply says, "as it is written", customarily quoting the Old Testament in support of his doctrine. In an earlier chapter we have shown that the text bears the sense, "The Redeemer shall come with respect to Sion". And He *has* come, as corresponding Scriptures bears witness (e.g. Isa. 28:16; 1 Pet. 2:6). The effect of His coming in "turning ungodliness from Jacob" and fulfilling the covenant to "take away sins" is made plain in other Scriptures and was proclaimed by the Gospel (Dan. 9:24; Matt. 2:21; Acts 3:26; 13:23, 32, 38-39; Heb. 8:12; 10:16-17).

The word "until" cannot be used in support of the substitution of "so" by "then", simply indicating, as it does, continuedness, fixing attention on the whole duration, and referring to the space of time intervening. It does not say that after Gentile fulness the "blindness" of the "part" will be removed, and that this is the salvation promised. If this were the intention it might well be asked, what of the many since Christ and since Paul who have passed into eternity, the blindness of unbelief still upon them? The answer was already supplied by the Lord Himself (John 8:21-24). In an earlier chapter examples of the use of "until" were given. In this Epistle we find the word in 5:13, which does not imply that sin was no longer in the world after the law; and in 8:22, which does not mean that the groaning of creation was discontinued after the apostle's time. Consistently, therefore, the word here does not declare blindness relieved after the incoming of the Gentiles.

In the words of Dr. Pieters, "It is important not to read Romans 11:26 as if it said, 'and *then* shall all Israel be saved'. The apostle does not say that. He says, 'and *so*'—after this manner—which involves no succession of time, but refers to the regathering, whether of many individuals or of a great body of people together, perhaps, at the same time that the Gentile fulness is being ingathered". Thus, Gentile Christians are warned against conceitedness, as before against highmindedness (11:20), as though thinking they alone were to come into the blessing of God; Israel's blindness is only "in part", and neither Jews nor Gentiles have Gospel advantage the one over the other: "there is no difference" in their guiltiness of sin or in the grace of salvation (Rom. 3:22-23; 10:12). And it is "through your (Gentiles) mercy that they (Jews) also may obtain mercy" (11:31); that is to say, by the instrumentality of believing Gentiles shall all Israel be saved.

If, therefore, "they are not all Israel which are of Israel" (9:6), then the "all Israel" (of 11:26) cannot include those who are the "not Israel" of this determining premise. It seems clear in the course of the apostle's reasoning in these three chapters that the "not all Israel" are the non-elect, "the rest" under judicial blindness (11:7), the "part" (11:25). It is equally clear that the "all Israel" (11:26) are the non-blinded, "the election of grace" (11:5), the reservation which has never ceased whatever the fluctuation of the people's fortunes, and which remains "at this present time" (11:5). "All Israel" are the equivalent of "their fulness", the elect of the nation. The elect out of all nations are the "fulness of the Gentiles". Therefore, simultaneously with the incoming of the fulness of the Gentiles through Gospel effectuality, Israel's elect are being ingathered, and will be, unto *their* fulness, by the same means. "Fulness" in neither case is a nation or nations as such. In neither case does it mean all without exception. Two conclusions are certain: one respecting the universal principle of "faith which cometh by hearing" the Gospel; thus, while God is able to ingraft the branches, this is conditioned by "if they abide not still in unbelief" (10:16-21; 11-23). The second is that no salvation is promised to the Jews subsequent to the incoming of Gentile fulness: these are simultaneously accomplished.

As before observed, to claim as prophetic fulfilment any return from among the nations in a state of non-repentance and unbelief is contrary to the fundamental condition laid down by Moses. The insistence that the Israeli state to-day is the Lord's doing in preparation for their conversion at His coming cannot be sustained. If, as Christian Judaisers hold, Romans 11:26 and the closing chapters of Zechariah are mutually explanatory, even then, the "all Israel" of Romans 11:26 cannot be the nation in entirety, for "two parts shall be cut off and die", and the "third part" only purified "through the fire'". These only are God's people, the remnant (Zech. 13:8-9). God's aggregate is determined by His distinguishing grace. The "firstfruit" are those gathered to the Christian Church at the beginning, even as the apostle himself desired that he might be instrumental, "if by any means I might save some of them" (11:14-16; Jas. 1:1, 18; Rev. 14:4). The full harvest, "the lump," will have been ingathered simultaneously with the incoming of Gentile fulness. Thus it is demonstrated, and will be, that "the gifts and calling of God are without repentance" (11:29). He means what He says, and we need not, therefore, be "ignorant of this mystery" for He also says what He means.

— — — — — — — — — — —

At many points premillennialism appears to misconstrue the testimony of Scripture. We quote again from a recent article: "God is still on the throne: we pray that soon He will send back His dear Son to reign publicly until all His enemies are under His feet". This, of course, is another example of millennial earthly kingdom fallacy. The Scriptures do not assert that Christ will be "sent back" by descent to earth "to reign publicly" and so to subjugate all His foes, but that upon His ascension after the cross He "sat down" at God's right hand in heaven where He reigns perpetually until the conquest is finished. And all is due to His victory in death and resurrection.

The words addressed by God to His Son, "Sit Thou at My right hand until I make Thine enemies Thy footstool" appear by quotation and adaptation a number of times in the New Testament. In their first occurrence David recognizes that his promised Messianic Son is also his sovereign Lord, but he did not predict for Him a reign on earth, but in heaven (Psa. 110:1). By His use of this inspired writing the Lord Jesus "put to silence the ignorance of foolish men" (Matt. 22:44-46; Mark 12:36; Luke 20:42-43). His introduction, "What think ye of Christ? whose son is he?" is a vital matter still.

'What think ye of Christ?' is the test
To try both your thought and your scheme;
You cannot be right in the rest
Unless you think rightly of Him.

It is to be noted that David associates with this enthronement His entering upon His Melchisedekan priesthood, and continues "at Thy right hand" even in "the day of His wrath'" (Psa. 110:4-5). It is here "within the veil" that He entered for us, "made an high priest forever after the order of Melchisedec" (Heb. 6:20; 7:1-4). This investiture was His merited reward as Son of Man and Son of God testifying His vicarious and finished service on earth. Because and by means of this the habitable world to come is not made subject to angels, as this world was, but to Him, and though "we see not yet all things put under Him, we see Jesus Who was made a little lower than the angels for the suffering of death, crowned with glory and honour". There He ministers and administrates, bringing to its glorious issue "the eternal purpose," "bringing many sons to glory," the uncountable myriads of His redeemed of all time (Heb. 1, 2).

In this "administration of the fulness of times", introduced at His first advent, to be completed at His second advent, all things in heaven and earth are to be headed up in Him. *During* these times of restoration of all things spoken by the prophets He abides in heaven which has welcomed Him. Due to the victory of His cross, the princes of this world are *in process of* being brought to nought (Eph. 1:10; Gal. 4:4; Acts 3:21; 1 Cor. 2:6). So complete, so universal, so certain, so final will be the ultimate issue of His finished conquest on the cross, that the Gospel often reiterates David's words in one form or another, "Sit Thou at My right hand until I make Thine enemies Thy footstool" (Acts 2:34-35; Heb. 1:13). There, glorified, He is "expecting" this crowning victory in earth and heaven and hell (Phil. 2:10; Heb. 10:13). It is sometimes spoken of as though already accomplished, so certain it is (Heb. 2:8; Eph. 1:22; cf. Rom. 4:17). In this association also He is made Head over all things to the Church which is His fulness, and at His coming He will in fitting resemblance transfigure her "according to the power whereby He is able to subdue all things unto Himself" (Eph. 1:23; Phil. 3:21). It is in this context of resurrection and transformation at His coming that the Scripture says, "For He must reign till He hath put all enemies under His feet", and the context would seem to confirm that the second pronoun refers to God the Father, agreeably with David's statement and New Testament quotations (1 Cor. 15:25-28). The Son, however, is always Executor of His Father's will.

Appropriately to this great subject of resurrection at His coming, and His putting down of "all rule and authority and power," the Scripture continues, "the last enemy that shall be destroyed is death". Death's final destruction will be by force of resurrection, and

another quotation is given that *"Then* shall be brought
to pass the saying, Death is swallowed up in victory";
an expression as full and final as can be. Paul fixes
thus the last enemy's destruction at the second coming,
when the Church will be resurrected and glorified.
John fixes the same event at the final judgment after
the thousand years of Christ's heavenly reign when
death shall be cast into the lake of fire. This explains
the significance of the striking word "swallowed up in
victory". Following this the apocalyptic vision is of "a
new heaven and a new earth" which includes in its
description of the banishment of all evil "there shall be
no more death". The original prophecy has this very
context (Isa. 25:8). There can be no question, therefore, that this is the time when death shall be destroyed,
"swallowed up in victory".

"He must reign" (1 Cor. 15:25) is interpreted by
millennialists of a post-coming kingdom to be "set up"
on earth with Jerusalem and the Jews figuring centrally, for which, to reiterate the quotation above, God will
send back His Son to reign publicly until all enemies
are under His feet. Interpolations are not uncommon
with dispensationalists. For example, there is no
mention of a millennial reign in 2 Pet. 3, yet such
elasticity is ascribed to a word that judgment simultaneous with the day of His coming is said to begin, then
be arrested for a thousand years, and then finished at
the end! No one would ever have guessed this on
reading Peter, but the millennial program would disintegrate without some such qualification. Similarly
here, no mention is made of a millennial reign; the
argument for it is based on a "particle of succession",
a word meaning "moreover, after that, furthermore"
("then" in 1 Cor. 15:24, compared to "afterward" in
v. 23). Thus the "reign" is made to intervene between
the Coming and "the end".

But what saith the Scripture? In resurrection Christ
was first fruits and "afterwards (as to resurrection) they
that are Christ's", and when? "at His coming". "Then",
that is, furthermore, in succession upon the Coming,
"the end." But the dispensational arrangement is

different, and the expression is made to mean, "His coming; then cometh the millennial reign, and then the end". The obvious meaning of the text as given would be, "Christ's reign must and will continue until every enemy has been conquered" (Phillips). The apostle's language and argument envisages Christ as already reigning upon His resurrection and ascension, and the Scriptures, above cited, agree with this, "Sit Thou at My right hand". Otherwise (as with judgment in 2 Pet. 3), an "arrestment" must be introduced, death destroyed in part at His coming, continued in measure during His reign, and destroyed fully at the end. Against all such manipulation the Scripture stands. The last enemy, death, the destruction of which is post-millennial, "swallowed up in victory", determines that the Second Coming also must be post-millennial, for the Scriptures are never contradictory but ever corroborative, and how otherwise, is 1 Cor. 15:26 compatible with Rev. 20:14; 21:4?

We observe, therefore, that David, Peter, Paul, John and the Lord Himself declare that Christ, as a reward of His cross, is now invested with total authority in heaven and in earth (Matt. 28), is majestically and omnipotently enthroned at God's right hand until all enemies are made His footstool, the last being death itself. There is no promise that He will vacate the throne in heaven before this task is completed; no question of God "sending back" His Son, thereby vacating heaven's universal throne, (for "the heavens do rule") and during a temporal earthly reign accomplish the universal subjugation of His foes. God means what He said, and His reigning Son knows what He said and knows what He meant by what He said. He is, therefore, "expecting"—not to be sent back to do a thousand years' contract on earth, but —waiting above until that which is determined shall "succeed to Him". At His first coming He "finished" the work and said, "Father, I have glorified Thee *in the earth*". When He comes the second time, it will be in celebration of a work finished *in heaven*, and so "in His times He shall show Who is that blessed and only Potentate, the King of kings and Lord of lords".

DOUBTFUL ORIGINS OF
DISPENSATIONAL
OPINIONS

IN ORDER RIGHTLY to divide the word of truth, "distinguish the dispensations". But who determines the dispensations, and what are they? Biblically and historically, two have been commonly acknowledged. They are presented in the Testaments, Old and New, B.C. and A.D., divided and united by the advent of Christ. Broadly they concern the covenants of the first man and the second, public and representative men, both "Adam"; Israel and the Church; Moses and the prophets and Christ and the apostles; the covenants of works and of grace; the law given by Moses and grace and truth which came by Jesus Christ; God who hath spoken through the prophets and in His Son; in time past and in these last days; in ministries unto condemnation and justification; the Spirit of Christ in the prophets beforetime testifying His sufferings and glory and the gospel now preached with the same Holy Spirit sent down from heaven; sin reigning unto death through the law and grace reigning through righteousness unto eternal life in Jesus Christ our Lord; the former, the preparation for the latter and the latter, the fulfilment of the former; the law our schoolmaster unto Christ and Christ the object of the law unto righteousness.

These two scriptural dispensations or administrations accord with the principles advanced in previous chapters; namely, that God means what He says in the Old Testament and says what He means in the New Testament, or as otherwise expressed, the New in the Old concealed and the Old by the New revealed; or again as Paul writes, "that was not first which is spiritual but that which is natural, and afterward that which is spiritual". To invent a third dispensation or to multiply them involves a reintroduction of the first and a subdivision of the second, the divorcing of that which God has joined together, building again the things abolished (Gal. 2:18).

The popular Scofield Reference Bible gives seven dispensations, the Companion Bible (Bullinger) has its own additions and divisions with a self-claim to be "unique". There are further products, some unto "strange doctrines and commandments of men", for error rides best on the back of truth.

By inspiration God has given His Word. He promised to those to whom His Spirit should come guidance into all the truth; not, however, without their own diligent and sincere searching the Scriptures whether the things taught and heard are so; whether God's meaning or man's is given in explanation of what God says.

> *I keep six honest, serving men,*
> *They taught me all I knew;*
> *Their names are What and Why and When,*
> *And Where and How and Who?*

> —RUDYARD KIPLING

We do well to ask of views and theories propounded, not only what are these but whence came they? The writer has found much assistance from these "honest serving men" in this general examination of inspired principles of prophetic interpretation. In this concluding chapter are set down some of their findings in respect to the doubtful origins of dispensational opinions.

"When these particular doctrines were announced about a century ago they were declared to be *rediscovered* truths which had been lost since apostolic times" and "can be traced back directly to the Brethren Movement which arose in England and Ireland about the year 1830". The Movement "had its beginnings at a time when there was great interest in the Second Advent. The Rev. Edward Irving had stirred London by his flaming eloquence, declaring in sermon after sermon that the Lord might come at any moment" (Dr. Oswald T. Allis in *Prophecy and the Church*). It has been affirmed that these teachings are not to be found in the earlier history of the church (Dr. Rendle Harris). Both Futurists and Simple-Futurists, followers of John Nelson Darby and Benjamin Wills Newton (who differed on pre- and post-tribulationism) claim, as did Irving, the divine bestowment at that time of new light upon prophetic Scripture, especially the Book of Revelation.

The general consent of "the Fathers" cannot be claimed in support of dispensationalism; the late Sir Robert Anderson, a dispensationalist, wrote a strong warning against Irvingism, and also criticized patristic theology. The late Dr. Handley C. G. Moule, remarking upon the history of opinion on the Lord's Return, century upon century, points out the diversity of interpretation which existed and recurred. With repetition he bade his students "observe the fact that some of the amplest prophecies of coming blessedness *on earth* in the Old Testament are applied in the New Testament, *not* to a future millennial age but, to that of the gospel" (*Outlines of Christian Doctrine*).

That there was "in the latter part of the eighteenth century and the beginning of the nineteenth, a very decided revival of evangelical truth in Europe and America, resulting in a widely diffused desire to spread the knowledge of the gospel among the nations and the Jewish people, is attributable to the Lord's great mercy" (B. W. Newton). Nevertheless, a movement or work of the Spirit of God may be vitiated by the Evil One, and divine intervention in the church for her good has often suffered thus, and we are admonished not to be ignorant of his devices. Faithful men and the evangelical causes they serve are not immune from the temptation to "turn everyone to his own way", that is, the way of his liking. The illustration of the gipsy woman is apt. Observed to throw a stick into the air and watch its descent, repeating the action several times, she explained that the stick pointed the direction she should take, but she added, "it will point that way, and I want to go this way"! We have to be on guard lest the way we take in prophetic interpretation is the way we ourselves wish to take, whether it may not be a case of, "My people love to have it so". Professor F. W. Newman, fellow with Darby, said of him, "he only wanted men to 'submit their understanding to God', that is, to the Bible, that is, *to his own interpretation*" (*History of the Plymouth Brethren*).

The ministry and influence of the Rev. Edward Irving was chiefly responsible for the beginnings of popular Second Advent dispensational teaching. The seed then sown became rooted in the Brethren Movement, and spreading down the century, it yields today its harvest of systematized futurism regarded in some quarters as fundamental. Indeed, the acceptance of the N.T. spiritualized interpretation of the O.T. has been met with the charge of modernism. Yet associated with and branching from advent dispensationalism have been departures from the historic faith of God's elect.

An earlier alternative to the Protestant Reformers' and Puritan theologians' prophetic interpretation is attributed to "the Jesuit Ribera (A.D. 1580) whose aim was to disprove the claim of the Reformers that the Pope was antichrist" (*Allis*). "To protect the Papacy and to confuse the Protestants as to the true meaning of the book of Revelation. The scheme is not to be commended for obvious reasons. The early church Fathers cannot be said to be futurists as everything to them was future" (*Dean Alford*). "There is now a first issue copy of Ribera's Futurist commentary in Cambridge library, and futurist commentaries since then are based on it" (*L. R. Thomas*). "Under the stress of the Protestant attack there arose new methods on the papal side, and their authors were the Spanish Jesuits, Ribera and Alcazar" (*Encyclopaedia Brittanica*). Edward Irving, in pursuing his dispensational revelation, regards as providential his discovery of a later treatise on the subject, which he translated into English, presented as the work of a converted Jew, Ben Ezra, but who proved in reality to be another Spanish Roman Jesuit, Lacunza. It is not infrequently remarked by tolerant futurists that "the Lord has His dear saints in the Roman communion". Maybe, but there stands written the challenge, "Come out of her my people, that ye be not partakers of her sins, and that ye receive not of her plagues: for her sins have reached unto heaven, and God hath remembered her iniquities" (Rev. 18:4, 5).

The Phenomenal Rev. Edward Irving

"It is no strange thing that there should be a boiling over or effervescence when a movement of revival is on foot. This there was in connection with the great Scottish movement of over a century ago. It took place in the errors of doctrine and irregularities of worship and church life that attended the kindred movements associated with the names of *Edward Irving* and John Campbell. Irving bequeathed to the world as his legacy that system of Catholic Apostolicity, as it called itself, which rested for authority on the basis of ecstatic utterances and half-hysterical speakers with tongues".

Referring to sound theologians of the Scottish pulpit we read, "of that class a few were taken up with *pre-millennial ideas,* and this affected their preaching to a greater or less extent. The members of this school were men like the brothers, *Andrew and Horatius Bonar.* In the formative years of their college career they came under the spell of the meteoric message of Edward Irving before his excesses in doctrine had led him far from the beaten track. And as he laid stress on the pre-millennial dating of the second advent they imbibed this form of the Chiliastic hope. It may have been of somewhat slighting reference to this school and its fanciful hopes that the older evangelicals used to call the young pre-millennial set, the Evangelical Light Infantry".

"In regard to the Lord's coming again, perhaps, the most influential book was the post-millennial treatise written by *Dr. David Brown* when he was minister in

Glasgow. Dr. Brown died as principal of the Free Church College in Aberdeen. In his early life he had been assistant to *Edward Irving* in London, and shared in his prophetic views. With his change of judgment and conviction on these contested questions, he became, by reason of his volume on the Second Advent, the leading opponent of the pre-millennial reading of unfulfilled prophecy. This work of his ran into seven editions and it a book of permanent value" (Dr. John Macleod in *Scottish Theology*).

"*Edward Irving* was appointed in 1822 to a poor, struggling congregation in London, Caledonian Church in Hatton Gardens. In a few months the miracle took place. London was set ablaze. Every notable in the city crowded to hear this golden-tongued preacher. Canning, the prime minister, referred in the House of Commons to Irving's sermons as being the acme of oratory. The new preacher attracted all kinds of intellectual and literary people, none more so than the poet, Coleridge. In a few years his people, gathered from every quarter and every sect, moved out and built the large church known as Regent Square Presbyterian Church. Irving became immensely interested in prophecy, and particularly in the second coming of Christ which he believed to be immediate" (Dr. James Black, Free St. George's, Edinburgh).

"The beginning of the third decade of the nineteenth century was a time of religious revival. A movement of this type centred around the picturesque personality of *Edward Irving*. At twenty-seven years of age this brilliantly gifted man became assistant minister in the great Dr. Chalmers' parish in Glasgow. Seven years later he was called to the principal Church of Scotland pulpit in London. His preaching took London by storm. His popularity was phenomenal beyond all precedent. The cultured classes of the metropolis thronged his church. But popularity did not quench his spirituality. He was surrounded by many God-fearing and devoted men and women who shared his aspirations, and meetings for prayer were frequent and prolonged. The burden of their cry was for a renewal of the Pentecostal gifts. Ere long one and another among them became suddenly endued with a supernatural power under which they uttered spirit-given words, sometimes in an unknown dialect, but usually in their native tongue" (Sir Robert Anderson, K.C.C., LL.D.).

IT CAN BE GATHERED from his recorded experiences that Mr. Irving became firmly and fully convinced, by circumstances which appeared to direct his way, of a providential confirmation of his prophetic views and teachings. The Ben Ezra translation is dated, Caledonian Church, January 17th, 1827. The work is entitled, "The Coming of Messiah in Glory and Majesty," and the "discourse" is addressed "to the Church of Christ of all denominations". Quotations are necessarily abbreviated.

"My soul is greatly afflicted because of the present unawakened and even dead condition of all the churches with respect to the coming of our Lord Jesus Christ which is, as I believe, close at hand. I have always deemed it an honour to be instructed by good and wise men, but when this instruction hath proceeded without instrumentality of man's teaching, my acknowledgements are due unto the Holy Spirit—remarkably the case with respect to the great truths of the second advent. *When I obtained this light* I did not communicate it to anyone until not a shadow of a doubt was left upon my mind. Perceiving that the time was near at hand, I felt it an immediate duty to make known that sure conviction."

"Last Christmas (Dec. 25th, 1825) purposing to warn my flock against indulgences to which at that season we are all exposed, I chose for my text, 1 Thess. 5:4-7—and found that I had insensibly wandered far into that subject near to my heart, and upon the day commemorating the first advent I was maintaining the doctrine of the second advent. It was a day to be remembered in my ministry. I found it necessary to take up certain strong positions, of which these were the chief:

First, that the present visible church, the mixed multitude, all their sects, this body of baptized men, everyone of whom should have been a saint, standeth threatened in the Scriptures because of its hypocrisies, idolatries, superstitions, infidelity and enormous wickedness, with such a terrible judgment as hath not hitherto been, which fearful judgment I judge to be close at hand.

"*Secondly*: When the Lord shall have executed this, He will prepare another testimony, and will turn His Holy Spirit unto the Jews, giving the promised days of refreshing, in which He will likely use His election according to grace among the Gentiles; but chiefly, I believe, by the sending of Elijah, awakening, refining, occasioning that great warfare when Antichrist shall fall at Armageddon. The faithful among the Gentiles, expecting the Lord to deliver them, raised from the dead or changed, all gathered unto Him; the faithful among the Jews, prepared for the coming of the Lord to settle and establish them forever in their own land".

"*Thirdly*: When the land shall have been cleared of intruders, and the Jews perfected by suffering for its habitation, He shall lead them into it with a mighty, outstretched hand, sit upon the throne of David judging and seeking judgment, and send forth the law from Zion, rule among the nations the Prince of universal peace, using His risen saints. Thus, Satan being cast out, the heavenly Jerusalem the dwelling place of His elect church; the Jerusalem on earth with the house of Jacob and all the nations, shall enjoy the millennial reign of righteousness".

"These three points I opened and defended from sabbath to sabbath with all boldness, yet with fear and trembling. *So novel and strange a doctrine* could not fail to call down upon my head all forms of disappointed and sorely-afflicted expostulation. I have begun this 'preliminary discourse' by giving an exposition of the doctrine I have been teaching to show the wonderful coincidence with the doctrine in this book, which I now present to the churches using the English tongue".

"The book, *The Coming of Messiah in Glory and Majesty*, first printed in 1812 in Spain in three volumes, suppressed by the Spanish government, came to England in 1816 by the circuitous route of the Spanish colonies. A clergyman of the Church of England, labouring amongst Spaniards, receiving from a Roman Catholic friend that copy of the Spanish edition from which this translation is made. God had given me the discernment to perceive that it was the master work of one of His most gifted servants. The doctrines of the Romish Church now and then appear, but this I say with the full perception of the capital and fundamental points on which we differ, transubstantiation, the mass, the seven sacraments, the hierarchy, the central unity of the Church of Rome; yet perceiving that the Papacy will furnish the great strength and supply of the infidel power in the persecution of the true church of Christ, that it will stand up against the Lord and His Anointed, and not be destroyed but by the brightness of His coming."

"Upon enquiring who this 'converted Jew' Juan Josafat Ben Ezra actually was, our friend informed us that the name was taken for a covert or disguise, and his true name was Emanuel Lacunza, a Jesuit, who had taken refuge in Italy. Born in Chili, 1747, sent to the college of Jesuits, expelled with his order, established his residence in Italy, where in retirement with his books he died in 1801.

"Brethrenism", writes Blair Neatby, "may be held to derive its very existence in part from the new studies on unfulfilled prophecy to which the unsettlement of men's minds, consequent on the long agonies of the Napoleonic wars, gave rise. Prophetic meetings were established in 1827 at Aldbury Park, Surrey, seat of the well-known Henry Drummond. Irving took part, and to Aldbury Irvingism traces its rise. Lady Powerscourt attended, and 'was so delighted with them that she established similar series at Powerscourt House near Bray in County Wicklow. These lasted till 1833'. He quotes from 'a graphic account', when each present was called to speak in turn on a given subject. 'Mr. Darby spoke last, and often for hours, touching on all that had been previously said'. He names some in attendance and adds, 'there were clergymen present, and Irvingites'."

Delay in his translation of Ben Ezra was occasioned by Mr. Irving's engagement with the Aldbury conference, of which he has written his own account, dated,

Jan. 17th, 1827: "I have said that this work was to have been my Christmas offering to the Church, and now two months have passed beyond the stated time. The cause of this delay I hold myself called upon to give."

"There arose last summer amongst students of prophecy in London a desire to compare their views, and we held meetings as we could find opportunity. One of our number thought well to invite ministers and laymen whom he knew to be interested in prophetic studies to his house at Aldbury Park, Surrey, on the first day of Advent for a full week to deliberate upon questions which do most instantly concern Christendom. There assembled about twenty men of every rank and church and orthdox communion. In honour of our meeting God so ordered it that Joseph Wolff, the Jewish missionary, should also be of the number. We spent eight days in close and laborious examination of the Scriptures upon these six great heads:

First, the doctrine concerning the times of the Gentiles, *Secondly*, the duty of ministers, etc., towards the Gentile churches. *Thirdly*, the doctrine concerning the present and future condition of the Jews. *Fourthly*, the duties growing out of the same towards the Jews. *Fifthly*, the system of the prophetic visions and numbers of Daniel and the Apocalypse. *Sixthly*, the doctrine concerning the future Advent of the Lord. And *lastly*, the duties of the church and of the world arising out of the same.

Mr. Irving then explains their unity of view, "though we were for the most part strangers to one another, we believed in common that the present form of the dispensation was commensurate with the times of the Gentiles, which again are commensurate with Jerusalem's being trodden under foot, and of the Jews' dispersion; that the restoration of the Jews would introduce a new era altogether into the church and world, while this is the dispensation of the Church only; that the conclusion of the latter in great judgments and the commencement of the former in great mercies, was nigh at hand, yea, even at the very door. All being agreed that the 1260 and 1290 days of Daniel were accomplished and the remaining 45 begun; at the conclusion of which the blessedness will be fully arrived, which may open upon us any day; and we are to look for the second advent of the Lord in person to raise the dead bodies of His saints and to reign with them upon the earth; all agreeing that in view of these things there was required of us the greatest vigilance . . . as we are admonished in the sixth vial under which it was the universal opinion we are now living ready for the last great and concluding vial of wrath".

In relating the order of proceedings Mr. Irving says, "No appeal was allowed but to the Scriptures of which the originals lay between us, in the interpretation of which, if any question arose, we had the most learned eastern scholar in the world to appeal to and a native Hebrew, Joseph Wolff".

The years have passed and proved the speculations inaccurate. It is noticeable what especial and sometimes sentimental respect is paid to the supposedly superior knowledge of a Christian Jew, not because he is a Christian but because he is a Jew, whereas the Scripture makes no such distinction. A comment, not irrelevant at this point is as follows: "Premillennialists often ignore the vitally important fact that chiliastic views were extensively circulated in the early church through such Jewish or Jewish-Christian writings as Enoch, 4 Esdras, Assumption of Moses, Ascension of Isaiah, Psalms of Solomon, Baruch, writings such as neither Jews nor Christians regarded as canonical, Judaizing tendencies were very strong even in apostolic times as is made clear by the attitude of Jewish Christians to the Gentiles (e.g. Acts 15) and especially by the epistles to the Galatians and to the Hebrews" (Dr. Oswald Allis in *Prophecy and the Church*). The bias of Hebrew-Christians towards the futuristic type of Judaism dies hard. The church still has need of the warning given by "a Hebrew of the Hebrews" against "Jewish fables" (Titus 1:4). "It is the Spirit that quickeneth, the flesh profiteth nothing". Paul knew this and so testified. The "gains" he abandoned for Christ may all be described as "Jewish" (Phil. 3:1-7). The burden of the apostle's prayers for his racial kinsmen did not concern their earthly national status, but their spiritual and individual salvation, his own conversion being the pattern for all who thereafter should believe on Christ to life everlasting (Rom. 10:1-4; 1 Tim. 1:16).

Among the brief appraisals of Rev. Edward Irving given above is one from Sir Robert Anderson, K.C.B., LL.D., himself a dispensationalist, whose speeches and writings championing the verity of the Scriptures against higher criticism and religious scepticism were highly valued. We remember to have heard him in our youth to much profit especially on the platform of The Bible League, as well also in the perusal of some of his works. We quote Sir Robert again upon this further development of Irvingism. An outbreak of tongues manifestations was current at the time of his writing on "Spirit Manifestations and the Gift of Tongues" published by the Evangelical Alliance in 1909. He refers to the solemnity of the times and of "a tendency to make the great truths of divine revelation subordinate to subjective spiritual manifestations, and to emotions and experiences which such manifestations are fitted to produce. The first enquiry which will suggest itself is whether any light can be derived from similar religious movements in the past. And we shall find what we seek in events recorded by men whom those of us who are now getting on in life count as their contemporaries."

Sir Robert Anderson then proceeds to quote from "a rare book entitled *Narrative of Facts* concerning the Unknown Tongues and Spiritual Manifestations in Members of the Rev. Edward Irving's Congregation, and Other Individuals, and formerly in the Writer himself", published in 1833 by James Nisbet & Co. The significance of statements of this kind will be appreciated by all who were acquainted with their author, Mr. Robert Baxter. I enjoyed his acquaintance for many years and often met him in Christian work. I had heard of his connection with Irvingism, but his *Narrative of Facts* never came into my hands until a few weeks ago. As I knew him Robert Baxter was a typical English Parliamentary lawyer, reserved, slow of speech, and noted for soundness of judgment. And as I have read (in his own account) of his pouring out a torrent of unpremeditated words sometimes for two hours at a stretch, and of his cramming a handkerchief into his mouth at private prayer, lest his 'inspired' bellowings should disturb the household, my distress and amazement are unbounded that anyone could suppose the spirit which energised him was divine."

"Robert Baxter was mercifully delivered from his supernatural 'power', and in his *Narrative* he writes: "I have been much confounded by the fact that Christ was preached in such power, and with such clearness, and the exhortations to repentance so energetic and arousing, that it is hard to believe the person delivering it could be under the delusion of Satan. Yet so it was, and the fact stands before us as a proof that the most fearful errors may be propounded *under the guise of greater light and zeal for God's truth.* Satan is permitted to sustain and accomplish his delusions as "an angel of light. 'As an angel of light'—these words recur as a refrain throughout the narrative."

Here I may mention that on my visit to Toronto shortly before the death of Dr. T. T. Shields, he remarked that he had had in his possession a significant record bearing upon the origins of popular dispensationalism, which he had allowed someone to borrow without its having been returned. The reference was to Baxter's *Narrative of Facts.* I said I also possessed a copy and he bade me be sure to bring it on my next visit! Alas for us, but not for him, ere long he was called to be with Christ. In earlier controversies it was said that J. N. Darby's introduction to the idea of an imminent Coming was at one of Irving's tongues meetings. Others also, and not alone those who followed the Darby line, may have been similarly initiated; the comparison is significant. "The study of unfulfilled prophecy was a prominent feature of the Brethren movement from the first. Bellett had his interest in the subject greatly enlarged during a visit to London in the beginning of 1828, of which he communicated the results to Darby, only to find that Darby's 'mind and soul had travelled rapidly' in the same direction" (Neatly's *History of the Plymouth Brethren*).

Mr. Robert Baxter commences his "Narrative" with the introduction: "In the following narrative I may lay myself open to the charge of egotism in supposing my doings and misdoings to be worthy of public attention. It is not my individual stumbling which can hurt the church, or my recovery that can help the church; but it is the exposure of the cunning craftiness of Satan, which may be made useful to the weak members of the church, and that craftiness working in the most unworthy individual, may lay bare his subtle influence over the more prominent and respected victims of his delusion. The Narrative will necessarily involve the conduct of many who, like myself, though more excusably, have been deceived".

Excerpts from
THE NARRATIVE OF FACTS

IN AUGUST 1831, in the midst of the feeling of awe and reverence produced, I was myself seized upon by the power, and to give forth a prophecy that the messengers of the Lord should go forth, publishing to the ends of the earth the testimony of *the near coming of the Lord Jesus.* When I had put back the declaration of *His instant coming,* I felt myself openly rebuked.

In the midst of prayer the promise in Malachi 4:5 and in Luke 1:17 was brought before me, and that the Lord is now pouring out upon His church the spirit and power of Elias *to prepare for the second coming of Jesus.* I was made to cry out with great vehemence that the coming of the Lord should be declared.

September 1831. Is there not in the outpouring of the Spirit manifested in the midst of us, an especial testimony to the speedy coming of Christ, and the Lord's judgments upon the earth? Isa. 40, the testimony individually laid upon John the Baptist was unto a revelation of Christ which will make every eye to see Him. We look for *some manifestation of the spirit and power of Elias before the Second Advent.* I would also hint the enquiry as to the cry, "Behold, the Bridegroom cometh", which must go forth through the slumbering church.

The continual witness of the Spirit is that His servants

go forth to bear through the earth the testimony of *the coming kingdom*, working with the power of that kingdom, so bearing the testimony of Elijah until they are, like Elijah, *translated without seeing death;* testifying to the world of the translation of the saints, as Noah testified of the ark, and finally *to be rapt from the earth into the presence of Jesus.* In Malachi 3 and 4 the message is as Matt. 24, "in an hour when ye look not for Him", and this is preparatory to "the great and dreadful day"; not to "the acceptable year" but "the day of vengeance of our God".

The voice is one from the beginning, with John the Baptist, confirmed by Christ, borne by apostles and disciples, confirmed by the Holy Spirit sent down from heaven. It hath lain in the church as a candle hidden, but now the Lord is stirring up His people to ask in faith for the fulness of the testimony. The voice will continue crying in the wilderness until the church enters into her rest. The time of rest is at hand. The prophecies were that the Lord was *at hand, the morning star* arising among us, and *the signs* of His coming all around us.

The call to "stand out and be separate" was often repeated. The declarations of the two witnesses (Rev. 11) were again repeated, and very distinctly we were commanded to "count the days", 1260, appointed for testimony, at the end of which the saints would go up *to meet the Lord in the air.* An opinion had been advanced in some of Mr. Irving's writings that *before* the second coming of Christ and the day of vengeance, the saints would be caught up to heaven, and would thus be saved from the destruction of this world, as Noah was saved in the ark, as Lot from Sodom . . . (Matt. 24:41) were brought to me in the power: this is the translation of the saints whilst the rest of the world are left in their usual occupations.

The witnesses' 1,260 days set forth *three years and a half* from the beginning of its delivery *up to the translation of the saints.* The "utterance" was most distinct to count from that day (Jan. 14th, 1832) 1,260 days and 3½ days (Rev. 11:11) which would end on June 2nd, 1835. The same thing was again and again declared. The midnight cry, "Behold, the Bridegroom cometh" was the declaration of the second coming, the wise and foolish virgins were awakening at it; lamps without oil make the professors. Fearful denunciations of judgment were given, and *the reiterated testimony* that within three and a half years *believers would be caught up to Him, and the world delivered over to the judgments of God.*

Waiting for the expiration of the three and a half years, the power came in the revelation and opening up of scripture. Constrained to read the 12th chapter of Revelation, was just as light flitting across the mind. The sun-clothed woman, the spiritual church contradistinguished from the visible (professing) church; the being with child was interpreted of the spiritual church, *bringing forth testimony* to the second coming of the Lord Jesus. The dragon was Satan influencing all powers in church and state *to devour this child, that is to quench the testimony.* The same child brought forth *was the testimony.* Caught up to God, the Spirit sealing the testimony as His Own. The woman fled into the wilderness was the spiritual part of the church. The war in heaven was the power of Satan put forth against the power of the Spirit of Christ.

It was revealed that while the spiritual church would have victory over Satan, the visible church and the world would be subject to his delusions, as "having great wrath because he knoweth that he hath but a short time". The overcoming by the blood of the Lamb and the word of their testimony, and they loved not their lives unto the death was shown as our way to victory; yielding our tongues and giving heed to the testimony of the Spirit. Great strength and comfort seemed to arise out of this interpretation.

2 Thess. 2:6. "He who now letteth" was declared to be the Spirit of God, and the taking of this power out of the way was *the taking away of the Spirit* from the visible church. The revelation of the man of sin, Satan ruling in the church, receiving that worship which belonged to God, showing himself that he was god; not to invalidate its application to the papacy. At the end of the three years and a half *God would take away His Spirit and His church* altogether from the earth, then the personal man of sin would stand forth exercising all the mighty power and working of evil spirits, claiming for himself the worship of all nations. The person who should be so energized was at a subsequent meeting declared to be young Napoleon.

"When the Son of Man cometh shall He find faith on the earth"? was inferred to be the time when God would sit in judgment upon the churches, and punish by taking away *His Spirit,* for their wicked quenching of the Spirit. Concerning this casting off of the visible church, God's purpose was to bear His last warning and prepare a people before the great and terrible day of the Lord. This revelation of the shortness of the time would serve to awaken the church. The prophecy was then of the development of the man of sin in the person of the young Napoleon as before detailed.

The broad line of distinction was continually kept in view in all the utterances. The visible was considered discarded, and the seduction of the enemy was turned towards *the discarding of Baptism and the Lord's Supper.* The spiritual ministers would baptize with the Holy Ghost and fire, and no longer with the baptism of water. In reference to Rev. 3, the utterance was that Christ was now knocking by His Spirit for His people to realize that which the bread and wine typified in the Lord's Supper, that thus the antitype displaced the type, and bread and wine be laid aside.

This morning a clergyman from Ireland had come expressly to enquire, favorably disposed but startled by the doctrines. I was made more and more peremptorily to warn. It is not a little remarkable that the call being given for all to depart who did not receive the word spoken in power as the word of God, the clergyman professed his faith in the work. Whilst under the awe of the presence of the supernatural power, he was so overcome as to profess full faith in it and believe himself to be really receiving it.

The characteristic to which I now allude is *the spirit of separation* which marks out a line by the reception or rejection of the utterances: all who bow to them are received, those who cannot are not acknowledged. The effect of this is, it casts off *under the name of Babylon* the great mass even of orthodox professors, and raises up a little church which does receive the utterances into the distinctive title of "The Church". Extreme secrecy is enjoined, and the manifest shrinking from public examination, with bitterness of denunciation and hastiness of spirit, found in the manifestations of the power. Many times have I been appalled at the stern and remorseless denunciations under the power.

One circumstance of these manifestations cannot but force itself upon observation: the continual use made of the doctrine of the second advent of our Lord, the leading theme of the utterances. The nearness of it, its suddenness, its fearful judgments were the continual arguments used to excite our minds. Alas, the hollowness of our hearts, which drank in flattery and seduction, and persuaded us we were drinking in the sincere milk of the word and growing in love and meekness! I have seen by woeful experience that if a warning is disregarded, *Satan in a little time contrives some system of explanation* to do away with the doubts and misgivings which it has created, and we are more fully given over to his power than if the warning had never been sent us.

Irving's Tongues and Advent Testimony

"Futurists and dispensationalists are the same although divided into the 'simple' and 'extreme' groups of interpretation. Ribera the Jesuit popularized Futurism, for the literalists in England welcomed its presentation and propagated it there and in America" (G. H. Clement, Hamilton). It is, however, to Edward Irving that the new-fashioned theories which became systematized into the futuristic scheme must be attributed. The trend and tendency of his prophetic thinking and preaching, and his ensuing experiences which he regarded as of God's providence, eventuated in the spirit manifestations and gift of tongues, from the authentic record of which we have copied. These were "novel and strange doctrines", to use Irving's own description, precedent to the Brethren "new-found revelation". Although the passage of years has proved the teaching unreliable, with some parrotry it is still repeated by pulpiteer and printed preacher. In the "Narrative" quotations above there appear the following:

Advent testimony and preparation commissioned by the "power". The Imminence of the Return of Christ. The Pre- Mid- or Post-tribulation Coming. The Rapture of the saints prior to the revelation in judgment. Babylonian apostasy of the professing Church. Removal of the Holy Spirit with the rapture of the true Church. The appearing and reign of the Man of Sin. The prevenient ministry of re-appeared Elijah. The symbolism of the woman and man-child (Rev. 12) a special end-time testimony to the truth, persecuted but preserved by God. Christ to sit on David's re-established throne in Jerusalem, and the Jews restored in a millennial kingdom. The discarding of the ordinances, baptism and the Lord's supper, for their spiritual counterparts. The contriving of some subterfuge to buttress theories when met with doubts and misgivings. Fellowship with or separation from believers determined by their acceptance or rejection of the oracle.

Easily recognizable in present day advent testimony is the substance of the Irvingite tongues utterances, whether the type of futurism be "simple", "extreme" or "mystery". Here are features of its most popular form, generally attributed in its beginnings to J. N. Darby and his Brethren colleagues but traceable to the earlier manifestations. With certain of these Newtonians concur: the Babylonianism of Christendom, Elijah's re-appearance with Moses, the end-time special testimony, sometimes known as "the Pearl testimony" adapting thereto the parable of Matt. 13. For this we are referred to B. W. Newton, but the "tongues" appear to have introduced the idea. Again, the "Mystery" teaching, as it is called, initiated by Dr. E. W. Bullinger, (as Dr. Oswald Allis remarks, the logical sequence of dispensationalism) finds its forerunner in the same Irvingite association; "a system which denies us baptism and the Lord's supper as carnal ordinances, and stands forth as one of the grave but masked perils of today" (D. M. Panton in *The Dawn*, on "Bullingerism"). Exclusivism and sophism also were prominent in these originals and are with us yet (Jude 19; Rom. 16:18b). Satan's "craftiness of working" and "subtle influence over prominent and respected victims of his delusions", which Mr. Robert Baxter exposed from his own experience and observation, still require our enlightened watchfulness.

In our investigating pursuit of this subject in the foregoing articles we have endeavoured to submit to the Scriptures, to the New Testament as interpreting the Old, and as being self-explanatory in its comparative and cumulative testimony, The Scriptures are the infallible authority and the final arbiter. "Six honest men" have furnished us with things new and old out of the treasury. Sometimes question has been answered with question, and thus we conclude:

If Irvingism, the source of modern dispensationalism, being evil, is to be eschewed, are the prophetic revelations which emerged from it to be espoused as divine? "Came the word of God out from you, or came it unto you only?" (1 Cor. 14:36). What "if the light that is in thee be darkness?" (Matt. 6:23). "Who can bring a clean thing out of an unclean?" (Job 14:4). "Doth a fountain send forth at the same place sweet water and bitter?" (Jas. 3:11). "Do men gather grapes of thorns, or figs of thistles?" (Matt. 7:16). "A good tree cannot bring forth evil fruit, neither can a corrupt tree bring forth good fruit" (Matt. 7:18). "Either make the tree good, and his fruit good; or else make the tree corrupt and his fruit corrupt" (Matt. 12:33).

MAY TRUTH BREAK FORTH
FROM CONTROVERSY

IT HAS invariably done so. We share the desire. Thus introduced, a critical review of our *Gospel Witness* articles, entitled *Prophetic Studies,* is appearing in the magazine *Watching and Waiting,* organ of the Sovereign Grace Advent Testimony, London. The reviewer is Mr. James Payne, a Strict Baptist pastor known to me for many years. The S.G.A.T. upholds "Simple Futurism" as set out in the teachings of Mr. B. W. Newton, Dr. C. Y. Biss, Dr. Tregelles, Mr. David Baron, etc. In their view the second advent is post-tribulational and pre-millennial, broadly, with minor differences, the modern dispensational position. It may be remarked that Mr. Payne does not write as representing his denomination.

The reviewer kindly acknowledges that in the past he had profitted by my ministry. That, of course, was when, as others and like himself, I mistakenly thought I had "arrived". But by the compelling force of truth, further studied, I travel along its way with open mind, as expressed in my articles. This is the blessing I wish for my reviewer and for all. Truth is liberating from bondage to men.

There is danger in selective quotation. I hope the editor of *Watching and Waiting* will recommend its readers, as I have requested, to peruse *The Gospel Witness* articles, and not form a judgment by the review only as to what was said and meant. Without this, truth may itself remain captive.

I am grateful to *The Gospel Witness for* allowing me these further pages. I greatly value Dr. Shields' appraisal of an earlier brochure, of which the articles are a more detailed extension. *"The Gospel Witness* says Amen to the principles enunciated. We suggest that our readers not only read them, but study them diligently with the scripture references given" (see Introduction, May 30th, 1963).

Our reviewer's touchstone by which our articles are judged of their scripturalness is the system of prophetic theories he has espoused, and these represent the "truth" he would have "break forth". I repeat that our main guiding principle is that God means what He says and says what He means. But the meaning of what He said in the Old Testament is stated in the New Testament. We repel as unworthy of *Watching and Waiting* and its reviewer, the comparison with Swedenborg, Tillich, Gnosticism, Higher Criticism and Modernism. It is not the first time in this magazine that the unjustified comparison has been made. I must, however, acknowledge the re-assuring comment of my friend. I am not past redemption, for "I am sure," he says, "Mr. Wilmot will share in the millennial blessedness of all His saints." Knowing what he means by the millennium, I cherish no such expectation. I shall be abundantly satisfied, if the God of all grace shall call me to His eternal glory in Christ Jesus, and I may share with patriarchs, prophets, martyrs, and redeemed sinners of all generations, the heavenly country, the inheritance incorruptible, undefiled, that fadeth not away; and though lost among the ten thousand times ten thousand and thousands of thousands, to find myself also "lost in wonder, love and praise", and with the uncountable multitude "around the throne of God in heaven, singing glory, glory, glory."

The New Testament supplies ample examples of divinely-intended spiritualisation. But liberty may not be taken to wrest Old Testament quotations used in the New Testament of the First Advent, and transfer their fulfilment over the centuries and millenniums to the Second Advent, and label that prophetic *truth*. It is recommended that "we must not interpret the New Testament in opposition to the prophecies of the Old Testament". (B. W. Newton). The New Testament, of course, is not in opposition: it is the exposition of the Old Testament. In this respect the New Testament is not "supplemental" but fundamental, and apostolic illumination is pre-requisite to interpreting the prophets.

"It is with relief," says the review, "that we turn back to the simplicity of the scriptures when read in their literal and obvious sense", and "if we de-literalise a part of scripture, do we not blunt it as an instrument wherewith to combat those who would deliteralise the whole?" Let us apply the argument to a few examples and learn how unreliable it may be:

According to the literal and obvious sense of Isaiah's prediction, Messiah should have been named Immanuel, for this is what God said. But according to the divine sense, the prophecy was fulfilled in the name Jesus, by which God explains what He meant (Isa. 7:14; Matt. 1:21).

The obvious sense of Hosea's reference, verified in the context, is the Israel nation's deliverance from the Egyptians, whereas in the divine sense the prophecy was fulfilled in the childhood of Israel-Messiah, the Son of God. "Out of Egypt have I called my son" (Hos. 11:1; Matt. 2:15).

The disciples, judging by the literal and obvious sense expected Elijah as Messiah's forerunner, for the prophet had so said. But God's sense and meaning, affirmed the Lord Jesus, was realized in John the Baptist (Mal. 3:1; 4:5; Mark 1:2, 3; Luke 1:16; John 1:21; Matt. 11:13, 14; Mark 9:11-13; Luke 17:10-13).

The Lord Jesus, in the temple precincts, issued the challenge, "Destroy this temple and in three days I will raise it up." By the literal and obvious sense the reference was to Jerusalem's temple, and they held it against Him to the end. Even the disciples learned not the divine sense, that He spake of the temple of His body, until His resurrection (John 2:18-22; Matt. 26:61). Similarly, it may be remarked, the divine sense of temple in certain New Testament passages may mean the church (e.g. 2 Thess. 2).

Having warned them to beware of the leaven of Pharisees and Sadducees, by the literal and obvious sense

Christ appeared to speak of bread deficiency. But the literalist disciples required to understand that His sense and meaning was to beware of doctrine (Matt. 16:6-12).

Claiming to be Himself the true manna, the bread from heaven, Christ said, "the bread is my flesh". Judging by the literal sense, the people murmured, "How can this man give us his flesh to eat?" But His sense and meaning were the spiritual sustenance His death would provide, His life-giving gospel. "The flesh profiteth nothing: the words that I speak are spirit and life" (John 6:63).

To the Samaritan woman the obvious sense was that thirst-quenching water must be drawn from the well; but how, since the well was deep, and He had nothing to draw with? Christ's sense, of course, was spiritual, the experience of salvation, "a well of water within springing up into everlasting life" (John 4:13).

God had said through Moses, "Thou shalt not muzzle the ox that treadeth out the corn." The sense was literal and obvious, and the Israel farmer believed that God meant what He said. By inspiration Paul gave the spiritual sense, that by what He said God meant the Church should support her gospel preachers, and that Moses wrote the injunction in the Old Testament law "altogether" for our sakes under New Testament grace (1 Cor. 9:10; 1 Tim. 5:18).

The literal and obvious sense of the ordinance given in Eden was expressed thus: "therefore, shall a man leave his father and mother and shall cleave unto his wife." But the apostle, quoting the very words, gave the sense divine and spiritual and sublime. "This is a great mystery, but I speak concerning Christ and the church" (Eph. 5:32).

The following passages which have come under "review" we take for comment in their scripture order:

This prophecy (Isa. 40) is quoted by Luke (ch. 3) as fulfilled in John the Baptist's ministry. Notwithstanding Luke writes that John ministered "as it is written" in Isaiah's prophecy, and God's meaning given of the Old Testament text is "see the salvation of God", our reviewer defers this to be the Second Advent, changing the italicised "it" of Isaiah to "Him". Howbeit, this supposed simultaneous universal vision of Christ's glory at the Second Coming is scarcely compatible with the view that converted Israel in the millennium will evangelize the nations "who have not heard His fame *nor seen His glory*" (Isa. 66:19). It will be seen, however, that John the Baptist did not so interpret the prophet's words, but warned the unbelieving Jews to "flee from the wrath to come" (Luke 3:1-9).

Further, the word "together" which our reviewer emphasizes, is given, "alike", and does not imply universal vision in the sense that "every eye shall see Him" at once, but the introduction of the gospel dispensation wherein Jews and Gentiles *alike,* i.e., without distinction by faith see His salvation and glory (John 1:14; 2 Cor. 5:6). Moreover, the quotation of this passage by Peter confirms that the words have reference to the effects of preaching the gospel (1 Peter 1:24-25).

The prodigious measurements of the temple and city, considered with the symbolism which pervades the prophecy, we regard as ideal rather than actual. We quoted Fairbairn, Lightfoot, Jamieson, Fausset and Brown, that "the Septuagint substitutes cubits for reeds to escape the immense compass given to the whole. The vast extent is a feature marking the ideal character of the temple". Our reviewer ventures to say, "This is incorrect", and for his literalism is forced to rely upon the cubit in preference to reed. He appears to follow R. B. Cave's charts and outlines. Bullinger would surmount the problem by the suggestion that the millennial land will be greatly extended and become "a magnificent territory bounded north, south, east and west by the Euphrates, Nile, Indian Ocean and Mediterranean". (Ezekiel 40.48).

R. B. Cave surmises that the sacrificial difficulty will be overcome in that the restored Jewish nation will commence their millennium with literal sacrifices, so fulfilling Leviticus, but will later learn the sufficiency of the one sacrifice of Christ as the Church apprehends it today! Strange subterfuge this, when the gospel of Messiah's finished atoning work will already have been preached to generations of Jews, as well as Gentiles, since the First Advent; stranger still when the Epistle to the Hebrews has forewarned them of the apostasy of continuing animal sacrifices now abolished. And, perhaps, strangest of all that our reviewer should claim that these are "entirely new institutions, and not a return to the rites and ceremonies of the law". Ezekiel prescribes burnt, meat, drink, sin, peace offerings; feasts, new moons, sabbaths; the slaughter of lambs, bullocks, goats, rams; the service of Levites, passover, unleavened bread, indeed, altogether the ordinances of Moses, of "making reconciliation for the house of Israel". It is clear from Israel's history that after decline and apostasy, when their rulers repented and reformed, the restoration of sacrifices, feasts, and law obedience generally followed being officially enjoined. Ezekiel also prophesied, therefore for the guidance of the nation on her return from the 70 years' captivity. This was the concern of Daniel, Haggai, Zechariah, Malachi. There is no comparison between sacerdotalism of this type and the simple ordinance of the Lord's Supper, nor is the former called memorial as is the latter. And, indeed, the New Testament declares that such sacrifices are memorials of "sins untaken away". Second Advent "memorials" are incongruous for Christ will no longer be absent. Moreover, such "institutions" were rather *memorials* of Moses than of Christ. Ezekiel is in accord with this, for Christ had not yet "appeared to put away sin by the sacrifice of Himself".

That the prophet and his companions in the office should employ ideal terms and figures; that his descriptions of the temple, city, country, should exceed their post-captivity attainment, is not surprising when we recognize the prophetic movement was always towards the goal in Christ, and the gospel with its sublime promises and expectations unto perfection incite always to a going on, and we must ever say, "not as though I had already attained, either were already perfect, but I follow after, reaching forth unto those things which are before; I press toward the mark" (Phil. 3). So also with the prophets built upon Moses.

Daniel's dream interpretation of successive empires from Babylonian to Roman, represented in the image, concluded with the prediction that "in the days of *these* kings" (Nebuchadnezzar to Caesar) God would set up a kingdom never to be destroyed or left to other people, but to break in pieces and consume all these kingdoms, and itself stand forever" (Dan. 2:44). In relation to the "image" God's instrument was represented as a "stone" (consistently in scripture the figure of Christ) not hewn by man but "cut out of the mountain without hands" that is, by act of God. This would smite the image on its feet, representing the Roman Empire, so that the entire image would be "broken in pieces" and become as chaff scattered by winds. For whereas these kingdoms each in succession inherited the characteristics of the former, and the last of the whole, the kingdom of God would inherit nothing in this manner; it would rather consume; yet would the world of mankind continue. And so, of this One "like the Son of Man" it was said, "all people, nations and languages should serve Him" (Dan. 7:14).

The words are almost identical with ultimate gospel achievement, *"the uttermost part of the earth"*. It is here that my millennialist reviewer's criticism is itself like a smiting stone, myself the target, for he says, "It is astonishing how blind to obvious facts godly men can be when they have first rejected one part of the scripture", which part is not specified. Daniel says that Christ's kingdom is to "fill the whole earth". On this ground he puts forward the smiting time far, far beyond the last of "the days of these kings" in which it is said the stone would fall and God's kingdom distinguished in character from the disintegrated empires, be inaugurated. To satisfy the terms Futurism invents the resuscitation of the Roman Empire, and our reviewer reasons that at His first advent Christ "came not to destroy men's lives but to save them". This is obviously irrelevant. In His plan for universal salvation He also destroyed the oppressive systems described, scattered Israel among the nations, and commissioned His Church to preach the gospel to every creature, even unto *"the uttermost part of the earth"*, which He is to possess. Thus, when He comes the second time "He shall send forth His angels and they shall gather together His elect from the four winds, from *the uttermost part of the earth* to the uttermost part of heaven." And in glory He will amass an uncountable multitude redeemed out of all nations, kindreds, peoples, tongues. Is His kingdom which "shall fill the whole earth" to be understood in terms of *terra firma* or in the souls of men? Of what interest is the earth to Him, save in the inhabitants whom He redeemed unto Himself? Old John Trapp's comment might be appropriate about such as "have heaven commonly at their tongue-ends, but the earth continually at their finger-ends".

The review appears to invalidate the interpretative authority of scripture by substituting application and illustration for fulfilment. Our reviewer remarks that the prophet "cannot be a fulfilment unless the Exodus was either vision or allegory". But Micah, by the Spirit was a *direc-

tive to God's intended gospel fulfilment of the Exodus history. The passover lamb was no allegory or vision or illustration; it was typical, and Christ was its fulfilment. The inspired prophet, in advance of Christ's perfect redemption, declared the spiritual objective in the historic deliverance, fore- and forth-telling the true Deliverer then to come. Therefore, Micah introduced his evangel with, "According to the days of thy coming out of Egypt will I show unto him marvellous things" (Mic. 7). More than a prophet's or preacher's illustration here. The spiritual and evangelical consummation is more marvellous than the historical event, though both were supernatural. The Spirit inspired Moses and the Prophets built upon Moses, and by His superintendence there is a progressive preparation unto Christ and the New Testament.

A comparison with the repeated patriarchal promise where the "Seed" in the second mention is Christ, the Blesser of "all the families of the earth" (Gen. 28:14) would suffice to show that our Lord, as His apostles, looked beyond limited racial bounds to the seed of faith, making all distinctions void (Matt. 8:11; Luke 13:29). Our reviewer, according to dispensational custom, transports this foreview to the millennium. He says when Abraham and his seed possess the land this shall be. How clearly the context establishes his error! The centurion's faith the Lord commended as exceeding that of Israel, and upon this, He forecast world-wide gospel success "from East, West, North and South". Nor can we overlook the contextual contrast of pronounced judgment upon unbelieving Israel. But the millennialist's programme reverses this, giving first commendation of the faith of the Jews, and thereafter, and by their means, the salvation of the world. Together with this prophecy of the many coming from North, South, East, West into the kingdom our Lord announced, "*But* the children of the kingdom shall be cast out into outer darkness." This is how the prediction arose. The response to the gospel of underprivileged nations is more highly commended than that of the nation of privilege. Our reviewer concedes that "hereafter" (John 1:51) bears the sense "from this time forth", yet he asserts that it so used "to fit in with my thesis". "Physician, heal thyself"! Other meanings given are, "from now on; even now; this present; this day; henceforth; with the idea of a point of departure." Never once do they indicate the possibility of "a point of departure" millenniums ahead to the Second Advent, whenever that certain event of uncertain time may occur. It is also translated "henceforth" and "now" as well as the repeated "hereafter" (Matt. 26:64; Matt. 23: 39; Matt. 26:29; John 14:7; 15:15; 13:19; Rom. 6:6; 2 Cor. 5:15; Eph. 4:17). To postpone the "point of departure" a couple of thousand years would make nonsense of any of these scriptures, even Matt. 26:64 which first names the ascension.

The explanation seems apparent. Speaking of Nathaniel, "an Israelite indeed", the Lord recalled the character of Jacob. Jacob's vision of ascending and descending angels had assured the pilgrim, this "outcast man and a lonely", of providence vouchsafed which was responsively acknowledged. And how truly the angels ministered to him throughout (Gen. 28:12; 31:11; 32:1; 48:16)! So the Lord Jesus, the true "Israel", Whose name was called upon Jacob (Gen. 32:28; Isa. 49:3; see again Gen. 48: 16) — the mediatorial Redeemer, represented by the "Way" Jacob observed in his dream; the Son of Man, Who "as a homeless Stranger to this world came, an outcast Man and a lonely", His was the attendance of ministering angels from birth to death, Who also escorted Him to glory. The Gospels tell the story. Angel ministers were seen as already present with Jacob and with Jesus as the statement would indicate, "ascending and descending". Futurism, however, would introduce another "gap" of a couple of thousand years, between "here" and "after", ere the angels attend upon the Son of Man. Mr. Payne feels sure that I have "not yet seen heaven open and the angels of God ascending and descending upon the Son of Man". Not, indeed, in the imagined millennial sense whatever vision he thinks that may be: he says not how. But certainly in the spiritual vision of faith. For sightless literalists we may well utter the prophet's prayer: 2 Kings 6:17. Do we not now "see Jesus crowned with glory and honour"? And in the Gospels we see Him, when "made a little lower than the angels for the suffering of death", and His Father commissioned them to attend Him from Bethlehem to Olivet, and now we see Him exalted to the right hand of the Majesty on high, "angels being made subject to HIM."

Any post-Christian reinstitution of ceremonial and sacrificial worship after the Mosaic pattern, based on Ezekiel and claimed for the millennium, described in the

New Testament as "shadows" and "beggarly elements" done away in Christ, would conflict with our Lord's statement that from the time of His first advent those only are acceptable who worship in spirit and in truth (John 4) Our reviewer rejoins, "all did this even in the Old Testament else they did not worship at all" and that "the *form* of worship is the *only* difference. It should be remembered that the old-time worship though of divinely appointed form, the sanctuary in general being described as "worldly", and the ordinances as "carnal", was imposed only "until the time of reformation"; that is, the first appearing of Christ, and the sanctuary and ordinances were "figures of the true" and "the shadow of good things to come". The "reformation" arrived with Christ, and it were a backsliding if not apostasy to return to the dark ages of ceremonial "shadows" when it is already declared that "the darkness has passed away and the true light now shineth". In his own Church Letter our pastor-reviewer asks: "Is it not a fact that the nearer the heart of any Christian is to the Saviour, so will there be less regard for showy forms and ceremonies?"

Nothing is said in the criticism of our Lord's timepointer: "the hour is coming (repeated) and now is when the true worshippers shall worship the Father in spirit and in truth" (in a true spiritual manner (cf. John 5:25). Thus He anticipated His own atoning removal of the veil, the consecration of the new and living way, the sealing Pentecostal enduement, so that "through Him we both (Jew and Gentile) have access by one Spirit unto the Father", and "we are the circumcision who worship God in the Spirit, rejoice in Christ Jesus, and have no confidence in the flesh" (Phil. 3).

We quote the following from a writer, himself a millennialist, which *Watching and Waiting* will not dispute: " 'The hour cometh and now is' tells of the passing of the dispensation of shadows thrown forward to forms and ceremonies of the law which, at their best, were but 'the example and shadow of heavenly things', and which, while they outlined the coming light, yet concealed it from man's view. The heavenly temple of which Christ is the Priest, had now replaced those 'holy places made with hands'. Worship must be *no longer* that of the external details of a material ritual, but the inward service of the heart. All this is taught in the word, 'true'. This was *a new truth, a truth as astonishing as new.* Through the ministry of the one heavenly High Priest, God would seek such to worship Him. This the law had never given any hint of, indeed it could not do so. It was 'weak and unprofitable' " (Dr. C. Y. Biss).

All the prophets since the world began, Peter says, have told of these "times", "these days", the ground of which is expressed in the prophetic testimony that Christ should suffer (Acts 3). "Times of refreshing", therefore, since these are "times of restitution", are blessedly promised to the penitent. At the end Christ shall come again. His mediatorial enthronement in the heavens continues while the times of restitution proceed. Such is the meaning here. "During", therefore, befits "until" (Dr. E. Henderson on Ezekiel, 1855). The dictionaries confirm this for they give us the force of "until", "while", "continuously" with the accomplished "end" in view. It is not said or even implied that Christ will vacate heaven in a Second Advent, to inaugurate millennial "times of restitution"; but that the heavens have received Him while those "times" proceed unto their completion. To that end He was invested upon His resurrection victory with "all authority in heaven and in earth". This is the power whereby "He is able even to subdue all things unto Himself" including the glorifying of His church "who mind not earthly things" and "whose citizenship is in heaven" (Phil. 3: 20, 21).

Christ is yet engaged upon an unfinished work in heaven. Upon its accomplishment He will arise to judgment: "We see not yet all things put under Him, but we see Jesus crowned with glory and honour." The Jews were urged by their apostle-preacher to buy up their present opportunity. The children of the covenant made with Abraham, Peter assures them, includes not only Jews, but "all the kindreds of the earth". But the gospel, Peter said, was first preached to the Jews. If despised, judgment and not mercy, will be first pronounced upon them "in the day when God shall judge the secrets of men by Jesus Christ" (Rom. 2:9, 11, 16).

Judaising Christians were disturbing the peace of Gentile believers by imposing the rites of the law. The Church with apostles and elders came together "for to consider of this matter" (Acts 15). Peter explained how God "a good while ago" gave the gospel to the Gentiles through him (before Paul was inducted to this ministry). James presiding, after hearing Paul and Barnabas, reminded them that "Peter had declared how God at the first (for the first time through Peter) did visit the Gentiles to take out from them a people for His name" (as well as from the Jews). The president thereupon affirmed that "to this agree" the prophets and quoted Amos, "After this I will return and build again the tabernacle of David." To "agree" is "to say the same thing", therefore, apostolic Gentile evangelisation was the fulfilment of prophecy including that of Amos. "I will return" does not announce the Second Advent; the word is simply, "turn back or turn again". and is used of God's turning to sinners in the grace of salvation.

The distinction made between the literal rebuilding of the temple, which some claim to be the meaning here, and the tabernacle, was simply to indicate that a passage like this cannot be so played with. If there is to be a literal restoration, then "tabernacle" is not temple (1 Chron. 16:1; 28:6). I am glad to note that my reviewer, however, resorts to a kind of spiritualisation here; he calls it "metaphorical", but insists that the fulfilment of Amos will, nevertheless, be literalised in a Davidic regime yet to be restored. Consulting Amos, it will be seen that James' "after this" is the equation of Amos' "in that day"; that is, the day not of restored nationhood after a Second Advent but of her scattering among the nations. That is the immediate context of Amos, while "all the sinners of My people shall die by the sword", the remnant (as the "grain" preserved) is spared, "and all the Gentiles which are called by My name, saith the Lord Who doeth this" (Amos 9:9-12; cf. Luke 21:24). The immediate and the ultimate in Amos's last verses are fulfilled in the post-exilic return and in the gospel of Christ. The current events being discussed — the Jews in the judgment of their dispersion, the Gentiles in the mercy of their conversion — agreed accurately with the prophecy quoted. Its fulfilment was present before their eyes. There was no hint of postponing it to an indefinite future.

We venture to say that if Pastor James had been present to advance his claim that Amos was not speaking the same thing as the apostles, but of another far, far distant visitation of the Gentiles, of uncertain date after a Second Advent, President James may have called him to order and pointed out that there existed no "agreement" between that surmise and the current situation, which they had gathered to determine, and determine which they did.

Our reviewer detects "confusion" here. As well say David's Lord cannot be David's Son, or shepherd and door, or sacrifice and priest, or the church cannot be both building and bride, as that Abraham cannot be both father and heir (Rom. 4). With regard to the covenant promise Abraham is "heir of the world". With respect to the principle of faith, he is father of all "who walk in the steps of that faith". The New Testament reference to heirship arises from "thou shalt be the father of many nations" (Gen. 17), while of the promised seed, the children of faith, Abraham is father. Since the promise is of a seed universal (as well as in particular of Christ) he is said to be "heir of the world"; that is, the world as in John 3:16, not materially but of redeemed mankind. God thus explains through Paul what He meant in promise and covenant to Abraham.

So vital is it that God's promise to the patriarchs should mean them to inherit Canaan in their resurrected state, that if not, our friend suggests he might even be fearful of his own salvation! "Doth His promise fail?" If he would but accept their testimony he might banish his fears! They *"declared plainly"* that they sought a heavenly and not earthly country, "strange" or foreign, to them. It is well to mark that in the initial promise the land with its defined territorial boundaries was not to Abraham personally, but to his natural seed (Gen. 15:18-21), while Abraham's own death and burial were forecast. When repeated to Abraham personally, and then to Isaac, and later to Jacob, the significant qualification "everlasting" was attached both to the covenant and to Canaan (Gen. 17:7, 19; 48:4). Nor can the promise be called "unconditional" (Gen. 22:12, 18; 26:5). Everlastingness precludes a temporary Canaan inheritance of a thousand years, and must, therefore, be understood as the New Testament explains it, a type of the eternal "country", the true "rest" into which believers enter now, and permanently enjoy (Heb. 4:11). David also understood the promise to be perennial and not millennial (1 Chr. 16: 15-18; Ps. 105:8-11). Stephen later noted that God gave Abraham in Canaan "not so much as to set his foot on, yet He promised" (Acts 7:5). But is it not significant that Stephen began, "the God of *glory* appeared unto Abraham?" Are we to receive or revise the patriarchs' own confessed expectation? "Flesh and blood cannot inherit the kingdom of God, neither doth corruption inherit incorruption." But Mr. Payne's parallelism is rather nebulous; namely, that "eternal, spiritual and immortal beings as angels, do constantly minister in this sin-cursed world"; that the Lord Jesus also in Old Testament Christophanies and after His resurrection were visitants. So with the immortalized patriarchs! Yet he also adds, "Abraham and his seed must possess the land *as God promised*". How fanciful the wriggle from the difficulty becomes! The "seed" possessed and inherited the land (may we say literally?) as the scripture intended, in their mortal estate, but the fathers themselves are to inherit only as visitants after the fashion of ministering angels! But the patriarchs believed God and looked for heaven. We may not impose on them, confessed strangers and pilgrims on the earth, a leasehold of nine-hundred and-ninety-nine plus years, when they are more than satisfied with a freehold of eternal glory (Heb. 11:8-16; Col. 3:2).

Believing Jews and Gentiles are incorporated in the Church. The Jews were accorded Gospel priority. Salvation is of the Jews because of them by divine decree the Saviour came. The parable is of two olive trees, good and wild, natural and spiritual (Rom. 9-11). Some Jews, as branches, were broken off because of unbelief. In their stead, Gentiles wild by nature but by grace spiritually privileged, were ingrafted. God is able to ingraft Jews again on one common indispensable condition, that "they abide not still in unbelief". Many have been, are being ingrafted. These are the election of grace. Possessing Palestine is not in the picture; national salvation is not the subject. The church is in view (as in Eph. 3, under another figure). The tree is not the branches (cf. John 15). No difference is suggested between the branches in the tree; all receive of the same sap of life. Gospel faith in Christ is the essential requisite. Concludingly we read, "And so all Israel shall be saved." These are the totality of saved Jews throughout all generations, according to the apostle's introductory governing principle exemplified from her history, covering Abraham, Isaac, Jacob, Moses, David, Isaiah, Hosea, Elijah, and "at this present time". The "fulness" of Gentiles are God's elect taken out for His name; the "fulness" of Israel likewise are "the election" of the Jews. These all, without distinction, are "called", being "vessels of mercy prepared unto glory". A "part" of Israel is "blinded" judicially; these are set in contrast with "the election". Gentiles must not be boastful against the Jews as though all were cast off and entirely, but humble and seeking their salvation. It is a reciprocal ministry. The Jews are scattered among the nations. God knows His elect, and His Gospel is the instrument which discovers them: a shepherd finding lost sheep. Mercy is thus shown to Gentiles, and abounds through them in mercy shown to Jews. And SO (it does not say *when* or *then*) in this manner, through the incoming of the Gentiles in their fulness "all Israel shall be saved". There is, therefore, in view, combined and total "fulness" in Christ, the body complete (Romans 9 to 11; specially 9:18, 23, 24, 27, 29; 11:5, 7, 12, 16-26; also John 12:37-43; Acts 13:40-48; 28:25-28; Eph. 1:23).

The following sentences from a sermon by Dr. T. T. Shields are apposite:

"I believe that from among the Jews 'all Israel shall be saved' according to the scriptural definition that 'he is a Jew which is one inwardly, and circumcision is that of the heart, in the spirit, and not in the letter.' Millions of Israelites have died in unbelief, and whether of Jews or Gentiles the Word stands, 'If ye believe not that I am He, ye shall die in your sins.' If, then, you understand by 'all Israel shall be saved' that everyone of the seed of Abraham through Isaac's line after the flesh shall be saved, you will be driven to believe in some kind of purgatory where those who have already died will have a second chance, for beyond all question, countless thousands have died in unbelief. On the other hand, if 'all Israel' means only all Israel then living when their blindness shall be ended, it follows that they will be saved on a principle favouring them above all generations of Israelites which have preceded. There is not a word here about the salvation of Israel as a nation after the flesh, not a word about their being established as a Jewish State or earthly kingdom. It had been written, 'The deliverer shall come out of Sion'. Is this the second coming? Was not the stumblingstone laid in Sion? And was He not a stumblingstone because Israel had no eyes to see? The same Person in the same

Sion was no 'stumblingstone' to believers, but 'the power of God and the wisdom of God' " (*The Gospel Witness*, February 9, 1939).

The context (1 Cor. 15), as the review says, is that of resurrection. Resurrection involves death's defeat: "Christ, the first-fruits, afterwards they that are Christ's at His coming." Were our reviewer correct in interposing a millennium, the parallel should read, After the coming the millennium, and after the millennium the end. But as the resurrection of Christ and of His people are conjoined as firstfruits and harvest, so also the coming and the end are joined in this parallel. "They that are Christ's" anticipates gospel effectiveness between His resurrection and theirs. For "they" must be evangelized, outcalled and ingathered through successive generations of time, determined by God but not disclosed to men. The assumption that an unmentioned millennium divides the coming from the end is artificial. "He must reign" is not an earthly post-advent imperative, but a pre-advent necessity. But no intervening period is mentioned between the Coming and the end. It is the dispensationalists' imperative! Consider the wealth of scripture statement concerning His present occupancy of the throne of God in heaven, and His complete authority over all creatures. Jesus, the name high over all in earth, and air and sky; angels and men before Him fall and devils fear and fly. "The early Christian labourer when asked in derision, 'Where is your carpenter god now?' answered, 'Making coffins for His enemies!'" (Dr. R. McCaul, in *The Inside Story of G.A.R.B.C. Dispensationalism*).

Concluding the argument, Paul explained that at the full harvest of resurrection, the saying written "shall be brought to pass, Death is swallowed up in victory". A sentence more expressive could not be found of the complete abolition of death: "the *last* enemy that shall be destroyed." This is at the *End*. Consequently, no allowance is made for arrested judgment, a millennium of abounding animation on earth between death swallowed up in victory and death totally destroyed, which denote the same thing. The two are mutually inclusive. Therefore, death's destruction is the consequence of the Second Coming of Christ and the resurrection, and is at the End which follows. All other enemies will then have been subjugated, and at the last judgment death shall be "cast into the lake of fire" and "all things made new", "there shall be no more death". Moreover, both contexts convey the comfort, "God shall wipe away all tears from their eyes". These are not pre- and post-millennial repetitions of death's judgment. Indeed, at the Second Coming every case will have been decided for time and for eternity (Isa. 25:8; 1 Cor. 15:54; Phil. 3:21; 2 Pet. 3:4, 9, 10, 12, 13; Rev. 20:11; 21:1; 22:11, 12).

Assuming that the prophecy of Christ "as a priest upon his throne" (Zech. 6:13) is distinct from His present priestly office "on the right hand of the throne of God", it is said that His induction as King-Priest after this "order" awaits the Second Coming. But the Hebrews epistle recognizes His royal priestly ministry as now in being, He is now as Melchizedek, "first king of righteousness and then of peace" (Heb. 7-10). How better and more briefly could one state the meritorious basis of righteousness and the consequent blessing of peace—the Gospel of His life-obedience, atoning death and risen mediation? That He has entered upon this royal "order" of priesthood is clearly announced. What God said in the Psalm of David (Psa. 110) He confirms with the meaningful exposition of the New Testament Hebrews. The prophecy "He shall build the temple of the Lord" in His Own words is given, "I will build My church" (Zech. 6:13; Matt. 16:18; 1 Cor. 3:16; Eph. 2:21; 1 Pet. 2:5; Rev. 3:12; 22:16). See also other First Advent fulfilments from Zechariah, as Branch and Dayspring, the King's entry into Jerusalem, the sword smiting the Shepherd, the look upon the pierced One, the opening of the sin-cleansing fountain, etc. But now He has ascended on high, a Priest upon His throne (Zech. 3:8; 6:12; Luke 1:78; Zech. 9:9; Matt. 21:5; Zech. 13:7; Matt. 26:31; Zech. 12:10; John 19:37; Zech. 13:1; 1 John 1:7).

It would appear that the extended exposition of Christ's Melchizedekan priesthood embraces the fulfilment of the promised new covenant. The "sum" of the things spoken here about Melchizedek and Christ is stated thus: "We have *such* an high priest Who is set on the right hand of the throne of the majesty in the heavens", not after Aaron, but Melchizedek. The passage thereupon proceeds to describe the "more excellent ministry" of the new covenant, quoting the terms in full. This He executes in regeneration by His Spirit, the impartation of the divine nature, the unction of the Holy One so that "ye need not that any man teach you", thus "from the least to the greatest" with distinctions removed, mercy ministered, sins and iniquities forgotten. This is indeed a Gospel feast, far superior to the bread and wine which Melchizedek in his typical ministry brought forth for Abraham and his men.

> What food luxurious loads the board,
> When at His table sits the Lord!
> The bread how rich, the wine how sweet,
> When Jesus deigns His guests to meet.

We have regarded as identical with this "nation" (1 Peter 2) that to which the kingdom would be transferred when "taken from" the self-condemned wicked husbandmen, the Jews. The "Stone" context and the prophetical quotation supporting it, which doubtless Peter heard from his Lord's lips, are also the context of this "holy nation" ascription. The nation is the church. Our reviewer disputes this. "The sojourners of the *diaspora,*" he says, are addressed, being thus reminded that they are "still God's holy nation" from which he reasons that the Jews are yet to be nationally saved. For ourselves, we have not found a single scripture in the New Testament which promises salvation to the Jews *as a nation.* In his very next verse, the apostle, referring to Hosea, describes them as "in time past not a people". But they "are now the people of God"; that is, by individual faith in the Lord Jesus within His church. There is no other way. Hence, not to earthly nationhood are they saved, but to an incorruptible, undefiled and unfading inheritance reserved in heaven, the reverse of that on earth which was taken away. So at the end these same addressees are assured of their being called unto God's eternal glory. Now, Paul, quoting the same prophet Hosea, clinches the matter with the words, "even us whom He hath *called,* not of the Jews only, but also of the Gentiles"; and Peter, in agreement with Paul, adds to the fourfold status, including "an holy nation", He hath *"called* you out of darkness into His marvellous light." No New Testament epistle is addressed to Jews because they are Jews, but because they are Christians, and the same may be said of the Gentile writings. Any difference is of approach, but the truth and the end are the same (1 Peter 2:9, 10; Rom. 9:24, 25; Matt. 21:41-43; 1 Cor. 9:10-23).

Christ's First Advent initiated the day of grace: the activity of grace was known before. Hitherto, sin had reigned unto death, but now grace reigns through righteousness unto eternal life. This is the characteristic of the present divine administration. This is the time of acceptance unto salvation without distinction as to race (Isa. 49:8; Rom. 1:16; 2 Cor. 6:2). With the Second Advent will be introduced the day of judgment, not that God's judicial acts were before unknown, but as the especial characteristic of that day. Then privilege and opportunity for all without partiality will terminate. Then, in the equitable balance of divine economy, Jews and Gentiles will face the Judge of all the earth "with Whom there is no respect of persons". Now, between the Advents waits the longsuffering of God, "Who is not willing that any should perish but that all should come to repentance" (Rom. 2:5, 16; 2 Thess. 1:10; 2 Pet. 3:7, 9, 15).

Upon such judgment, timed at the Second Coming, a new universe will be created. This, and not a millennial reformation, is "the regeneration". This is the expectation of all the redeemed according to God's "promise" (2 Pet. 3:13). How are these new inhabitants of a new universe described? In an epistle occasioned by a Jewish problem, the closing word is, "In Christ Jesus, neither circumcision availeth anything nor uncircumcision, but a new creation", and earlier, "but faith which worketh by love" for such is the evidence of divine regeneration (Gal. 5:6; 6:15). Not to be "in Christ Jesus" is to have no hope (Eph. 2:12, 13). By circumcision the Jews are meant; by uncircumcision, the Gentiles (Gal. 2:7, 8). Therefore, neither Jews nor Gentiles as such, neither the nation called Israel nor other nations as such, are of any account with God. A new creation with Him is essential and indispensable, and that is "in Christ Jesus", redemptively in union with Him. Neither favoured Jews nor far-off Gentiles avail anything. The new creation avails everything. Upon these is His benediction of peace, and they are called "the Israel of God" (Gal. 6:16). Upon them God bestows the ancient significant title. They are the "holy nation" of Peter, "the one new mankind" of Paul, and being in Christ, His name is called upon them. He is "Israel"; He is Christ. This only availeth or prevaileth with God, and so again emerges the meaning of what was spoken to the patriarch (Gen. 32:28; Isa. 49:3-6; Gal. 6:15-16; Eph. 2:15; 1 Pet. 2:9). Christ, the true Prince, hath prevailed, and His people, "the Israel of God", prevail in Him. A new creation, they will be the inhabitants of the new world "wherein dwelleth righteousness". His promised Second Coming will introduce it: though derided by scoffers, the delight of the saints.

Of course this scripture (Rev. 20) is authoritative and is not anti-millenial! If, however, by the thousand years is meant the Darby - Newton - Scofield popularized Jewish millennium, then, I suppose I am anti-millennial. My reviewer's other "passing millennial references" in the New Testament are not specified. Moreover, his description of this as "Christ's personal reign *on earth*" and the added copied criticism, "if there is no reign of Christ *on earth* as in Rev. 20, why not join the higher critics?" are inept for this one and only millennial passage says nothing about a reign *on earth*. The scene is in heaven. A natural, earthly economy which, though reformed, would be after the first Adam, cannot supersede the spiritual, heavenly administration of the last Adam, the regeneration. "The world passeth away, but he that doeth the will of God abideth forever."

The numeral, thousand, he says, must be regarded with "literal exactitude". But may it not be that symbolical numerals as in the Apocalypse are not intended to be understood as in historical and chronological records? "The thousand years," we are told, "must be taken in their literal and obvious sense," to be consistent, therefore, so must the rest; e.g., the repeated 144,000, the measurements of city and wall, 12,000 furlongs, 144 cubits, the winepress of blood 1,600 furlongs. Armageddon's cavalry of two hundred millions! The numerical figures and the symbolical figures are related as constituents used by the Revealer for signification. But we have already noticed how "literal exactitude" is waived when faced with the literally extravagant.

To correct "confusion" my reviewer calls in the aid of dictionary antitheses. Words, however, are often to be understood by their use; they have been described as counters of exchange. Whatever may be said in opposition I would repeat that objects of figurative intent were really very literal, and fulfilment is not necessarily the complement of vision and allegory. In "that which is first is natural" the reference is to the first man, the first Adam. The contrast, "that which is spiritual" refers to the second

Man, the Lord from heaven, the last Adam. Other associations of these terms are "earthly" and "heavenly". Adam was natural, and he was literal, not an imaginary being. He was also figurative, and being thus spoken of, natural and figurative are not in opposition. The selfsame doctrine is given in both scriptures (Rom. 5:14; 1 Cor. 15:46). The Lord Jesus Christ is spiritual, a life-giving Spirit. He is also literal, not figurative. He is the Reality, the Fulfiller. And, arising from this first instance it will be found that the appointed types and figures and patterns and shadows in God's revelation of old were natural and literal and figurative. Even a vision consisted of substantial images of things, and an allegory was drawn from tangible existences and events. Well-known examples spring to mind: the passover lamb was natural and literal and typical and figurative, the Lamb of God was the spiritual, evangelical fulfilment, for "Christ our passover was sacrificed for us." The wilderness rock was natural and literal, and surely figurative, for "they drank of that spiritual rock which followed them, and that rock was Christ". Human wisdom is no arbiter of divine words.

One is impressed with the evidently paramount importance to dispensationalism not only of a pre-millennial advent, but to put it another way for emphasis, of a post-advent millennium. It is as a keystone. Drop their thousand years from the scheme, and it would disintegrate. Yet this conception, "of the earth, earthy", was unknown to Christ and His apostles. The scriptures do not affirm that the millennium is introduced by the Second Advent or that Christ comes to inaugurate an earthly reign. The thousand years of Revelation 20 are made to be the duration and scene of matters of prophecy and promise in the Old Testament interpreted as, e.g., a nationalised Israel, a Jerusalem metropolis, a renovated world. But not a single scripture is found to establish this. This applies equally to New Testament passages, including quotations thus put forward from the present Gospel dispensation of grace to an invented age of government, to be contained within the same time limitation. Millennialism presents its greatest problem when divine qualifications are considered. Dr. Shields was wont to quote his father as saying, "God is a great packer: He can pack an oak tree into an acorn." But how shall everlastingness be packed into a thousand years? He is the everlasting God, and a millennium to Him is but as yesterday, and as a watch in the night (Psa. 90). We would direct you to a few specimen scriptures, quoting only the pertinent sentences, but commending meditation upon the entire context:

"I will establish between thee and Me an *everlasting* covenant, and I will give unto thee and to thy seed after thee, all the land of Canaan for an *everlasting* possession" (to Abraham, and so to Isaac and Jacob, Gen. 17:7-8).

"The eternal God is thy refuge and underneath are the *everlasting* arms; and He shall thrust out the enemy from before thee" (Moses' blessing, Deut. 33:27).

"Be ye mindful of His covenant, the word which He commanded to *a thousand generations* (forty millenniums?) with Abraham, unto Isaac, to Jacob and Israel for an *everlasting* covenant, saying, unto thee will I give the land of Canaan, the lot of your inheritance" (David at return of ark, 1 Chron. 16:13-18).

"He hath remembered His covenant forever, the word which He commanded to *a thousand generations*: an *everlasting* covenant, saying, unto thee will I give the land of Canaan" (The Psalmist of the patriarchs and Israel, Psa. 105:6-11).

"The desert shall rejoice and blossom as the rose . . . And the ransomed of the Lord shall return, and come to Zion with songs and *everlasting* joy upon their heads: and sorrow and sighing shall flee away" (Isa. 35. cf. Rev. 7:17; 21:4).

"Israel shall be saved in the Lord with an *everlasting* salvation; ye shall not be ashamed nor confounded *world without end*. Look unto Me and be ye saved all the ends of the earth. Unto Me every knee shall bow, every tongue shall swear" (Isa. 45:17, 22, 23. cf. Rom. 10:1, 9, 10, 11, 26; 14:11; Phil. 2:10-11).

"I will make an *everlasting* covenant with you, even the sure mercies of David. Instead of the thorn shall come up the fir tree, and instead of the briar the myrtle tree: and it shall be the Lord for a name, for an *everlasting* sign that shall not be cut off" (the curse, not millennially but eternally removed, Isa. 55:3-13; cf. Acts 13:34, where the apostle declares them Gospel mercies which he preached).

"For a *small moment* have I forsaken thee, in a little wrath I hid my face from thee for a moment, but with *everlasting* kindness will I have mercy on thee, saith the Lord, thy Redeemer" (Isa. 54:7-8; cf. the New Testament parallel: 2 Cor. 4:17).

"In their land they shall possess the double: *everlasting* joy shall be unto them. I will direct their work in truth, and I will make an *everlasting* covenant with them" (Isa. 61:7, 8). (As with the patriarchs, the land was evidently to be typical of the heavenly country, not for a thousand, but years without end).

"The Son of Man . . . there was given Him dominion and glory and a kingdom, that all people, nations and languages, should serve Him: His dominion is an *everlasting* dominion which shall *not pass away,* and His kingdom that which shall *not be destroyed.* And the kingdom and dominion and the greatness of the kingdom under the whole heaven, shall be given to the people of the saints of the Most High, Whose kingdom is an *everlasting* kingdom, and all dominions shall serve and obey Him" (Dan. 7:14-27; Heb. 12:25-29).

"O the depth of the riches both of the wisdom and knowledge of God! how unsearchable are His judgments, and His ways past finding out! For of Him and through Him and to Him, are all things, to Whom be glory forever. Amen" (Rom. 11:33-36).